D1542029

nonsense

nonsense

ASPECTS OF INTERTEXTUALITY IN FOLKLORE AND LITERATURE

susan stewart

THE JOHNS HOPKINS UNIVERSITY PRESS

BALTIMORE AND LONDON

This book has been brought to publication with the generous assistance of the Andrew W. Mellon Foundation.

Copyright © 1978, 1979 by Susan Stewart
All rights reserved. No part of this book may be reproduced or transmitted in any form or by any means, electronic or mechanical, including photocopying, recording, xerography, or any information storage and retrieval system, without permission in writing from the publisher. Manufactured in the United States of America

The Johns Hopkins University Press, Baltimore, Maryland 21218
The Johns Hopkins Press Ltd., London

Library of Congress Catalog Number 79-4950
ISBN 0-8018-2258-0
Library of Congress Cataloging in Publication data will be found on the last printed page of this book.

contents

preface

Two dangers threaten
the world—order and disorder.
Valéry

This is an essay into the relationships between two universes—
the universe of common sense and the universe of nonsense. Like horses
and carriages, it seems that it is difficult to have one of these universes
without the other. And because it is also difficult to speak, to stand
on a common ground, without partaking in one or the other of these
universes, this essay has returned continually to the problems of its own
assumptions. Hence two questions that may be the same question underlie this study of nonsense. First, how is it possible for us to talk
about something while, at the same time, we are caught up in or implicated in that something? And second, how do we use what we've got?
Both of these questions are "how" questions, questions concerned with
ongoing activities in social life. They are questions about the relationships between acts of classification and acts of transformation, relationships between the ways in which we organize, disorganize, and
reorganize the world. Simply put, the essay looks at common sense
as an organization of the world, as a model of order, integrity, and
coherence accomplished in social life. And nonsense is considered as
an activity by which the world is disorganized and reorganized. The
essay sees common sense not as a stable ground for social process, but
as an ongoing accomplishment of that process—acts of common sense
will shape acts of nonsense and acts of nonsense will shape acts of
common sense. Thus I have assumed that organization is always a reorganization brought about by disorganization, that change and
learning are continual and continuous, characterizing the very "nature"
of social life.

My particular focus in this study has been upon the relationships
between common sense and fictions. I have used a concept of inter-

textuality to describe these relationships. In part 1, "Common Sense and Fictive Universes," I outline an intertextual construct premised on the assumptions that common sense is an ongoing accomplishment of social life; that common sense is a set of interpretive procedures used in creating everyday life situations; that fictions and play are texts standing in a paradoxical and dependent relationship to texts manufactured by using common sense; that the varieties of play and fictions are arranged through common-sense reasoning in relationships of decreasing reality to the texts of common sense; and that the outer limits of this arrangement are characterized by nonsense and its concomitant categories of fate, chance, and accident.

In part 2, "Making Nonsense," I have looked at several ways of transforming common sense into nonsense. These operations stand in a paradoxical relationship to common sense, either by pointing to some inherent leak or contradiction in common-sense reasoning, or by using procedures in contradiction to common-sense procedures. The procedures we have available to us for making nonsense indicate that our repertoire of ways to interpret experience—to form the boundaries of the texts of experience—includes procedures that cancel each other out, procedures that are contradictory and paradoxical. Because of this ambivalence in our procedures for interpreting experience, we cannot characterize the world prior to these procedures as being intrinsically one of order or disorder. My concern here has been with the social manufacture of order and disorder. While I have outlined five ways of making nonsense, I have not wished to present a taxonomy of nonsense procedures. Our ways of making nonsense will depend upon our ways of making common sense, and the interpretive procedures used in making common sense are assumed to be continually in process and emergent.

Throughout this essay I have relied mostly upon verbal art for my examples. This is because I have wanted to talk about a set of genres that infuses both "everyday" and "exceptional" contexts; because, to some degree, this set of genres relies upon a common language; and because such a common language highlights the variations in interpretive procedures between common sense and nonsense. My examples also are chosen for the most part from a "Western" tradition, although I have considered the integrity of such a tradition to be an outcome of practical reasoning more than a historical reality. The procedures used in making common sense as well as the procedures used in making nonsense so clearly parallel certain linguistic devices and the methods of formal logic that I am skeptical of any claim that they are cross-cultural or universal. The richness or paucity of examples is a matter of availability and preference. I, too, have used what I have at this place in time.

The conclusion to the essay, "Change's Sensibility," returns to the problems of change and function with which the essay began. Here I have presented a critique of the idea of learning as abstraction and leisure, hoping to show that this idea is an outcome of common-sense thinking and that change and learning are going on all the time and all the way down the line in our experience of social life. The conclusion discusses parallels between paradoxes of nonsense and other paradoxes in social life.

As a folklorist, my concern has been with the relationships between the interpretive procedures used in making a wide variety of fictions and the interpretive procedures used in making "reality." Folklore and literature—oral and written fictive forms—themselves often reveal devices of borrowing and transformation common to other borrowings and transformations in social life. In cultures where folklore is considered to be the province of one class and literature the province of another, a study of the relationships between folklore and literature may be revealing of the ways each class perceives its relationship to the other. In other words, the organization of fictions will have to do with other forms of social organization. But my concern in this particular study has not been with who owns fictions so much as with the relationships between an array of generic forms. Rather than cutting between "folklore" and "literature," I have cut between "realities." For example, proverbs and the novels of realism are seen as standing in a metonymic relationship to common sense, while riddles and nonsense literature are seen as standing in a paradoxical and metaphorical relation to common sense.

Returning to the problem of a common ground, I continually have tried to emphasize that this essay itself is caught up in the interpretive procedures it is about. Common-sense reasoning continually attempts to sway the reader. As for the procedures of nonsense, this essay often turns back upon itself and cancels itself out, shifts the horizon of its concern, chooses from a set of examples that threatens infinity and exhaustion, assumes a simultaneity of fictions available to both author and reader, and continually arranges and rearranges a common set of ideas. In keeping with this essay's tradition, I must remind the reader that a preface is really an afterword, a final attempt at making everything "fit," to say what was left unsaid in the text. And, within this tradition that is not yet here nor there, I will say in conclusion that what has been left out and not said, what does not and cannot fit, has been the true concern and delight of writing this essay.

acknowledgments

My deepest thanks to those four teachers who served as advisors to this study: Stanley Fish, Barbara Kirshenblatt-Gimblett, Barbara Herrnstein Smith, and John Szwed; if I ever had an ideal reader in mind, it was a medley made of the four of them.

Part 1 has benefited from a careful reading by Roger Abrahams, and Michael Holquist's enthusiasm for simultaneity helped give shape to chapter 6. I am grateful to Jeanne Flood for making the resources of the Widener Library available to me, and to the children of Rutland and Coppin Elementary Schools, Baltimore, Maryland, for being so generous with their oral tradition. Finally, I would like to thank my husband, Daniel Halevy, who was no help at all with the middle, but who helped me to begin and end it.

I · common sense and fictive universes

1 · making common sense

THE SENSE OF COMMON SENSE

When one wonders how to begin to talk about something, etymology appears, a way to start an argument that places all of history within the subject at hand. The word comes to swallow the world. The word comes to carry its own ontology, its own reward for being. As a device it bears the stamp of the cultural; its causality is synthetic. Jean Paulhan has suggested, "The word itself tells us so: etymology, *etumos logos*, authentic meaning. Thus etymology advertises itself and sends us back to itself as its own first principle."[1] Each word becomes burdened by an infinite regress of meanings. The word becomes text—manifold, diffuse, scattered over history. And history becomes the horizon of a range of possible contexts.

The problem of etymological proof is a problem of decontextualization. The word lifted out of history has only itself as recourse. The word becomes its own last resort. And this is the beginning of nonsense: language lifted out of context, language turning on itself, language as infinite regression, language made hermetic, opaque in an envelope of language. As Wittgenstein put it, "When a sentence is called senseless it is not as it were its sense that is senseless. But a combination of words is being excluded from the language, withdrawn from circulation."[2]

Ironically consider the etymology of *nonsense* in English:

1. That which is not sense; spoken or written words which make no sense or convey absurd ideas; also, absurd or senseless action.
   Often used exclamatorily to express disbelief of, or surprise at, a statement.
   > (1614 B. Johnson *Bart. Fair* iv, iv. Here they continue their game of vapours, which is Nonsense.)
   b. In particularized use: A piece of nonsense.
   > (1643 Visct. Falkland, etc. *Infallibility* (1646) 98 Every new nonsense will be more acceptable . . . than any old sense.)
   c. *No nonsense*: no foolish or extravagant conduct; no foolery or humbug. Chiefly in phr. Stand no nonsense (also used as adj.).
   > (1821 *Sporting Mag.* VIII, 233. Smith would stand no nonsense.)

2. Absurdity, nonsensicalness.
> (1630 W. Bedell in *Ussher's Lett.* (1686) 421. I shewed the false Latin, non-sence, injustice of it.)

3. Unsubstantial or worthless stuff or things.
> (1638 Cowley *Love's Riddle* iv Wks 1711, III, 113. Our Desires . . . are Love's Nonsense, wrapt up in thick Clouds.)

4. A meaning that makes no sense.
> (1650 Weekes *Truth's Conflict* i, II. This is to put a nonsense upon the place, and to destroy the savor that is in it.)

5. Want of feeling or physical sensation. Obs.
> (1621 in T. Bedford *The Sinne*, etc. A i b. Disquietness of Conscience (growes) into a numbdnesse or non-sense.)

6. *Attrib.* and *Comb.* as *nonsense-proof* adj., *-talker*, *-writer*; nonsense-book, a book of nonsense or nonsense verses; nonsense-name, nonsense verses, verses consisting of words and phrases arranged solely with reference to the metre and without regard to the sense; also *nonsense-song*, etc.
> (1887 *Spectator* 17 September 1251, Lear's Nonsense Books.)

  b. That is nonsense; full of nonsense; + in the 17th century often used as *adj.* = Nonsensical
> (1621 Burton *Anat. Mel.* ii, iv. I.V. (1651) 375. A few simples well-understood are better than such an heap of nonsense confused compounds.)

And *nonsensical*:

That is nonsense, of the nature of, or full of nonsense; having no sense, absurd; of persons; a nonsensical, absurd or trifling thing. "Nonsensify," to make nonsense of, "Nonsensification," the production of nonsense.[3]

In the nineteenth century *nonsense* could mean "money" or a "fiasco" in slang.[4]

What is the meaning of this range of meanings, a tentative construct riding on the surface of the word itself? In every case, nonsense depends upon an assumption of sense. Without sense there is no nonsense. Here is a connection with "money," a conventional system of exchange. Like language, money is a confidence game society plays with and against itself. Like a "fiasco," nonsense is a failed event, an event without proper consequence. Nonsense stands in contrast to the reasonable, positive, contextualized, and "natural" world of sense as the arbitrary, the random, the inconsequential, the merely cultural. While sense is sensory, tangible, real, nonsense is "a game of vapours," unrealizable, a temporary illusion. While sense is "common" and "down to earth," nonsense is "perfect," "pure," an untouched surface of meaning whose every gesture is reflexive.

From this comes the problem of definition, the problem of "the scope of the investigation." Nonsense always refers back to a sense that itself cannot be assumed. The locus of the investigation must be in the nature of the *not* that stands between the domain of common sense and the domain that takes its identity as "not common sense." And thus I am concerned in this essay with acts of classification, what is nonsense and what is not nonsense, and with acts of transformation, how sense becomes nonsense and nonsense becomes sense.

Most uses of *nonsense* in the discourse of everyday life have to do with engaging in acts of classification. Nonsense is that which should not be there. We say "Cut out that nonsense," "Knock off the nonsense," "Enough of that nonsense," or "That's just a bunch of nonsense." Nonsense becomes that which is irrelevant to context, that to which context is irrelevant. Nonsense becomes appropriate only to the everyday discourse of the socially purposeless, to those on the peripheries of everyday life: the infant, the child, the mad and the senile, the chronically foolish and playful. Nonsense becomes a negative language, the language of an experience that does not count in the eyes of common-sense discourse.[5] Nonsense is an impediment, an infirmity, to such discourse, for nonsense confuses the proper schedule for "time's marching on." Nonsense wastes our time. It trips us up. It gets in the way. It makes a mess of things.

While this cutting-out gesture has to do with how we use nonsense in everyday discourse, we can at the same time ask what it is that nonsense "does for us" in everyday discourse, in other words, what might be the function or functions of nonsense. Here it may be helpful to make a distinction between use and function. In traditional anthropological terms, "use" refers to the situations in which a phenomenon is employed in human action; "function" concerns the reasons for its employment and particularly the broader purpose or purposes it serves.[6] In everyday discourse, nonsense is used as a category that is both negative and residual. Like its companion categories of Fate, Chance, Accident, Miscellaneous, and even *etc.*, it gives us a place to store any mysterious gaps in our systems of order. By providing such a place, nonsense can be seen to function as an aid to sense making. Without nonsense, sense would not be "measured," sense would itself threaten infinity and regression. Whereas earlier, on the basis of etymology, we concluded that nonsense depends upon sense, we can now say, on the basis of function, that sense depends upon nonsense.

Consider what Richard Hilbert has called "a limiting task," a task in which "from a member's view, there is no possible available method for evaluating the 'true state of affairs.'" Hilbert writes:

This is to distinguish it from cases of sense-making in which members are able to resolve difficulties and contradictions and thus to document the objective and non-contradictory nature of Reality. This is also to distinguish it from cases in which members, though unable to resolve contradictions are nevertheless able to withhold judgment and to hypothesize possible methods of further investigation, methods which for one reason or another are determined to be temporarily or permanently beyond members' practical reach. Thus for members involved in a limiting task, the impossibility of resolving difficulty and contradiction is an *essential* impossibility in that all imaginable methods of reconciliation can only be imagined to fail.[7]

Put in everyday terms, to be confronted with a limiting task is to be "up against the wall," "in a jam," "at wit's end." In a recent study, Hilbert created a situation of limiting tasks by giving members of a large undergraduate sociology class five versions of an event and a set of instructions to find out "what really happened" by putting together the five versions. The five versions were actually randomly selected stories in no way derived from any common event. In a last resort gesture, Hilbert's students classified the assignment as "nonsense." Since they saw no possible way to reconcile the accounts, they chose to disregard the entire assignment. What is important here is that it was not the hypothetical event or any part of the "real world" in which the students found themselves, but the *assignment* that was classified as nonsense. By saying that the assignment was an impossible one from its outset, the students were able to say that "nothing happened." The legitimacy and rationality of sense making was left uncontaminated, unthreatened, since there was no actual nonsense event.

In accord with Hilbert's findings, we can regard members engaged in sense-making activities to have three ways of dealing with contradictions: (1) they can resolve them according to some sense-making principle, (2) they can put them off to a later date when "more information" will be available, or (3) they can classify them as nonsense and thereby limit their influence to another domain, a domain that is not any "real world." Thus Hilbert presents us with a model in which nonsense rescues common sense by providing a residual category for storing disorder.

This is a rather neat argument: nonsense arises out of sense-making activities and ultimately serves the interests of such sense-making activities. But function, like etymology, can be seen as a cultural and not a "natural" argument. Surely the "purposefulness" of nonsense, which is achieved by ascribing a function to nonsense, stands out as another marker for the message "common sense at work here." It is easy enough to show that the function of any given phenomenon is to see that that phenomenon or some other phenomenon keeps on functioning. It is perhaps impossible to see function in any other way. This argument is naive only to the extent that it assumes an inevitability and naturalness to these processes, assumptions that blind us to the kinds of "work" that go into accomplishing such processes.

And so we are brought to a certain crisis, a crisis of "method" and its correlative "subject." Any investigation into common sense must take its own procedures as subject and, at the same time, must be subject to its own procedures. It is perhaps Alfred Schutz's phenomenology that has most clearly articulated this crisis. In Schutz's essay "Common Sense and Scientific Interpretation of Human Action,"[8] he discusses the respective tasks of the natural and social scientists. The natural scientist is concerned with designating constructs that will supersede the constructs of common-sense thought, hoping to determine which sector of the universe of nature, and which facts and events within that sector, will have import for his specific purpose. These facts or events *in* nature do not have relevance structures as such. In contrast:

> The facts, events and data before the social scientist are of an entirely different structure. His observational field, the social world, is not essentially structureless. It has a particular meaning and relevance structure for the human beings living, thinking and acting therein. They have preselected and preinterpreted the world by a series of commonplace constructs of the reality of everyday life, and it is these objects which determine their behavior, define the goal of their action, the means available for attaining them—in brief, which help them to find their bearings within their natural and socio-cultural environment and to come to terms with it.[9]

Cultural systems involve a "humanistic coefficient."[10] While natural systems may be objectified, may be seen to operate independently of the desires, purposes, and interpretations of men, cultural systems are ontologically defined by such desires, purposes, and interpretations and cannot be taken into account outside of their human universe.

The investigation is of necessity about itself, involved in a gesture of reflexivity. We must deal with constructs of "the second degree"—that is, "constructs of the constructs made by actors in the social scene."[11] This means that our concern is also with the nature of the investigation, that our constructs are themselves reflexive models of the procedures for making constructs. Method thereby becomes subject and subject becomes method. Let us take this essay into nonsense as a case in point. The discourse I am engaging in as I write this page is "common-sense" discourse. Complete sentences, paragraphing, margins, footnotes, titles, the author's true name—all say, "I really mean this, this counts," as do ideas presented as if they were contingent upon one another and quotations from the past that are "brought to bear" upon the text. Such writing becomes concerned with creating a plausible context within which its discourse can make sense to its readers.[12]

The two procedures I am interested in investigating do not occupy a domain different from the domain of this writing. The manufacture of common sense and the transformations by which nonsense is made out of common sense belong to the same social universe. Just as the investigation is not taking place "out there" in some other, unstructured world, so is it not creating another world. Rather, the goal is an interpretation of activities in the social universe that accomplish sense and nonsense. The investigation itself is inextricably rooted in that social universe. The "method" is reflexive and critical: "to take a theoretic stance toward the everyday world is to stand back from, to reflect upon, to re-view the experience taken for granted in the natural stance,"[13] the stance of actors in the everyday lifeworld.

Sense making may be seen as a primary activity of everyday life, that is, as an activity that is a feature or goal of a wide range of social behaviors. All "practical action" is organized along principles of sense making, of rationality, and, at the same time, is an accomplishment of those very principles. In other words, I am not granting a status for "sense" or "rationality" outside of those sense-making activities. Principles of sense and rationality are ongoing accomplishments of social life. I do not mean by this, however, that members are involved in making order out of some primary chaotic state of the world. Rather, as ethnomethodologists have pointed out, to invoke a notion of a primary, meaningless, yet "really real," reality out of which social reality is constructed is itself to engage in legitimating sense-making procedures.[14]

The domain of common sense may be typified as a domain of situations in the everyday lifeworld. This typification itself is derived from common sense since, as noted above, the adjectives we use for common sense, "ordinary," "down-to-earth," "grounded in," "just plain," all refer to this lifeworld. Schutz has said that this world is characterized by a set of fundamental assumptions that we further assume to be intersubjective, that is, held equally by members. These assumptions are "unquestionably given": that the structure of the world is constant, that the validity of our experience with the world is constant, and that our ability to act upon the world and in the world is constant.[15] Our experience of the lifeworld thus depends upon assumptions we hold regarding our position as actors within and upon the world, regarding the nature of the world, and regarding the nature of our actions in the world. These assumptions allow us to suspend any fundamental distrust of the everyday world, indeed, to take it for granted.[16]

And to take common sense for granted is not simply a matter of willing suspension of disbelief. It is also a matter of economy. We may assume that what is not made manifest in everyday discourse, what is left unsaid in situations, is not necessary to or needed for the situation to proceed. It would indeed be nonsensical for us to make explicit what can remain implicit, to make a continual retreat back to assumptions. This may be why, in thinking about common sense, it is so difficult to think of "examples," for an example is brought to the fore whenever a rule needs to be illustrated, whenever the rule itself is problematic. To bring forth an example is to make the rule suspect. When situations proceed according to "rules" that are implicit and thereby not properly "rules" at all, the situation is not seen as "rule governed," but as "natural." This is how nature is made pervasive. To give an example of the natural is to point to the natural as a cultural category, to imply a "not natural" domain that coexists with the natural and thereby weakens the stance of the natural.

The assumptions that allow us to take common sense for granted come to us through tradition, through what Schutz called "the stock of knowledge at hand." This stock of knowledge is available to us in an ever-emerging form throughout our lives. Tradition lends us a set of expectations that are stratified in terms of typification and relevance, for evaluating what will count and not count in forming the horizon of any situation. By placing the origin of typification and relevance in tradition, we can avoid considering them as natural features of the world and instead see them as artful accomplishments of the social process.[17] It is not that the everyday world has become a social world by having the social process impose features upon it, but that the everyday world is a social and intersubjective world from the outset.

This conception of the everyday world is highly dependent upon a notion of indexicality,[18] which we may see as a notion of context. The significance of events in the everyday lifeworld is created by assuming a contiguous relationship between "text" and "context," between meaning and the occasion of its manufacture. Schutz's notion of contextual determinancy linked the process of making meaning in everyday life to what he called "the here and now of existence": "All my goals and objectives form a hierarchical order and originate in my 'biographically determined situation.' The latter is also the source of my systems of relevancy, both my permanent ones and those that are transient, shifting with my 'purpose at hand.' The system of relevancy that prevails at a given moment depends upon the goals I am pursuing and, also, as mentioned before, determines my typifications."[19] All concrete human events may be seen to be dependent upon their situations. Their meaning will be contextually determined. The members of the situation will choose from a plan of action determined by their "stock of knowledge at hand" and their "purpose at hand." Accomplishing common sense has to do with an agreement regarding the horizon of the situation, an agreement regarding what is relevant or appropriate to the situation in light of this horizon, and a mutual procedure for achieving an appropriate outcome of the situation—a procedure that, again, depends upon typifications and relevance structures that are socially manufactured. None of this is accomplished privately. We must see our situation as "intersubjective," holding to an idea that others share in a "vivid present" and that this present is a matter-of-course, accessible to everyone else in the same way in which it is accessible to us. We take it for granted that we can "stand in each other's shoes," and we take it for granted that others see their activities as possessing the same degree of taken-for-grantedness.

The idea that meaning is contextually determined may be stated in terms of Wittgenstein's notion of meaning as use: "For a large class of cases, though not for all, in which we employ the word 'meaning,' it can be defined thus—the meaning of a word is its use in the language."[20] Here again we may note the irony of etymology, the word bringing evidence to itself as word, outside of context—the attempt to find a meaning that transcends particular historical situations. While this idea that meaning is use in particular contexts has been impressively expanded by ordinary language philosophy, speech act theory, and sociolinguistics,[21] it should be qualified. The idea is important in that it demonstrates that the meaning of an utterance is not identical through the changing occasions of its use. But, at the same time, we cannot assume that we have a unified, occasionless notion of context. This critique of the "context" schools has been brought by Jacques Derrida in pointing out the limits of an ordinary language notion of context when talking about writing,[22] and by Harold Garfinkle: "Not only does no concept of context-in-general exist, but every use of 'context' without exception is essentially indexical."[23] Context is determined through interpretive procedures that have evolved through prior experience with "contexts" and "texts."

We cannot assume that the horizon of the situation remains the same for all members in all situations. The attempt to outline a contextual "environment" will only result in an infinite regress of significant features. The horizon of the situation is something that is accomplished in interaction. "What anyone knows" in determining this horizon is a complex set of shared assumptions for proceeding. This has been readily demonstrated in Garfinkle's famous "ad hocing" study where students were asked to describe common conversations by writing on the left side of a sheet of paper what was said and on the right side of the sheet of paper what they understood was being talked about. The explanation on the right-hand side of the paper branched out into an infinity of explanation. The exercise was frustrating to the students and eventually seen as a fault in the instructions of the assignment.[24] In concluding this study, Garfinkle wrote:

For the conduct of their everyday affairs, persons take for granted that what is said will be made out according to methods that the parties use to make out what they are saying for its clear, consistent, coherent, understandable or planful character, i.e. as subject to some rule's jurisdiction—in a word, as rational. To see the "sense" of what is said is to accord to what was said its character "as a rule." . . . the appropriate image of common understanding is, therefore, an operation rather than a common intersection of overlapping sets.[25]

Common sense will be both an accomplishment of the situation and an aid to accomplishing the situation. Again, common sense as a subject continually dissolves into a kind of method. And common sense, when used as the method for any investigation, must be viewed with suspicion, must be made *subject* in the investigation.[26]

Going back to the distinction made earlier between use and function, we can consider typification and relevance as two procedures used both to organize interaction in general and to engage in interaction in light of any particular "purpose at hand." Accomplishing the situation involves classifying and stratifying elements of significance. Articulating the boundary between text and context will have to do with determining levels of inclusion and exclusion, with hierarchically organizing what will count and not count in determining the situation. To employ these operations is to be common-sensical. And put in broader functional terms, the employment of typification and relevance serves to substantiate our notion of ourselves as historical beings, our confidence in social categories and hierarchies in a system of rationalities based upon typification and relevance, and, finally, our confidence in a taken-for-granted world perceived in terms of these same rationalities. In the common-sense world, immediate interests guide our constructs, the portion of the stock of knowledge at hand that we will use in any particular situation. And, at the same time, the connectedness, orderliness, and importance of the stock of knowledge at hand in relation to—in felicitous fit with—the situation substantiates our belief in the connectedness and orderliness of the larger context of the everyday lifeworld.[27] The use of common-sense operations, operations that are socially derived and distributed, will lead to the accomplishment of a purpose at hand and a common-sense world within which that purpose at hand takes on significance and direction. At every point we are engaged in manufacturing common sense as well as in employing it.

On any level, theorizing may be seen as the creation of a possible society. Therefore, when I speak of a "we as members," I mean members of a situation rather than members of a society. To posit a society prior to its members would be, again, to engage in accomplishing a rationality appropriate to the activities of everyday life rather than to those of the investigation. "Society" is an outcome of our belief in intersubjectivity, in a belief that others are participating in the same reality with the same approximate stock of knowledge at hand. Society, as larger context, does not "lie behind" immediate situations, reflected in them as in a mirror. Rather, the discourse of social interaction resolves situations and accomplishes situations. Vološinov discusses this society-accomplishing function of discourse as an ideological function: "Whatever kind it be, the behavioral utterance always joins the participants in the situation together as co-participants who know, understand and evaluate the situation in like manner. The utterance consequently depends on their real, material appurtenance to one and the same segment of being and gives this material commonness ideological expression and further ideological development."[28] Society may be seen as an outcome of situations as much, or more than, as a ground for situations. Just as I was not concerned with the ontological status of the "real" world prior to members' interpretations, so am I not concerned with the status of a society prior to members' interpretations. Society, as a model of order, production, and connectedness, is an outcome of the common-sense reasoning of everyday life.

This is why any attempt to define society must dissolve into process. As Theodor Adorno has emphasized, "Its laws of movement tell more about it than whatever invariables may be deduced. . . . The object meant by the concept society is not in itself rationally continuous. Nor is it to its elements as a universal is to particulars; it is not merely a dynamic category, it is a functional one as well."[29] To see society as a function and outcome of members' interactions is to get away from a position that reifies common-sense notions about the individual, social life, and, perhaps most of all, change. Common-sense thinking must see the lifeworld as a stable and ordered phenomenon in order to get on with the business at hand. An investigation that accepts this as the nature of the everyday world will then be in a quandary with regard to explaining changes in our perception of the world. But this is to confuse levels of analysis. A constant, coherent, "rational" world is an outcome of members' activities. It is an ongoing accomplishment. It is ongoing since the biographical situation of individuals and the stock of knowledge at hand are always "in process." To take stability as the basis of an investigation is simply to engage in employing the same rationalities as those that we employ in everyday life.

Rather, process may be seen as the order of things and change may be seen as a way in which we interpret that process, indeed, go about categorizing, typifying, evaluating, and making relevance of that process. To say "something changed" is to make a mark, to organize social time. Change cannot be assumed outside of interpretation. It may be seen as an outcome of what Hans George Gadamer has called "the historicity of understanding":

Just as the individual is never simply an individual, because he is always involved with others, so too the closed horizon that is supposed to enclose a culture is an abstraction. The historical movement of human life consists in the fact that it is never utterly bound to any one standpoint and hence can never have a truly closed horizon. The horizon is, rather, something into which we move and that moves with us. Horizons change for the person who is moving. Thus the horizon of the past, out of which all human life lives and which exists in the form of tradition, is always in motion. It is not historical consciousness that first sets the surrounding horizon in motion. But in it this motion becomes aware of itself.[30]

This essay will assume that the concepts "real world," "individual," "society," and "change" are functions and products of situations, of social process.

AN INTERTEXTUAL CONSTRUCT

What are some of the interpretive procedures used in accomplishing these two domains of social life, common sense and nonsense? From the preceding discussion, we might see the domain of common sense as being "the real": a domain experienced through the senses, through the "actually happened." Conversely, we can see nonsense as a "not real" domain, a domain of the "never happened," even more, a domain of the "could not happen."[31] My concern is not an investigation into the objective status of the reality and not-reality of these two domains—rather, it lies with the procedures by which these domains are manufactured.

The material examined here is discourse, that is, language as social event; not language as some contained and abstract "fact," nor as a product of some individual psyche, but rather language as discourse, accomplished in social process. I shall not be concerned with determining psychological motives, processes, or effects, nor with looking at discourse as the product of an individual, for the point is that all language is considered here to be intrinsically social by virtue of its being an act of communication. Language is caught up in the intersubjectivity of the world from the outset; every utterance implies a listener and is both the creation and product of a social interaction. However, it is the very detachability of language from its context of origin that gives it this intersubjective force. Language can "make present" others who are physically absent, move one situation into another through the stock of knowledge at hand, even objectify the biographical situation by which the very notion of the self emerges.[32]

All discourse bears reference to a commonly held world. The discourse of common sense refers to the "real world." The discourse of nonsense refers to "nothing." In other words, it refers to itself, even though it must manufacture this "nothing" out of a system of differences from the everyday world—the common stuff of social life—in order to be recognized as "nothing." Any instance of discourse can be seen as a social event in that any utterance always implies and produces a possible listener, and, as well, a possible society. Conversely, social events can be seen as "textual" in that their borders, contents, and results are a matter of convention and interpretation that are themselves subject to the ongoing social process.[33] The interpretive work that we accomplish in "reading" any given social situation is analogous to the interpretive work associated with reading any other text. Specific rules for interpretation will depend upon culture-bound concepts emergent in the stock of knowledge at hand, and upon members' perceptions of generic differences between speech events.

I am therefore interested in social events as texts and texts as social events: in the event as accomplished through members' interpretive work and in the text as a product of social interaction, contingent upon social process. Again, the social world is assumed to be an interpreted world. Paul Ricoeur has stated this point as follows: "Like a text, human action is an open work, the meaning of which is 'in suspense.' It is because it 'opens up' new references and receives fresh relevance from them that human deeds are also waiting for fresh interpretations to decide their meaning."[34] This can be seen as a restating of Gadamer's point regarding the historicity of understanding. The meaning of interaction is not prior to, or intrinsic to, the interaction itself. It is emergent through members' ongoing interpretive work.

Alfred Schutz held that the everyday lifeworld is "a world of culture because, from the outset, the world of everyday life is a universe of significance to us, that is, a texture of meaning which we have to interpret in order to find our bearings within it and to come to terms with it."[35] Our stock of knowledge at hand, derived from our biographical situation and from tradition, influences not only the content and details of our interpretations, but also their style, the general lines along which the world will be constructed and understood. Interpretation is responsible not only for the "content" of the world, but for the hierarchical organization of content, the very shape of the world. Interpretation is not a process whereby some meaning "underlying" or "behind" the text/event is made evident, but a process in which meaning is manufactured and accomplished in light of the constraints of tradition, the stock of knowledge at hand. "Meaning" itself is not prior to social interaction, but is achieved in the course of social interaction.

Interpretation organizes, and is organized by, systems of relevance. As soon as there is a notion of style, there is a hierarchical arrangement of elements. Schutz wrote:

All our knowledge of the world, in common sense as well as in scientific thinking, involves constructs, i.e. a set of abstractions, generalizations, formalizations, idealizations specific to the respected level of thought organization. Strictly speaking, there are no such things as facts, pure and simple. All facts are from the outset facts selected from a universal context by the activities of our minds. They are, therefore, always interpreted facts, either facts looked at as detached from their context by an artificial abstraction or facts considered in their particular setting.[36]

Relevance and hierarchy are not features of "nature," but are the result of interpretive work in social life. Relevance provides us with a procedure for separating out domains of meaning that would produce contradictions if combined. This is the process at work in the first of the alternatives discussed above for dealing with contradictions such as limiting tasks: when faced with a contradiction, we can always make a decision of relevance in light of the stock of knowledge at hand and thereby "smooth over" the troublesome facet of the contradiction.

The idea of "domains of meaning" allows us to control contradiction in that it provides a set of universes that in some way are mutually exclusive and thereby will respectively tolerate the mutually exclusive aspects of the contradiction. This notion of domains goes back to William James's idea of "sub-universes of meaning," which Schutz adapted as "finite provinces of meaning." James was concerned with the ways in which often contradictory domains could be attended to, one at a time, as "the real." He contended that "only the reality lapses with the attention."[37] For Schutz, *meaning* was the key word in discussing these domains of social life, for such domains were the product of human interpretive activities: "We speak of meaning and not of sub-universes because it is the meaning of our experience and not the ontological structure of the objects which constitutes reality."[38] He suggested that each province of meaning has its own cognitive style with respect to which experiences within it are mutually consistent.

A notion of provinces of meaning allows members and investigators alike to manufacture and seek to uncover interpretive schemes for respective domains of reality. This is because interpretive schemes are themselves dependent upon specific situations and the hierarchical organization of such situations, and cannot be assumed to be uniform across varying domains of social life. It may be useful here to think in terms of George Boole's idea of a "universe of discourse,"[39] a range of ideas that is accomplished in social life. To contrast this range of ideas to other universes of discourse would emphasize contradictions between the domains. Subsequently, W. M. Urban has attempted to relate the idea of a universe of discourse to the study of communication systems: "The universe of discourse is nothing that exists or subsists independently of discourse or communication, but is itself created and fixed by the mutual acknowledgement of communicating subjects."[40] Following Urban, we can consider provinces of meaning—universes of discourse—to be sets of interpretive procedures that are internally consistent and, in some way or other, mutually contradictory. The universe of discourse calls for a "set towards the message," a procedure for manufacturing meaning consistent with a situation and purpose at hand. Each universe will be "finite" in the sense that attention to it will preclude attention to another universe of discourse at the same time and in the same place. But such universes are not "finite" in terms of their relationships to one another, for those relationships will be *intertextual.* The universes of discourse are involved in borrowing from one another and transforming one another at every step as they are employed in an ongoing social process.

The everyday lifeworld, while itself only one province of meaning, is at the same time most often designated as the domain of "reality." Special procedures must be built into our interpretive schemes in order to leap from this domain to any other. The everyday world acquires its paramount status because of the pervasiveness of its intersubjectivity, its taken-for-grantedness. Largely, it is a world where adult, wide-awake, interpersonal communication takes place, where "common," as opposed to "scientific," or "aesthetic," sense is manufactured. Perhaps most importantly, it is the world of work, of human action framed as "what really counts." In its taken-for-granted, doesn't-everybody-think-like-this, aspects, the everyday world encompasses much of what goes unsaid as well as what is said. It may be seen primarily as an attitude, assumed to be natural. It is our basic "set towards the message."

We can consider all other provinces of meaning to be modifications or transformations of the common-sense world.[41] This observation bears upon the relation of nonsense and common sense, reemphasizing my earlier point that nonsense is contingent upon the production of common sense. For we can thus regard the locus of the present investigation as being not in the content of the common-sense and non-sense domains, but rather in the transformative operations used in moving from one domain to the other, operations that, as noted at the beginning of this chapter, have to do with the "not" between domains.

In accord with the earlier discussion of texts as events and events as texts, we can now further characterize the relationship between domains as an intertextual one, a relationship whose nature and boundaries are determined by the interpretive work of members in an ongoing social process. The nature of the relationship between the domains of common sense and nonsense will be one that varies according to situation; to members' biographical situations, to the traditional stock of knowledge at hand, and to the "larger situation," the ongoing concept of society in general. There will be as many varieties of non-sense as there are varieties of common sense. Thus the focus of this investigation will be upon transformative operations used in discourse events rather than upon the content of those events.

We may also, in light of the previous discussion, consider absurdity and disorder as varieties of nonsense; for, as Bergson pointed out in *Les deux ordres et le désordre*, disorder and absurdity are "merely the want or absence of a particular variety of order" that is the order of common sense. He calls them "meaningless experiences" that serve to reify an order of a particular kind.[42] In that they work as nonsense works, as names for the absence or nonbeing of common sense, disorder and absurdity fall within the scope of this essay.

The concept of intertextuality relies upon two basic assumptions: first, that various domains of meaning are contingent upon one another, and second, that the common-sense world may be considered as a base from which other provinces of meaning are formed. Schutz set forth the following characterisitcs of the common-sense world: it is a world marked by a specific tension in consciousness, a wide-awakeness; by a specific epoché, that is, suspension of doubt; by a prevalent form of spontaneity, working, the bringing about of a projected state of affairs by bodily movements taking place in the outer world; by an experiencing of the working self as the total self; by a specific form of sociality, largely face-to-face intersubjective communication and social action; and by a specific time perspective, standard time integrated with a cosmic time held intersubjectively.[43] It is not only that the common-sense world is characterized by certain relations we hold to time, space, and causality, but that time, space, and causality are themselves constituted in the common-sense domain.

One important assumption that members hold regarding the common-sense world is that such a world is natural, that it has to do with the proper order of things, with what people know "instinctively" to be right and assume to be intersubjectively held, with an equal and uniform access to knowing. Hence the point I made above regarding the everyday lifeworld's encompassing of the unsaid as much as the said. We regard with suspicion any excessive signs of culture, of systematizing and rule making brought consciously to bear upon common sense. Common sense is assumed to be plain, simple, there "for anyone to see." This point is well made by Garfinkle in his study of the relationship between common sense and scientific thinking. While we can readily demonstrate common-sense assumptions and interpretations behind scientific methods, we cannot assume that the "rationalities" of science are the rationalities of common sense. Garfinkle concluded that "the scientific rationalities, in fact, occur as stable properties of actions and as sanctionable ideals only in the case of actions governed by the attitude of scientific theorizing. By contrast, actions governed by the attitude of daily life are marked by the specific absence of these rationalities either as stable properties or as sanctionable ideals."[44] To engage in scientific thinking is to manufacture a world in which scientific thinking will be rational, ordered, and purposive. To engage in common-sense thinking is to manufacture a world in which common-sense thinking will be rational, ordered, and purposive.

If members try to fit a set of scientific rationalities over a set of common-sense rationalities, the result is to exaggerate the senseless quality of the world of everyday life and to multiply what Garfinkle calls "the disorganized features of the system of interaction."[45] The juxtaposition of two or more systems of sense will point to the non-sensical character of one or more of them, for such a juxtaposition undermines the suspension of doubt needed to engage in at least one of the domains of reality.

Scientific thinking can be seen not only as based upon common sense assumptions but as being itself the product of social process and therefore subject to changes in its method, purpose, scope, and very shape by the ongoing nature of that process.[46] This essay is not concerned so much with the relationship between scientific and common-sense domains as with the relationship between what might be called an aesthetic domain and the common-sense domain. Often research depends upon a distinction between art and society that involves positioning these two provinces with an established and proper amount of distance between them prior to the investigation. It is an assumption of the present investigation, however, that art possesses what Vološinov called an "intrinsically social structure" as a product of social interaction: "Thanks precisely to that kind of intrinsically social structure which artistic creation possesses, it is open on all sides to the influence of other domains of life. Other ideological spheres, prominently including the socio-political order and the economy, have determinative effect on verbal art not merely from the outside, but with direct bearing upon its intrinsic structural elements. And, conversely, the artistic interaction of author, listener and hero may exert its influence on other domains."[47] The distance between real life and art is itself determined by historical, social process. The firm fixing of this distance is another functional move, appropriate to the search for social order.

Fixing this distance between the text of social life and the artistic text is a matter of determining the shape of an intertextual relationship —will the artistic text mirror the text of social life, will it distort the other text, reflect it, replicate it, reverse it, or multiply it? These are all questions of verisimilitude or *vraisemblance*; how is it that the text can gesture toward, make reference to, be construed as, a "real world"? At least since the *Cratylus*, writing has been seen as an area of conflict, a space where reality becomes problematic. Because of this focus upon the written word as betrayer of reality, the spoken word, speech in situations, is naturalized and accounted for, taken for granted and objectified as part of the reality of the everyday lifeworld. Julia Kristeva has seen an intrinsic connection between the manufacture of vraisemblance and the manufacture of sense: "Si 'vraisemblable' veut dire 'sens' en tant que résultat, le sens est un vraisemblable par la mécanique de sa formation. Le vraisemblable est le sens d'un discours rhétorique; le sens est la vraisemblance de tout discours." Kristeva argues that any sentence that makes grammatical sense will be accepted as one possessing verisimilitude, "tout énoncé grammaticalement correct serait vraisemblable."[48] To contend this, however, is to ignore the characteristic of speech that gives it its "realness"—its intrinsic part in the reality-generating conversation of society, its contextual baggage of "real life." Grammar alone is not enough. We may go back to the discussion of nonsense's impossible context, for fictions that are "realistic" employ a set of conventional devices to present possible, plausible, or potential contexts for themselves. The closer the discourse remains to the discourse of the everyday lifeworld, the more realistic it will be.

Realism partakes of the time, space, and causality, the ideology and the rhetoric, of the everyday lifeworld. Its descriptions approximate the distance of everyday life descriptions,[49] its field of action will be the field of the everyday lifeworld, its proper conclusions will be the proper conclusions of common-sense reasoning formed in common-sense experience. Realism as a mode thus depends upon an intimate relation between speaker and listener, writer and reader; it approximates the face-to-face situation where interpretation is emergent in interactions rooted in a common tradition. Its time is genuinely collaborative. Context envelopes speech. Context becomes foregrounded. And because of this dependence upon context, the content and field of realism will always be subject to social process. Perhaps this is why of all Western literary genres, the genres of realism seem to be most burdened by history, by standard intersubjective time and the limits of the everyday lifeworld. In this way the literary genres of realism are like those "scripts" from verbal art, such as personal experience narratives and gossip, which depend so much upon the collaboration of participants for the manufacture of their meaning, or like proverbs that rely so heavily upon situational and social contextual constraints.

It is important to remember, however, that such discourse is framed as discourse, and while the common-sense world infuses it, its transparence depends upon conventions and expectations that themselves are ongoing, conventions that articulate "This is a true story, worth telling." P. Florenskij has suggested: "Reality is described through symbols or images. Yet a symbol would cease to be a symbol and become in our consciousness a simple reality in its own right, without any relation to the thing symbolized, if the description of reality had as its object only reality: description must necessarily contain the symbolic nature of these very symbols; it must deliberately and consistently hold on to both the symbol and the thing symbolized."[50] Because of this symbolic nature of realism we can have realism that is more real than real life, which is truer to "Experience" than the actual flow of experience. And this is the place where realism and common sense always slip into ideology—with a conception of the real more real than real can ever be.

Fictions may also refer to merely possible contexts—contexts that may have been possible in the past or that may be possible in the future, but that cannot be projected upon the here and now of existence making up the present everyday lifeworld or any of its past manifestations. Myth and science fiction, for example, both present a kind of discourse that is "grammatical," but the contexts of the discourse lie behind, beyond, or before the range of everyday experience. Myth and science fiction, like many animal tales, are anthropomorphic. They present the stock of knowledge, the purposes at hand, of everyday life within the context of another world. In this sense, they represent the very pervasiveness of the common-sense world, the common-sense world's transference to, and adoption of, other domains of reality. Their very other-worldliness depends upon reference to the common-sense world, their otherness must of necessity be more a reaction than an invention.

When a fiction concomitantly presents two domains of reality as a set of voices in conflict with one another, irony results. In irony the text begins to demonstrate the relative nature of provinces of meaning. The text begins to split. Messages and contexts must be seen as part of a hierarchy of relations for interpretation to take place. What was left unsaid in the context of the everyday lifeworld—that one must abstract from context, lifting language from one context to another and thereby objectifying it, that one must choose from tradition in terms of relevance structures—begins now to "all talk at once." The ironic messages "Little did he realize" and "How could we have known" are comments upon the nature of relevance structures and the possibility of conflict between our expectations in social interactions and the conclusions of social interactions. They point to the tragedy of any attention that is focused—its essential incompleteness. With irony, common sense begins to be undermined. In terms of the work that irony accomplishes—a presentation of the relative nature of points of view, of the incomplete and only partially predictable nature of experience—we can see irony as a kind of metacommunication, a communication that bears a message about the nature of communication.

Irony emphasizes the textual, the interpreted, and the cultural, rather than the natural, status of social interaction. Thus it may be seen as linked to other parodies, satires, and burlesques of the everyday world; the specific taking in and taking over of one text by another. These genres show the possibility that intertextual relationships can be not only harmonious, but also in conflict. With such genres, speech begins to envelop context. What before was considered to be a matter of course now becomes a matter of discourse, subject to ongoing, ragged-edged interpretation. As Vološinov points out, "The form of irony in general is conditioned by a social conflict; it is the encounter in one voice of two incarnate value judgments and their interference with one another."[51]

Realism and myth stand in a contiguous relation to everyday life. With irony that contiguity is split, made reflexive. Metafiction can be considered to be a fourth type of discourse, making up the final level of this intertextual construct. Metafiction traverses and manipulates not only the domain of common sense, but the domains of other kinds of fictions as well. Its violation of common-sense principles of order, its foregrounding of the cultural nature of signification, its exposure of systems of interpretation as systems, its comments upon the nature of communicative modes, give it its status as a metafiction—a fiction about fictions—a fiction necessarily about itself. And, since the context of this type of fiction is impossible, hermetic, a place that cannot happen that is the fiction itself, we may see its intimate connection with nonsense. Such fictions are often marked off, delimited in social space just as nonsense is in conversation. The carnivalizing aspects of ritual, the novel that takes on all of language and the history of literature as its subject, many forms of children's speech play, all take place in a nonsense context, a context that is possible only when it is framed off as play. As nonsense, metafictions form the outer space of social life.[52] While the common sense of our intertextual construct arranges the language of realism in a metonymic, contiguous, relation to the language of everyday life, this metonymy becomes increasingly traversed as myth, science fiction, and fantasy shift its context and irony splits it into two levels. Metafiction continues the splitting with a reflexive gesture that threatens infinity. At the point of nonsense, common sense is scattered and dispersed, made relative to alternative systems of order.

ON FRAMING IN "LIFE" AND "ART"

Each level of textuality—realism, myth, irony, and metafiction—stands at an increasing distance from common-sense procedures and thereby decreases in realism. And each level depends upon the previous levels for both its content and its method. By this I mean that not only the subjects of other levels appear, but the procedures for organizing those subjects—the interpretive schemes available at any given level—appear as well. In this way, our interpretive procedures for each set of levels is increasingly reflexive and self-conscious, aware of the systematic, cultural, synthetic, and interpreted nature of reality.

It is an old argument in aesthetics that it is not the picture that makes art art, but the frame and the frame's implicit message "This is art." The frame focuses our attention not upon content alone, but upon the organization of content and the relationship between content and its surroundings. The idea of content itself is brought about by organizing interpretive activities. To determine what is or is not content and what is or is not context depends upon interpretive schemes guided by a purpose at hand.

Framing, in terms of both everyday life and investigatory procedures, implies metacommunication, for the organization of signification depends upon the use of signifying systems as well as communication about the nature of signifying systems. There is a point at which the notion of metacommunication is no longer useful, however, for communication even at its most "basic" common-sense level must always point to some other outside itself. This pointing will bear a critique of communication that is reflexive. Metacommunication has no choice—it must always speak; and metalanguage must always speak in language. The dilemma has been succinctly put by Segal and Senokosov in their discussion of the structuralist method:

Since structuralism operates constantly with sign systems, the problem of interaction between the object and subject of description is of vital importance; the problem of interaction is connected on a logical plane with the distinction between object and metalanguage. At the same time, particular attention is given to discovering the interdependence between the results of the investigation and the metalanguage of the investigation. . . . An important achievement of structuralism is to specify the concept of isomorphism and the hierarchy of systems with which human existence is connected.[53]

There is no place in which one can escape metalanguage or framing. An activity that was not framed would be the completely natural, would be prelapsarian, a point that itself must of necessity act to frame "the unframed." This activity would be a purely natural gesture at the other end of the spectrum of social process from the most impossibly social gesture—nonsense. The problematic nature of this "natural" gesture is foregrounded every time children play "copy cat." In this game one child will mime another child's gestures. If the victim crosses his legs, the copy cat crosses his legs; if the victim looks annoyed, the copy cat looks annoyed; if the victim says "stop it!" the copy cat says "stop it!" The victim becomes totally frustrated by the search for a completely natural gesture, a gesture outside of social life, outside of human communication and interaction—the gesture that is not socially adaptable. The "game" can only be ended arbitrarily. The social universe, the copy cat, always wins.

Framing therefore is not a useful concept if one wants to classify activities as either "framed" or "unframed." Rather, one can ask about the procedures for framing, the results and possibilities of framing. This has been done in quite different respects by Boris Uspensky in his *Poetics of Composition* and Erving Goffman in *Frame Analysis*.

Uspensky sees the reader's movement from the domain of the everyday lifeworld to the domain of the artistic text as a transition from one reality to another, a transition that creates the frame of the artistic text as much as it is guided by it. He writes: "In a work of art, whether it be a work of literature, a painting, or a work of some other art form, there is presented to us a special world with its own space and time, its own ideological system and its own standards of behavior."[54] But this "special world" both envelops us and does not envelop us. The confrontation with and participation in the work of art is as much a multiplication of realities as it is a transition between realities. And this multiplication necessarily leads us to entertain the possibility of multiple realities as much as it leads us to entertain the possible world of the art work. We may see visual art as largely a transformation of the space of the everyday lifeworld and verbal art and music as largely transformations of the standard time of the everyday lifeworld. But because of the interdependence of space and time, the arts in general involve a transformation of the here and now of common-sense reality. The structure of the everyday lifeworld—intersubjective and almost internally natural in its consistency—is modified as the reader steps into the "external," the reality of the work of art. Uspensky argues that the artistic text seems to possess the characteristics of a closed system: "Each world represents a unique microworld organized according to its own laws and characterized by its own spatial and temporal structure."[55] Thus each world presents a system of differences in relation to any other world. To step into the artistic text is to transform the external into the internal and the internal into the external. And each transformation opens up the possibilities of transformation itself.

Framing the artistic text will always imply framing the flow of everyday discourse as well. This framing may be done with a literal frame, with a curtain or a spotlight or a ring, with a culturally determined sense of "beginning" and "end," with times of day or season set aside for performance, or with set pieces such as "Once upon a time" or this Irish ending:

> They found the path and I found the puddle
> They were drowned and I was found,
> If it's all one to me tonight,
> It was all one to them the next night.
> Yet if it wasn't itself, not a thing did they lose
> but an old back tooth
> or some such gibberish.[56]

The frame makes the artistic text an artistic text. It is the boundary of the artistic text and everyday lifeworld, or the artistic text and any other province of meaning, that defines either domain. This is why the borders of domains and the rules of transformation between domains are of more concern here than any supposed "essences" of domains. The frame is a communicative gesture, an invitation. It lies between the external space of the common-sense world and the internal space of the representation. It is the scene of transformation.

The work of art itself may be divided into smaller "texts,"[57] each marked by changing frames, transformations from the internal to the external or the external to the internal point of view. Thus the creation of the artistic whole depends upon a process of framing both internal and external to the work itself. Because of this we have the possibility of metafictions such as representations within representations, frame tales with receding quotation marks, plays within plays, the novel as a carnival of discourse. The signifying· quality of the representation is thus emphasized. The discourse becomes a sign of a sign of reality; its conventional nature is foregrounded. This is why "a lesser degree of semiotic quality is naturally associated with a greater degree of realism (verisimilitude)."[58]

The framing activities that are used to create and engage in the artistic text are not specific to the aesthetic domain. Rather, we can consider framing to be an important device for articulating texts from contexts and for arranging texts and contexts in a hierarchical relationship throughout social life. Those features which Uspensky investigated in his study of the artistic frame—the relation of the discourse to time and space, point of view of actors, point of view of interpretive voices, relevance of background, relevance of degrees of description—are all features that members must interpret in order to accomplish any everyday life situation. It is not only that framing is a device that enables us to mark off "the real" from the nearly real, the nearly nearly real, and so on, but also that framing may be seen as a model of the kind of interpretive work going on in any social interaction. As Schutz wrote, "Every particular perception yields more than merely what it offers in genuine sense experience. Through every perception the object perceived appears, according to the point of view from which it is observed, under a certain aspect, from a certain side, in a certain orientation."[59]

It is not only that everyday life offers us a model by which we can make copies—imitations—in increasing distance from that model, but rather, if we see everyday life as a reflexive, ongoing process constantly copying, modifying, and rearranging itself throughout situations of interaction, it becomes clear that the activities we engage in when interpreting other domains of meaning are transferable to the domain of the lifeworld. The direction and economy of influence between domains of reality is itself a function of those domains, contingent upon social process. Thus Vološinov's point that it is in the ideological sphere that art has its deepest influence upon social life must be expanded, for art also presents a model for interpretation, for arranging perception, which at its profoundest point does not so much make its members "see into the life of things" as it enables them to remake the life of things.

From the work of Erving Goffman we can see framing to be a primary method for organizing experience, that "definitions of a situation are built up in accordance with principles of organization that govern events—at least social ones—and our subjective involvement in them."[60] Goffman makes much use of a notion of rule-governed behavior, but his exposé of the ways in which frame making can go wrong points to the ongoing nature of such rules. In other words, rules themselves are at least partially products of the events they set into motion, and the usefulness of breaking the rules (in Bergson's terms, providing the inappropriate rules) depends upon appropriateness conditions shifting from rule to rule as much as from situation to situation.

Goffman points out that, while we can see everyday activities as a model from which fictions, play, make-believe, and fantasy derive, the "reality" of those everyday activities is itself subject to the social process; it is always more or less real than what it is being compared to: "When we decide that something is unreal, the real it isn't need not itself be very real, indeed, can just as well be a dramatization of events as the events themselves—or a rehearsal of the dramatization, or a painting of the rehearsal or a reproduction of the painting. Any of these latter can serve as the original of which something is a mere mock-up, leading one to think that which is sovereign is relationship—not substance."[61] Again, framing is an activity common to the domains of both art and everyday life, and it is "common" to both domains simultaneously. Any gesture of framing will at once effect more than one domain of reality. Framing involves and, indeed, *is* the articulation of a boundary between domains, a statement of relationship between domains. To consider framing—the articulation of a field of interpretation and its relevant context from a surround of social life—as part of members' ongoing work in situations is to point to the artfulness and interpretive nature of such work.

We may see this notion of framing-as-representation as a kind of organization, a system of hierarchically arranged messages and contexts. "Representation" is another reality-generating device. It determines the boundary of the real, the next-to-real, the next-to-next-to-real, ad infinitum. The intertextual construct I have offered in this chapter, which outlines realism, myth, irony, and metafictions in decreasing order of "realness," depends upon a social construction of reality that places the real in the everyday lifeworld. It is important to note that this hierarchy of messages and contexts is itself an accomplishment of the social process, designed both to reify the real, the existing, order, and to provide alternative social space where any flaws in the machinery of interpretation can be repaired.

This construct is dependent upon a particular tradition that is, of course, largely a footnote to Plato. And the construct can work in the other direction of "realness" if so needed by members; it is at times useful to say that the everyday-life world's situations "don't count."

Examples come readily to mind simply from the way we sometimes talk about experience: "Chalk that up to experience," "We learn from our mistakes," "It's all behind me," are all messages that allow us to use standard time to devalue everyday life situations. They are a way of cancelling out and thereby also counting in parts of the biographical situation and stock of knowledge at hand. They are part of a world view that places "what really counts" in the future and allows the past to be constantly transformed through reinterpretation. Thus standard, intersubjective time comes with a relevance structure built into it, a relevance structure that helps to evaluate tradition and biography as they are brought to bear upon interpretation.

At the same time, in terms of ideology, the sources underlying members' actions in everyday life situations come as much from other domains of reality as from former everyday life situations. While censors may believe that only television, movies, children's literature, and pornography move us to certain plans of action in real life situations,[62] it seems more likely that we are moved by an entire barrage of types of discourse—proverbs, personal experience narratives, commercials, exhibits, music, and speeches[63]—throughout our lives. Our neighborhoods are full of Madame Bovarys, Cinderellas, Ebeneezer Scrooges, Constantine Levins, and wise fools as much as fictions are full of people from our neighborhoods. An interesting juncture of these domains appears in biographical literary criticism. As Boris Tomaševsky has pointed out, some ages have authors and others do not.[64] That is, the importance of the idea of "author" will vary historically and socially. But we might hypothesize that if there were no biographical criticism, aspiring authors would have no way to determine how an author should act. In face-to-face communities where performance is experienced firsthand this is not such a problem, but in other communities, biographical criticism becomes valuable and informative gossip. Fictions, as much as other kinds of social institutions, may be seen as an ongoing discourse that society produces about itself, constantly subject to members' interpretations.

My point is that this sytem of representation gives us a means for bringing about the apparition of any particular level of the intertextual construct. If we point to the base of fictions, we make everyday life the "relatively real." If we point to the base of everyday life, we establish the relative reality of other domains, including the fictive. Reality is thus a relationship brought about by members' interpretive activities, particularly by framing. This system of representation presents us with a kind of "unity." Demonstrating the unity of any phenomenon may be seen as the point of theory in general. If we have a representational theory of language, we can use it to point to some unified, equally accessible phenomenon that language represents—things, "the real world."[65] If we say that society is a representation of members' opinions of their ongoing activities, we have said that those activities are nonrandom, organized, even purposeful. Similarly, the idea of the fiction as representation perpetuates the notion of a world to be represented. It is thus the relationship between domains, in these cases a "representational" one, that defines the degrees of unity, reality, and purposefulness characterizing the domains. Theory is always a personification, an attempt to make the world behave as if it were "one of us"—predictable, reliable, orderly, and coherent. And "pure theory" is, of course, the person more real than real, the case that transcends all exceptions. Thus the intertextual construct itself must be resolved as an example of isomorphism; it is a construct that of necessity relies upon the interpretive procedures that are its subject.

PLAY AND THE MANIPULATION OF CONTEXT

The common-sense construction of reality takes place in contexts of everyday life situations. Common sense underlies and is an outcome of the interpretations created in and by these situations; it is rooted in the reality of this everyday world. These interpretations depend upon the immediate situational context, on such features of the interaction as "settings, participants, ends, act sequences, keys, instrumentalities, norms and genres."[66] Hence the here and now of existence typifying such situations is emphasized by a context of relevance that is itself "here and now" in scope. The discourse of such situations bears ostensive reference—it points to an immediate intersubjective ground of interaction. As Peter Berger and Thomas Luckmann, drawing from Schutz, have pointed out:

Language originates in and has its primary reference to everyday life; it refers above all to the reality I experience in wide-awake consciousness, which is dominated by the pragmatic motive (that is, the cluster of meanings directly pertaining to present and future actions) and which I share with others in a taken-for-granted manner. Although language can also be employed to refer to other realities ... it even then retains its rootage in the common sense reality of everyday life.[67]

But language is also characterized by its intertextual dimension, its detachability from a context of origin or immediate situation and relocation into other situations within the same domain of reality or into whole other domains of reality.

It is the language of everyday life that is transferred intact, transgressed, manipulated, traversed, and transformed to other domains of reality. Talking in one's sleep or gibberish or glossolalia[68] are all recognized as kinds of talk in contrast to the kinds of talk used in everyday life. Realism calls upon the organization of language in everyday discourse. But the recontexting of language, the reframing of language, demands different patterns of expectation, different rules of inter-action on the part of members. Each frame bears a set of procedures for interpretation that members manipulate in engaging the text.

Thus what is first of all transformed in the movement from one domain of reality to another—in the detachability of language—is con-text. And since context serves primarily as a way to organize interpreta-tion, the common sense characterizing the everyday lifeworld is transformed as well. Common sense is operative whenever a text relies, at least in part, upon the interpretive schemes of everyday life. Our common-sense expectations can thereby be seen at work in those texts we call "realistic."[69] However, at each intertextual level, with each transformation of everyday discourse, common-sense rules become more and more supplanted by discourse-specific rules of interpretation until common sense serves mostly in the articulation of differences between domains. In other words, common sense becomes the "not" of the discourse, the articulation of the discourse at hand from reality.

With changes in domains, the purpose at hand becomes transformed. In a poem a girl in a yellow dress may disappear over a hill, and because it is a poem, we do not proceed according to a projected plan of action affecting the immediate present and future. We do not ask, "That's a nice dress, I wonder where she bought it?" or say, "She seemed upset, I think I'll get in my car and try to follow her." As William Gass has pointed out in his *Fictions and the Figures of Life*, if we see a statue of a man on a horse, lifting his sword and pointing his left hand ahead, we don't try to figure out what he is pointing at in the environment surrounding the statue.

Earlier I suggested that framing could be considered as the articula-tion of a field of interpretation from a surround of social life: in other words, framing has much to do with the determination of a context and context-specific procedures for interpretation. How is it that the same message, the same behavior, can be framed so as to signify different sets of interpretive procedures? This was the question underlying Gregory Bateson's preliminary work on play and fantasy. Bateson wanted to know how animals engage in an interaction sequence of which the unit actions are similar to, but not the same as, those of certain other behavior sequences.[70] How is it that animals can engage in "fighting behavior" as fighting behavior, denoting what fighting behavior denotes, and as play, denoting something that is "not fighting behavior"?

Just as we can see culture as a stratification of categories, a shared understanding of procedures for communication, we can see play behavior as exhibiting a certain traversal and manipulation of those categories as stratified. Playing at fighting may be "not fighting," but it is not fighting on a different level of abstraction from other kinds of not fighting such as kissing, skipping rope, buying groceries, or singing

"Happy Birthday." Play involves the manipulation of the conditions and contexts of messages and not simply a manipulation of the message itself. It is not, therefore, a shift within the domain of the everyday lifeworld; rather, it is a shift to another domain of reality.

It was the "not really" aspect of play, play as "not really X behavior," which interested Bateson and his coworkers more than the nature of the "X" in this statement. Play has to do with the relationships obtaining between categories rather than the content of categories, although certain types of content may be privileged according to the particular system of categorization. Bateson saw a connection between the paradox of communication foregrounded by play—that a behavior can possibly not denote what those actions for which it stands denote—and the paradox of abstraction known as the Epimenides paradox.[71] Epimenides the Cretan, according to legend, emerged from his cave and said, "All Cretans are liars." Both play and the Epimenides paradox involve negative statements containing implicit negative metastatements, the negative metastatements having to do with a different level of abstraction, a different domain of reality:

I am a Cretan/I am not a Cretan
This is X behavior/This is not X behavior

The paradox of play also has to do with what Russell and Whitehead called the paradox of "the classes which are not members of themselves."[72] This paradox goes as follows: A class cannot be a member of itself (for example, "the class of popsicles" cannot be a member of the class, popsicles, for the class of popsicles cannot be a popsicle). But classes that are not members of themselves must be classes that are members of themselves. The class of "not popsicles" includes "the class of not popsicles," along with nails, hot dogs, bracelets, and rubber bands. Thus "the class of not popsicles" is a member of itself. The paradox in each case lies in the nature of the "not." These paradoxes are paradoxes of reflexivity, of self-contradiction. They are symptomatic, therefore, of epistemological paradoxes in which the mind, by its own operation, says something about its own operation, or the way in which language speaks in metalanguage or fictions through metafictions. All statements by a member of a class about the class to which it belongs tend toward the paradoxical. They are "vicious circles," the viciousness of every circle depending upon its paradoxical qualities of limitlessness and limitedness.[73]

Russell and Whitehead contended that one could avoid the paradox by distinguishing between levels of logical types. The paradox involved a confusion of levels of abstraction, they contended. Thus, "All Cretans are liars" and "the class of popsicles" are messages of a different logical type from other Cretanic messages and popsicles themselves and should be read as such. Ironically, however, Whitehead was later forced to recant this conclusion as a satisfactory way out of the paradox. In 1931 Kurt Gödel published his article "On Formally Undecidable Propositions of *Principia Mathematica* and Related Systems." Gödel demonstrated that any attempt to get out of the "vicious circle" paradox of the Epimenides or classes-that-are-members-of-themselves type was doomed to fail in that the statements of such a theory would themselves be implicated in the "vicious circle" as metastatements. In an address at Harvard in 1939, Whitehead acknowledged Gödel's point and said, "Our only way of understanding the rule (of logical types) is nonsense."[74] As a statement about statements, as a reflexive point, the "rule of logical types" posited by Whitehead and Russell is as self-contradictory as the statement of Epimenides. As a rule that erases its own context, it is indeed nonsense.

Once we see play behavior as a paradox in communication, and, indeed, the possibility of alternative domains of reality as paradoxes of communication as well, paradox appears not as an eccentric kink in the machinery of philosophy, but as an essential aspect of communication. Paradox in everyday life is resolved as Whitehead and Russell resolved it—by resorting to metacommunication, to a hierarchical arrangement of contexts and messages that allows us to proceed. Giving the message "This is play" involves exchanging one set of interpretive procedures for another, involves the recognition of communication as communication, and behavior as signification. Metacommunication is involved in giving instructions for its own reading, for reframing the text of the situation at hand. Its negative and paradoxical character comes from the implication that it is dependent upon some prior set of interpretive procedures, a set of procedures that it is contingent upon, about, and not about at the same time. With domains of reality such as play, ritual, and fantasy, behavior not only denotes what it would not denote in the everyday lifeworld; it carries a message about itself that says, "This behavior does not exist." Bateson says that these are the two peculiarities of play:[75] the messages or signals exchanged in play are in a certain sense untrue or not meant, and that which is denoted by these signals is nonexistent.

Paradoxes like these may be seen as critical devices, as ways of evaluating messages, as means of establishing a hierarchy of messages. The paradox establishes the limits of the domain of reality that it takes as its subject. As Rosalie Colie has observed: "One element common to all these kinds of paradox is their exploitation of the fact of relative or competing value systems. The paradox is always somehow involved in dialectic. Challenging some orthodoxy, the paradox is an oblique criticism of absolute judgment or absolute convention. . . . Like a tight spring, the implications of any particular paradox impel that paradox beyond its own limitations to defy its categories."[76] The paradox fractures the universe of discourse. At one and the same time it is part of the universe and has taken the universe as its subject. The message "This is play" and other metamessages split themselves in a reflexive gesture, transforming and reorganizing the boundaries of their own discourse. Because their movement is self-critical, it both centers and dissolves attention and thereby causes the "lapse in reality" that James predicted. The universe at hand becomes relative to what stands outside of it.

Through play an organism does not learn so much the content of categories of behavior as that there are sorts and categories of behavior, and that such sorts and categories can be manipulated, can support each other, transform each other, or cancel each other out. The metacommunication necessary for play involves a movement from one set of interpretive procedures to another, a movement "out of which the player discovers new possibilities for thinking, for codification of messages and so on. If you go on rigorously within one way of codifying—one onionskin structure—you go on unchanged," writes Bateson.[77] Bateson contends that play and its paradoxes are necessary for the survival of organisms, since adaptation occurs by loosening up the rules for communication. Play and other types of reframing thus prevent the organism from being trapped within one set of interpretive procedures. While on the one hand we have seen that reframing and representation involve the reification of a base "reality" (that is, the reality of the everyday life-world), on the other hand, the paradoxes of reframing and representation allow for the ongoing nature of the social process by continually exposing and evaluating the hierarchy of messages and contexts employed in social interaction. Bateson concluded from his research on play: "We believe that the paradoxes of abstraction must make their appearance in all communication more complex than that of mood signals, and that without these paradoxes the evolution of communication would be at an end. Life would then be an endless interchange of stylized messages, a game with rigid rules, unrelieved by change or humor."[78]

Such a game with rigid rules is indeed a feature of one domain of reality—the world of the schizophrenic. Bateson's concern with the adaptive possibilities inherent in the human capacity to distinguish between hierarchies of messages and contexts led him to consider schizophrenia as the inability to distinguish between such hierarchies. The schizophrenic is unable to resolve the contradictions and paradoxes inherent in communication by moving up or down to different levels of abstraction. Thus he or she is caught in a "double bind" of contradictory messages. Most "not" relationships become "proper not" relationships—for example, if you are not a floor, then you must be a ceiling; if you don't love me, you must hate me. Bateson's work with schizophrenia as a communication-based problem was presaged by Sylvano Arieti's study of schizophrenic language in his *Interpretation of Schizophrenia*. Arieti noted that schizophrenics often make identifications according to Von Domarus's Principle: "Whereas the normal person accepts identity only upon the basis of identical subjects, the schizophrenic accepts identity based upon identical predicates."[79] Thus mackintosh apples and fire trucks are the same thing since they are both red. Similarity is replaced by identification, and the world is turned into a metaphor that does not know it is a metaphor.

Jakobson's famous essay on aphasia[80] similarly contends that aphasia has to do with an inability to use either metaphor or metonymy. In similarity disorders, the aphasiac cannot use metaphor; he or she can only make semantic groupings based on contiguity. In this type of disorder, the aphasiac suffers from a loss of "naming," a loss of the ability to use words outside of an immediate context of origin. There is no detachability of context. The more indexical and dependent the message is upon immediate context, the simpler it is for this type of aphasiac to understand. Jakobson calls this defect "properly a loss of metalanguage," adding that "recourse to metalanguage is necessary both for the acquisition of language and for its normal functioning."[81] In a second type of aphasia, known as contiguity disorder, the aphasiac is unable to see metonymic relations. He or she exhibits a tendency to level the hierarchy of linguistic units; contextualization is not seen as a significant feature of any utterance. The extent and variety of sentences is reduced to a "word heap" as the aphasiac is unable to use metonymic principles of organization. The former disorder thus involves an inability to perform metalinguistic operations, while the latter disorder involves an inability to maintain the sequential aspect of linguistic units.

These studies of language disorders are revealing for an investigation into what characterizes language order and its correlative nonorder, nonsense. The procedures by which the schizophrenic or aphasiac "fails" to make sense are often the same procedures by which others succeed in making nonsense. In both schizophrenia and aphasia, disorder consists of an inability to distinguish between a hierarchy of messages and contexts that make up the various levels of abstraction featured in any interaction. Linguistic order depends upon a balance of metalinguistic and contextually rooted interpretive procedures. Jakobson has pointed out that fictions, as alternative domains of reality, may shift according to generic principles towards or away from each of the poles in this balance. He writes:

The primacy of the metaphoric process in the literary schools of romanticism and symbolism has been repeatedly acknowledged, but it is still insufficiently realized that it is the predominance of metonymy which underlies and actually predetermines the so-called "realistic" trend, which belongs to an intermediary stage between the decline of romanticism and the rise of symbolism and is opposed to both. Following the path of contiguous relationships, the realistic author metonymically digresses from the plot to the atmosphere and from the characters to the setting in space and time.[82]

He points out that the metonymic/metaphoric dialectic can be seen in the history of painting (cubism as the former, surrealism the latter) and film (D. W. Griffith as opposed to Chaplin).

In terms of the intertextual construct, realism depends upon metonymy, upon reference to context in a rule for interpretive procedures taken from the interaction sequences of everyday life. With succeeding intertextual levels, heightened reflexivity brings about paradoxes in communication and an increasing emphasis upon the metaphoric pole. Any radical shift toward the metaphoric or metonymic pole will result in nonsense, in language "disorder"; but nonsense most often results from what may be seen to be a radical shift toward the metaphoric pole, away from a contiguous relationship to the context of everyday life and towards the context of "nothing" symptomatic of the use of nonsense in everyday talk. Even when nonsense involves the preservation of metonymic relations at the expense of metaphoric relations, as in Lewis Carroll's poem, "Jabberwocky," where the conjunctions and prepositions are "spared" being turned into nonsense, the result is an exposure of metonymic relationships as purely systematic, as having no context outside of their own conventions.

Our conception of linguistic order depends upon a certain balance between that order's metaphoric and metonymic dimensions. These dimensions thereby provide ready-made axes for nonsense to use in making disorder. Metaphor involves principles of substitution and selection, metonymy involves principles of sequence. This metaphoric/metonymic distinction used by Jakobson in his study of aphasia is a pervasive one, common to the Frazerian distinction between sympathetic and contagious magic, Tylor's notions of metaphor and syntax, de Saussure's paradigmatic and syntagmatic dimensions, and Lévi-Strauss's models of harmony and melody in myth and his comparisons of totemic and caste systems. The metonymic axis, the axis of combination, has to do with relations of propinquity, while the metaphoric axis, the axis of substitution, has to do with relations of identity. It is important to note, however, that the poles are interdependent. Metaphor depends upon metonymy, upon a given order of things, since in its most general sense metaphor is "the relationship which obtains between entities of separate domains by virtue of the relationship each has with entities in its own domain."[83] Similarly, the ongoing social manufacture of metaphor results in new relationships of propinquity.

Metaphor may be seen as a device for reframing, for the decontextual-ization and recontextualization of messages. Like the message "This is play," it is itself a paradoxical message—in most cases a *catechresis*, a mistake on purpose. Like play, it has to do with a relationship between two semantic fields that simultaneously is and is not a traversal of domains.[84] Movements across contexts can be seen as movements towards abstraction. As opposed to generalization, which can be seen as an accumulation of similar contexts, abstraction has to do with hier-archical, "vertical," organization of messages and contexts. Abstraction is necessary for the use of metacommunication and the articulation of levels of logical types in any social interaction. Like most nonsense, a metaphor is not a violation of the rules of grammar, but rather, a violation of the rules of semantics. It is a procedure for the interaction of two domains that ordinarily (*ordinarily* being defined by members of the given situation) do not intersect. It is always an act in process, always involved in grouping, dismantling, and regrouping the semantic fields of social life. Because of its processural nature, we can have "dead metaphors." These metaphors are no longer what Dorothy Mack has called "fresh cuts" across semantic domains; rather, they serve as "short cuts" in social interaction.[85] Dead metaphors become part of the stock of knowledge at hand, the same stock of knowledge that is the necessary precondition for the construction of successful metaphors and for the detection of tautology and banality, irony, sarcasm, and parody.

As for "fresh cuts," the use of metaphor to present a novel way of seeing things, they are not used to smooth the flow of an interaction, nor are they as dependent upon context and common knowledge as short cuts are. When a metaphor is used as a "fresh cut" it opens up the field of interpretation, it creates a multiplicity of meanings. This is why a "substitution" view of metaphor is a fallacy—one cannot simply "plug in" a literal meaning to the metaphor's slot. The metaphor's equation of two disparate semantic domains creates what Mack has called "a whole range of possible shared attributes."[86] By abstraction, the metaphor presents another domain of meaning that is more than the sum of its component domains. Like fictions, metaphor involves the making of both "factual" and metacommunicative statements, yet it is neither. Neither is it true or false. Rather, it is subject to evaluation according to a set of evaluative procedures specific to its own domain. It presents a domain that is both "contrary to fact" and "another reality."[87] The way to "kill" a metaphor is to interpret it literally, to incorporate it into the stock of nonmetaphorical utterances and thus to substitute an everyday set of interpretive procedures for a metaphor-specific set of interpretive procedures.

Because metaphor has to do with the reorganization of a hierarchy of messages and contexts making up the semantic domains of the every-day lifeworld, every "fresh cut" will have a profound effect upon the social organization of experience. As reframing devices, metaphors are agents in forming the processural nature of social interactions. We may consider most social change to be a transformation from one "founda-tion metaphor" to another.[88] Similarly, an investigation into the social use of metaphor will be revealing not only for a study of the relation-ships between art and society, but also for an understanding of how transformations within the social process itself are enacted.[89] As Vološinov has pointed out, "A poet uses a metaphor in order to regroup values and not for the sake of a linguistic exercise."[90]

Earlier I suggested that nonsense results from a radical shift towards the metaphoric pole accompanied by a decontextualization of the utterance. Nonsense can be seen as an equation, an overlapping, of two or more disparate domains, the difference between these domains being a function of their use in the everyday lifeworld. In other words, non-sense can be seen as an activity that replicates the activities of both play and metaphor in that it has to do with common-sense relation-ships brought into a paradoxical is/is not status. But not all metaphor is nonsense. This is because metaphor is "rescued" from nonsense by contextualization. Thus in everyday life and the fictions of realism, which share a certain set of interpretive procedures directed towards situational contexts, a metaphorical expression like "He thought that the sun rose and set on her" makes perfect common sense. But in non-sense, the sun rising and setting on someone becomes nonsensically literal, so that the person is likely to get very hot or, at least, very tired from such a burden. In nonsense, metaphor "runs rampant" until there is wall-to-wall metaphor and thus wall-to-wall literalness. And metaphor, instead of having its causality rooted in everyday life situa-tions, becomes itself a kind of causality. Metaphors make "common sense" so long as they are taken as metaphors and contextualized as such. Once metaphors are removed from any possible context, they become part of a pure, metaphorical surface whose interpretive proce-dures are to some degree hermetic to that surface. The shift from the metaphorical to the literal typical of everyday life interactions is no longer possible. Once the sun begins to rise and set on someone's shoulders, other metaphorical, nonsensical contingencies result. This is the way in which nonsense is related to irony, which says that A is and is not equal to B at the same time that A is a false premise. Just as irony still depends upon an everyday life context for its "false premise" judgment of A, nonsense depends upon a common-sense domain of reality for its initial leap into a domain of the impossible context.

Once the impossible context is reached, the interpretive possibilities open up and nonsense, like metaphor, is characterized by a multiplicity of meanings. Constraints upon meaning can be viewed as contextual constraints. But nonsense, fettered mainly by its own ongoing, self-perpetuating context, becomes perhaps the most multiply-meaningful of fictions, while, at the same time, it becomes the least meaningful of fictions in everyday life terms.

The work of fictions and the work of play both involve: (1) a reframing of messages; (2) a manipulation of context that is a decontextualization and a recontextualization; (3) a set of procedures for interpretation that may or may not pertain to the everyday lifeworld; (4) metacommunication; (5) reflexivity (and therefore); (6) paradox; (7) representation; and (8) the "not really true" and/or the "not really here and now" —that is, a domain other than the everyday life domain. Both play and fictions are marked off from the everyday lifeworld, and this very marking off is a variety of metacommunication, a reclassification of the discourse being used. This reclassification implies a possibility of further manipulation, further reframing. The more clearly the metacommunication is marked, the more the transformation of the everyday lifeworld and the more "play-full" the discourse.[91]

Most work on play characterizes play by a set of features similar to those I discussed earlier as typifying any transition from one domain to another. Play is characterized by a particular leap from the world of everyday life, transforming its common-sense constraints upon invention and the boundaries of meaning. Play involves the construction of another space/time, another domain having its own procedures for interpretation. The transition to the "playground" is marked by a particular attention, a particular tension in consciousness that may be pleasurable. In all these characteristics, play overlaps with aesthetic activity. Susanna Millar has suggested that "a certain degree of choice, lack of constraint from conventional ways of handling objects, materials and ideas, is inherent in the concept of play. This is its main connexion with art and other forms of invention. Perhaps play is best used as an adverb: not as a name of a class of activities, nor as distinguished by the accompanying mood, but to describe how and under what conditions an action is performed."[92]

Many theories of play readily adapt themselves to a view of play as biologically functional, a view that says that play is a relief, a domain where attention can be focused on problems and adaptive alternatives can be safely "played out" without real life consequences. Similarly, what we may term a culturally functional view, the communications approach of Bateson, dissolves into a kind of biological functionalism as well, in that it sees play as an adaptive device, a device that develops the organism's capabilities of abstraction and reframing and thus helps it to "pull itself up by its boot straps." Brian Sutton-Smith's contention that "like universities, grammar schools, Head Start Programs, drama classes, art, music and poetry" games are schools in abstraction may be seen as adaptive in a similar way. According to Sutton-Smith, play and games allow us to use language and other skills outside of contexts where they can be supported by pointing or by the structure of the situation. In this way, humans begin to separate thought from common-sense contingencies and thereby to organize thought according to internal consistencies in thinking itself. This switch from a preoperational to an operational level of logic can be seen as a movement from *as is* thinking to *as if* thinking.[93] Like art forms, play confronts us with alternative conceptualizations—different in form, substance, arbitrariness, fictiveness, and temporality from other levels of living.[94] But the biological cannot be so easily separated from the cultural. It is no coincidence that the glorification of abstraction as an adaptive device takes place within a context where abstraction is valued as a mode of thinking in general, a mode appropriate to certain members at a certain point in social time.

Sutton-Smith's point again marks the role of play in permitting the detachability of contexts. Play involves a transition from the everyday lifeworld to another domain of reality—a transition from common-sense interpretive procedures to play-specific sets of interpretive procedures—and a movement that reorganizes the hierarchy of messages and contexts characteristic of everyday social interaction. In most play activities, the two major features of common-sense interpretive procedures, context and hierarchy, are transformed. All play involves a detachability of messages from their context of origin, the creation of a new play-specific space/time with its own rules of procedure, and a rearrangement of the hierarchical relationships characterizing common-sense discourse. While all fictions engage in these activities as well, nonsense may be seen as an exaggeration of these activities. More specifically, nonsense involves a transgression of common-sense interpretive procedures, a hermeticism in its establishment of another domain of reality, and—as we have seen in the case of nonsense and metaphor—not a simple rearrangement of the hierarchies of common-sense discourse, but a transgression of such hierarchies.

With these manipulations and transgressions, nonsense resembles the work of humor, where the notion of play takes on its shades of meaning as "free play" and "the play, or give" of something—its capacity to be stretched and manipulated. Earlier I discussed the "literalizing" of metaphor in nonsense. This process can be seen as the clash of two levels of abstraction, as an intertextual contradiction. Much humor derives from such intertextual contradictions, from the collision of two or more universes of discourse, and the humor of nonsense often comes from the contradictions that arise when the abstract and systematic nature of discourse is brought to the fore—nonsense is humor without a context as well as metaphor without a context.[95]

There are two methods by which humor can present an intertextual contradiction: On the one hand, humor can arise when difference is perceived between universes thought to be compatible. On the other hand, humor can result from similarity perceived between universes thought to be disparate. Puns, for example, are symptomatic of the first type of contradiction. While there is sameness on the aural level there is a splitting into difference on the semantic level.[96] An example of the second method of contradiction—the perception of similarity where there was thought to be difference—can be seen in the humor that depends upon an ongoing historical definition of the "not-human." In cultures where the other is perceived to be the animal, humor will result whenever men act like animals or animals act like men. It is interesting that Bergson's definition of humor as the mechanical encrusted on the living comes on the heels of the Industrial Revolution.

The structure of humor can be related to the structure of social interaction.[97] The child's early experience with humor is descriptive. It occurs without frame switching in ordinary discourse and derives its humor from something funny *in* the described event. The description itself is not funny outside of its content. Thus to a very young child, "Jenny fell down" may be uproariously funny. With early forms of speech play, the phonological component of language is most strongly stressed. This is already a move away from description and towards abstraction, towards attention to the message for its own sake. Language is used as language, and not simply as reference, and thus there is a reframing of discourse as performance, as "not common sense talk," as play. In genres such as riddles and other solicitational routines (like "Knock knock" jokes), there is a progression from description-based performances of the genre to complicated transformations of the generic frame itself. The developmental pattern is often seen to be one of increasing abstraction, of increasing skill with objectifying language. But the child has the ability to deal with metalanguage from the outset of his or her experience in categorizing discourse, and it may be more useful to think of these kinds of speech play as an array of more or less simultaneous possibilities rather than as a developmental pattern. Once the contexts of discourse can be specified, there is already a critique of discourse available to the child.

The objectification of language has to do with play with language.[98] As we move towards abstraction, we can begin to manipulate the conditions and contingencies of social interaction itself. This is the move from an intertextual level based upon common-sense interpretive procedures to the intertextual levels that pack alternative interpretive rules. Because the latter type of texts carry instructions for their own reading, they may be characterized as "ludic" texts, as texts bearing paradoxical messages regarding their own existence. Like play, they increasingly rely on metaphorical thought, and, often humorous, they reveal contradictions in the very processes of interpretation by which they are accomplished. In this they resemble "antilanguages," languages that M. K. Halliday has defined as no one's mother tongue, but that come into existence through reality-generating conversations that take their identity in contradiction to those of the everyday, and in most cases bourgeois, lifeworld. Antilanguages "create a reality which is inherently an alternative reality, one that is constructed precisely in order to function in alternation."[99]

In terms of the intertextual construct presented in this chapter, ludic genres can be characterized as any genres that involve a transgression of common-sense interpretive procedures either by presenting paradoxes of framing, or by juxtaposing two or more universes of discourse and thereby erasing a common-sense context. Certainly any of these procedures implies and necessitates the others, and each of them is a device for making nonsense out of the common-sense world. In "unpacking" the procedures for making nonsense, I will be concerned with such ludic genres, for the range of ludic genres at its most exaggerated, metaphorical, abstract, and systematic point may be characterized as nonsense. The "content" of nonsense will always shift as a result of the ongoing social process of making common sense. I will be concerned in the remainder of this essay with "how nonsense works," the interpretive procedures that members undertake and accomplish in reading and manufacturing the texts of nonsense.

It would seem to be possible to classify any genre in terms of "how it works." Certainly even realism is not a kind of effortless transparency of language, ready to be picked up like a pair of spectacles by a passer-by. Realism is a device that is accomplished in accordance with traditional techniques, with its own uses and functions by any group of members. Here we can return to the earlier distinction made between use and function. Consider this difference in the social use of myths and riddles: "Where myths prove the validity of land claims, the authority of social and cultural rules or the fitness of native conceptual classifications, riddles make a point of playing with conceptual borderlines and crossing them for the pleasure of showing that things are not quite so stable as they appear."[100] Ludic genres present a critique not only of conceptual classifications, but on the level of nonsense, of classification itself. This is the point where metaphor becomes the norm and is therefore literal again. In any of these forms—riddles, pranks, puns, jokes— multiple levels of order are played with, and are played against each other. And, as Bateson has pointed out, such play results in highlighting the paradoxes of communication in general, paradoxes that, once somewhere, seem to be everywhere. William Fry has contended that through such play we become aware of "levels of living" and keep from being locked into a single reality, the reality of the everyday lifeworld, as if it were a system that never changed:

As one is progressing through any particular portion of one's life, one is involved, on one level, in the explicit surface program. One is also involved, on many other levels, in the many conscious and unconscious programs that are implicit in the so-called "object" or "thing"—i.e. the "ongoing life process." It is as if we all lead many different lives at the same time, all on different levels of abstraction one from the other, and all interrelated comments on each other.[101]

His point emphasizes the intertextual nature of these levels of living. Each particular level will comment on, critique, and transform the other levels.

While in the first part of this essay I have focused on the dependence of nonsense upon common sense, it will become apparent as the discussion continues that common sense is dependent upon other domains of reality for its ongoing nature. This borrowing takes place not only because of the interpenetration of art and society on an abstract level, but also because the flow of experience in our everyday lives is continually reframed, reaccomplished, transgressed, and reified as we use the generic forms available to us at any given point in social time. Situations are turned into situation jokes, personal experiences become instances of a proverb or even a legend, pranks are transformed into narrative humor, riddles into jokes, and novels into parodies. The rules for conceiving reality are constantly in process. Once other levels of living become readily incorporated into the everyday lifeworld, once they are taken for granted, they become, so to speak, "dead metaphors." In this is the profound ring of Jacques Ehrmann's point that "the distinguishing characteristic of reality is that it is played."[102]

NOTES

1. Jean Paulhan, *La preuve par l'étymologie* (Paris: Éditions de Minuit, 1953), p. 12. Quoted in Fredric Jameson, *The Prison-House of Language: A Critical Account of Structuralism and Russian Formalism* (Princeton, N.J.: Princeton University Press, 1972), p. 6. See also Pierre Guirard, *L'Étymologie* (Paris: Presses Universitaires de France, 1972), p. 5: "Le term a été quelquefois pris dans son acception élargie par les rhéteurs antiques et les philosophes médiévaux. Étymologie signifie alors de la vérité; c'est un synonyme de philosophie."
2. Ludwig Wittgenstein, *The Philosophical Investigations,* trans. G.E.M. Anscombe (New York: Macmillan, 1953), p. 139e.
3. Definitions are taken from *The Compact Edition of the Oxford English Dictionary* (New York: Oxford University Press, 1971).
4. Eric Partridge, ed., *A Dictionary of Slang and Unconventional English,* 7th ed. (New York: Macmillan, 1970).

5. Here we might consider M. K. Halliday's notion of "anti-language" ("Anti-language," *American Anthropologist* 78 [1976]: 170–83). I am using *negative language* at this point because it seems that nonsense is not "against" language in the sense in which Halliday uses this term—as the language of an antisociety. Indeed, nonsense may be the only pure language. But nonsense does involve a negation of the systems of meaning that language is used to convey.

6. Alan Merriam, *The Anthropology of Music* (Chicago: Northwestern University Press, 1964), p. 210.

7. Richard Hilbert, "Approaching Reason's Edge: 'Nonsense As the Final Solution to the Problem of Meaning,'" *Sociological Inquiry* 47 (1977): 26.

8. Alfred Schutz, *Collected Papers*, 3 vols. (The Hague: Mouton, 1964), 1:5–13.

9. Ibid., 1:6.

10. See Florian Znaniecki, *The Method of Sociology* (New York: Farrar and Rinehart, 1934).

11. Schutz, *Collected Papers*, 3:xxix.

12. However, these procedures are specific to investigatory discourse. See Harold Garfinkle, "The Rational Properties of Scientific and Common Sense Activities," *Studies in Ethnomethodology*, ed. Harold Garfinkle (Englewood Cliffs, N.J.: Prentice-Hall, 1967), pp. 262–83, for a study of the lack of an absolute "fit" between common-sense and scientific rationalities.

13. Jack Douglas, *Understanding Everyday Life* (Chicago: Aldine, 1970), p. 15.

14. See Hilbert, "Approaching Reason's Edge," p. 26. This point has also been made by Melvin Pollner, "Sociological and Common Sense Models of the Labelling Process," *Ethnomethodology*, ed. Roy Turner (London: Penguin Books, 1971), pp. 27–40, and by the essays in Douglas, *Understanding Everyday Life*.

15. The discussion that follows in part 1 obviously owes a tremendous debt to Schutz's philosophy and, indeed, may be seen as a rereading of his work.

16. This is a fundamental difference between the procedures of phenomenological investigation and the procedures for acting in everyday life. Investigation is involved in *not* taking things for granted—in the Russian Formalists' terms, in "making strange."

17. See Garfinkle, *Studies in Ethnomethodology*, pp. 262–83.

18. This notion was most fully elaborated by Charles S. Peirce: "An index is a sign or representation which refers to its object not so much because of any similarity or analogy with it, nor because it is associated with general characters which that object happens to possess, as because it is in dynamical (including spatial) connection both with the individual object, on the one hand, and with the senses or memory of the person for whom it serves as a sign, on the other hand. . . . Psychologically, the action of indices depends upon association by contiguity and not upon association by resemblance or upon intellectual operations" (*Philosophical Writings of Peirce*, ed. Justus Buchler [New York: Dover, 1955], pp. 107–8).

19. See Aaron Gurwitsch's introduction to Schutz, *Collected Papers*, 3:xx.

20. Wittgenstein, *The Philosophical Investigations* (Oxford: Oxford University Press, 1958), p. 20.

21. For examples of these theories, see: J. L. Austin, *How to Do Things with Words* (New York: Oxford University Press, 1962); John Searle, *Speech Acts: An Essay in the Philosophy of Language* (Cambridge: At the University Press, 1969); Dell Hymes, *Foundations in Sociolinguistics* (Philadelphia: University of Pennsylvania Press, 1974).

22. Jacques Derrida, "Signature, Event, Context," trans. Tzvetan Bogdanovich (Paper given at the Congrès International des Sociétés de philosophie de langue français, Montréal, August 1971).

23. Garfinkle, *Studies in Ethnomethodology*, p. 10.

24. Harold Garfinkle, "Remarks on Ethnomethodology," *Directions in Sociolinguistics*, ed. John Gumperz and Dell Hymes (New York: Holt, Rinehart, Winston, 1972), p. 316.

25. Ibid., p. 320.

26. For a further discussion of common sense and scientific methods, see Henry Elliot, "Similarities and Differences between Science and Common Sense" in Turner, *Ethnomethodology*, pp. 21–26.

27. See Don Zimmerman and Melvin Pollner, "The Everyday World As a Phenomenon" in Douglas, *Everyday Life*, p. 99.

28. V. N. Vološinov, *Freudianism: A Marxist Critique*, trans. I. R. Titunik (New York: Academic Press, 1976), p. 100.

29. Theodor Adorno, "Society," *Salmagundi* 10–11 (1969–1970): 140–41.

30. Hans George Gadamer, "The Historicity of Understanding," *Critical Sociology*, ed. Paul Connerton (New York: Penguin Books, 1976), p. 120.

31. I use *could not happen* to articulate the nonsense context from those "not-real" domains where things should have happened, might have happened, could have happened, can only happen in the future, should happen, might happen, could happen, etc.

32. Vološinov, *Freudianism*, pp. 114–15, makes this point, as do Peter Berger and Thomas Luckmann in *The Social Construction of Reality* (Garden City, N.Y.: Anchor Books, 1967), p. 40.

33. This point is expanded upon in part 2 of this essay.

34. Paul Ricoeur, "The Model of the Text: Meaningful Action Considered As Text," *New Literary History* 5 (1973): 91–117. See also James Peacock, "Society as Narrative," *Forms of Symbolic Action*, Proceedings of the Annual Spring Meeting of the American Ethnological Society, ed. Robert F. Spencer (Seattle: University of Washington Press, 1969), p. 174: "A society's narrative forms often distill in strikingly clear and condensed fashion the patterns and principles that underlie the dramatic facets of its wider processes." Clifford Geertz suggests that "there are three characteristics of ethnographic description: it is interpretive, what it is interpretive of is the flow of social discourse, and the interpreting involved consists in trying to rescue the 'said' of such discourse from its perishing occasions and fix it in perusable terms," *The Interpretation of Cultures* (New York: Basic Books, 1973), p. 20.

35. Schutz, *Collected Papers*, 1:10.

36. Ibid., 1:5.

37. William James, *Principles of Psychology*, 2 vols. (New York: Dover, 1950), 2:283–324.

38. Schutz, *Collected Papers*, 1:207–39.

39. George Boole, *An Investigation of the Laws of Thought, On Which Are Founded the Mathematical Theories of Logic and Probability* (London: Walton and Maberly, 1854).

40. W. M. Urban, *Language and Reality* (London: G. Allen and Unwin, 1939), p. 203.

41. Schutz suggests that "this finiteness implies that there is no possibility of referring one of the provinces to the other by introducing a formula of transformation" (*Collected Papers*, 1:232). But later on the same page he says, "All other provinces of meaning may be considered its [the everyday lifeworld's] modifications."

42. Dell Hymes has pointed out to me that anthropologists, when faced with "inexplicable" aspects of culture, will often characterize such inexplicable aspects as being nonsensical. This is an academic example of the strategy that Bergson discusses.

43. Schutz, *Collected Papers*, 1:230.

44. Garfinkle, *Studies in Ethnomethodology*, p. 270.

45. Ibid., p. 283. Husserl made the same point in his essay "The Possibility of Cognition": "If we immerse ourselves in the sciences of the natural sort, we find everything clear and comprehensible to the extent to which they have developed into exact sciences. We are certain that we are in possession of objective truth, based upon reliable methods of reaching [objective] reality. But whenever we reflect we

43 / MAKING COMMON SENSE

fall into errors and confusion. We become entangled in patent difficulties and even self-contradictions. We are in constant danger of becoming skeptics, or still worse, we are in danger of falling into any one of a number of skepticisms all of which have, sad to say, one and the same characteristic—absurdity" (reprinted in *Rules and Meanings*, ed. Mary Douglas [Middlesex: Penguin Books, 1977], p. 200).

46. See Thomas Kuhn, *The Structure of Scientific Revolutions* (Chicago: University of Chicago Press, 1962); and Michel Foucault, *The Order of Things* (New York: Random House, 1970).

47. Vološinov, *Freudianism*, p. 115.

48. Julia Kristeva, *Sēmiōtikē: Recherches pour une sémanalyse* (Paris: Éditions du Seuil, 1969), p. 215.

49. This is why, as Roland Barthes has so often pointed out, the nineteenth-century novel's minute and "unmotivated" descriptions of everyday life have little more to say than "We are the real." See "L'Effet de Réel," *Communications* 11 (1968): 84–89, and *S/Z*, trans. Richard Miller (New York: Hill and Wang, 1974). Michel Butor has suggested that the copious description of objects points to the idea of the text itself as object (*Inventory*, trans. Richard Howard [New York: Simon and Schuster, 1961], p. 23).

50. Florenskij quoted in Boris Uspensky, *The Poetics of Composition*, trans. V. Zavarin and S. Wittig (Berkeley: University of California Press, 1973), p. 139.

51. Vološinov, *Freudianism*, p. 113.

52. I return to a specific discussion of these fictions in part 2.

53. Segal and Senokosov quoted in Uspensky, *Poetics of Composition*, p. xiv.

54. Uspensky, *Poetics of Composition*, p. 137.

55. Ibid., p. 167.

56. This is the ending to Old Mourteen's story in John Synge, *The Aran Islanders* (Boston: Brice Humphries, 1911), p. 133.

57. Uspensky, *Poetics of Composition*, p. 151–54.

58. Ibid., pp. 162–63.

59. Schutz, *Collected Papers*, 3:xiv.

60. Erving Goffman, *Frame Analysis: An Essay on the Organization of Experience* (New York: Harper and Row, 1974), pp. 10–11.

61. Ibid., pp. 560–61.

62. Or only television watchers, moviegoers, children, and the kinds of people who read pornography are likely to be so moved.

63. See Goffman, *Frame Analysis*, p. 562.

64. Boris Tomaševsky, "Literature and Biography," *Readings in Russian Poetics*, ed. Ladislav Matejka and Krystyna Pomorska (Cambridge, Mass.: MIT Press, 1971), pp. 47–55.

65. Samuel Weber has brought this criticism to Saussurean linguistics in "Saussure and the Apparition of Language: The Critical Perspective," *MLN* 91 (1976): 913–39, as has Derrida before him in *Of Grammatology*, trans. G. Spivak (Baltimore: Johns Hopkins University Press, 1974).

66. Hence Dell Hymes's mnemonic "SPEAKING" in Gumperz and Hymes, *Sociolinguistics*, p. 65.

67. Berger and Luckmann, *Reality*, p. 38.

68. "[Listeners to tongue speaking] fit the audiosignal into a previously prepared category, namely language," argues Felicitas D. Goodman, *Speaking in Tongues: A Cross-Cultural Study of Glossolalia* (Chicago: University of Chicago Press, 1972), p. 151.

69. This is not surprising in light of the more general point made before that the real is largely an outcome of common-sense interpretive procedures.

70. See Gregory Bateson and Jurgen Ruesch, eds., *Communication: The Social Matrix of Psychology* (New York: Norton, 1968).

71. Gregory Bateson, *Steps to an Ecology of Mind* (New York: Ballantine, 1972), p. 179. A comment on this paradox is made in Werner Herzog's film, "Jeder für Sich und Gott gegen Alle," about the Kaspar Hauser legend. When Kaspar Hauser is

presented with an Epimenides paradox and allowed one question in order to solve it, rather than employ a double negative solution, he says "I would ask him if he were a tree frog."

72. Bertrand Russell and A. N. Whitehead, *Principia Mathematica* (Cambridge: At the University Press, 1910). William Fry relates Russell's and Whitehead's theory to Bateson's work in *Sweet Madness: A Study of Humor* (Palo Alto, Calif.: Pacific Books, 1963), pp. 119-36.

73. Rosalie Colie, *Paradoxica Epidemica: The Renaissance Tradition of Paradox* (Princeton, N.J.: Princeton University Press, 1966), pp. 6-7.

74. Quoted in Fry, *Sweet Madness*, p. 131.

75. Bateson, *Ecology of Mind*, p. 103.

76. Colie, *Paradoxica Epidemica*, pp. 10-11.

77. Gregory Bateson, "The Message 'This is Play,'" *Conferences on Group Processes*, ed. Bertram Schaffner (New York: Columbia University Press, 1955), p. 216.

78. Bateson, *Ecology of Mind*, p. 193.

79. Sylvano Arieti, *Interpretation of Schizophrenia* (New York: Robert Brunner, 1955), p. 194. Arieti's study is bogged down, however, by Levy-Bruhlian assumptions about "paleological" and "primitive" thought, and certainly does not have the insightfulness of Bateson's communication theory approach.

80. Roman Jakobson, "Two Aspects of Language and Two Fundamental Types of Disturbance," *Fundamentals of Language*, ed. Roman Jakobson and Morris Halle (The Hague: Mouton, 1956), pp. 67-96.

81. Ibid., p. 67.

82. Ibid., p. 78.

83. Peter Seitel, "Proverbs and the Structure of Metaphor among the Haya of Tanzania" (Ph.D. diss., University of Pennsylvania, 1971), p. 54.

84. I. A. Richards, *The Philosophy of Rhetoric* (Oxford: Oxford University Press, 1936), p. 94. Richards was an early champion of an "interaction" view of metaphor. Metaphor is not simply a substitution of a decorative meaning for a literal meaning. Rather, metaphor is the result of an interaction between two separate domains.

85. Dorothy Mack, "Metaphoring as Speech Act: Some Happiness Conditions for Implicit Similes and Simple Metaphors," *Poetics* 4 (1975): 221-56.

86. Ibid., p. 236.

87. For an argument that art *is* metaphor, see Michael Polyani, *Meaning* (Chicago: University of Chicago Press, 1974).

88. See also Robert Nisbet, *Social Change and History: Aspects of the Western Theory of Development* (London: Oxford University Press, 1968).

89. See, for example, David Sapir and J. Christopher Crocker, eds., *The Social Use of Metaphor* (Philadelphia: University of Pennsylvania Press, 1977); Victor Turner, *Dramas, Fields, and Metaphors* (Ithaca, N.Y.: Cornell University Press, 1974); James Fernandez, "The Mission of Metaphor in Expressive Culture," *Current Anthropology* 5 (1974): 119-45; and idem, "Persuasions and Performances: Of the Beast in Every Body . . . and the Metaphors of Everyman," *Myth, Symbol, and Culture*, ed. Clifford Geertz (New York: Norton, 1971), pp. 39-60.

90. Vološinov, *Freudianism*, p. 116.

91. The relationship between art and play has long held a fascination for aestheticians. Friedrich von Schiller's pronouncement in his *Aesthetic Letters*, "Declare it once and for all, Man plays only when he is in the full sense of the word a man, and he is only wholly Man when he is playing," was recast in the nineteenth century by anthropologists, biologists, and aestheticians who wanted to find some function for the seemingly purposeless activities of art and play. Herbert Spencer presented a "surplus energy" theory, contending that play allowed the higher organisms to get rid of excessive energy. To a certain extent, Darwin also held to this theory. At the turn of the century, G. S. Hall contended that in the course of their development humans pass through the same evolutionary stages as those that appear in the history of evolution. Thus the content of children's play could be

correlated to successive stages in the evolutionary process. In *The Play of Animals* (1896) and *The Play of Man* (1899), the German philosopher Karl Groos argued that the biological function of play was to serve as a practice ground for survival. Morse Peckham's *Man's Rage for Chaos* (New York: Schocken, 1967) may be seen as a modern manifestation of Groos's position. Freud's notion of play as projection and sublimation may also be seen as a "mastery" theory, since Freud felt that play was a field where potential or actual situations were projected and controlled. The work of Johann Huizinga on play, first appearing as lectures in the 1930s, in published form in the early 1940s, and in English translation as *Homo Ludens: A Study of the Play Element in Culture* (Boston: Beacon Press, 1955), was an attempt to expand upon Schiller's notion of play as necessary for the development of culture. Although Huizinga's notion of play is largely agonistic, he regarded play as a cultural phenomenon with cultural functions rather than as a biological phenomenon. Early studies by D. E. Berlyne were concerned with the role play took in the exploration of novelty. His ideas about play as a process involving arousal, tension, and conflict resolution were put forth in *Conflict, Arousal and Curiosity* (New York: McGraw Hill, 1960). His theories have been further developed in Hans and Shulamith Kreitler, *Psychology of the Arts* (Durham, N.C.: Duke University Press, 1972). Jean Piaget sorted out play and imitation as two contrasting processes in order to link them to his notions of assimilation and accommodation. Play, according to Piaget, is associated with assimilation, the process by which an organism manipulates incoming information to match existing patterns. Imitation is associated with accommodation, the process by which the organism adapts its existing patterns to new information. See *Play, Dreams, and Imitation in Childhood* (New York: Norton, 1962). For Piaget, play is not an agent of change. Rather, it stabilizes novelty within a grid of existing categories. Brian Sutton-Smith has criticized the Piagetian notion of play, saying that it denies play any constitutive role in thought and assumes a reality prior to play, presenting thereby a "copyist epistemology" ("Piaget on Play: A Critique," *Child's Play*, ed. R. Herron and B. Sutton-Smith [New York: John Wiley, 1971], pp. 326–36).

92. Susanna Millar, *The Psychology of Play* (Baltimore: Penguin Books, 1969), p. 21.

93. Brian Sutton-Smith, "The Game As a School of Abstraction," *The Folkgames of Children*, ed. B. Sutton-Smith (Austin: University of Texas Press, 1972), pp. 442–48.

94. Kreitler, *Psychology of the Arts*, p. 28.

95. For useful reviews of humor theories, see D. E. Berlyne, "Laughter, Humor and Play," *Handbook of Social Psychology*, 5 vols., ed. G. Lindzey and E. Aronson (Reading, Mass.: Addison-Wesley, 1969), 3:795–852, and Patricia Keith-Spiegel, "Early Conceptions of Humor: Varieties and Issues," *The Psychology of Humor*, ed. J. Goldstein and P. McGhee (New York: Academic Press, 1972), pp. 4–34.

96. G. B. Milner presents a lively analysis of puns in "Homo Ridens," *Semiotica* 5 (1972): 17.

97. Conclusions in this section come from Martha Wolfenstein, *Children's Humor: A Psychological Analysis* (Glencoe, Ill.: Free Press, 1954); Barbara Kirshenblatt-Gimblett and Mary Sanches, "Children's Traditional Speech Play and Child Language," *Speech Play: Research and Resources for the Study of Linguistic Creativity*, ed. B. Kirshenblatt-Gimblett (Philadelphia: University of Pennsylvania Press, 1976), pp. 65–110; John McDowell, "Riddling and Enculturation: A Glance at the Cerebral Child," *Working Papers in Sociolinguistics*, no. 36 (Austin, Tex.: Southwest Educational Development Laboratory, July 1976); Richard Bauman, "The Development of Competence in the Use of Solicitational Routines: Children's Folklore and Informal Learning," *Working Papers in Sociolinguistics*, no. 34 (Austin, Tex.: Southwest Educational Development Laboratory, May 1976); and Catherine Garvey, "Some Properties of Social Play," *Play, Its Role in Development and Evolution*, ed. J. Bruner, A. Jolly, and K. Sylva (Middlesex: Penguin Books, 1976), pp. 570–83.

98. McDowell, "Riddling and Enculturation," p. 12.
99. Halliday, "Anti-Language," p. 575.
100. Elli Köngas-Maranda, "Riddles and Riddling," *Journal of American Folklore* 89 (1976): 131.
101. Fry, *Sweet Madness*, p. 53.
102. Jacques Ehrmann, *"Homo Ludens* Revisited," *Game, Play, Literature,* ed. Jacques Ehrmann, *Yale French Studies* 41 (1968): 56.

2 · some operations and affinities

The first chapter of this essay was concerned with assumptions, particularly with assumptions of common sense that are constitutive of, and emergent in, the everyday lifeworld. I have not been concerned with answering the question "What is common sense?" Rather, I have been concerned with analyzing "how common sense works." Briefly, I concluded that common sense is used to determine the parameters of everyday situations, including their functions and outcomes. Members bring to these situations an intersubjective tradition, and the aspects of this tradition that will be employed will depend upon the biographical situations of those involved and the particular purpose at hand. Common-sense activities are characterized by direction and hierarchy. They "get somewhere," as opposed to those activities that "are getting nowhere." And the shape of common-sense events will be determined by a mutually held idea of what it means for things to "work out well."

Because of the interpretive nature of common-sense activities, I have spoken of these everyday situations as texts. And because of the pervasiveness of everyday life, I have suggested that these texts manufactured through common-sense procedures serve as a basis for the generation of other texts at the same time that they are continually juxtaposed with and modified by such other texts. Two methods for accomplishing such modifications are play and metaphor, both of which are activities that produce texts that stand in a paradoxical relationship to the texts of common sense. I have emphasized the ways in which play and metaphor function as methods for criticism and innovation. The intertextual construct I have outlined moves from realism to myth to irony to forms of metafiction in an attempt to array the texts of fiction in increasing mimetic distance from the text of "reality." Because the construct recoups a common-sense model, it is itself suspect as an isomorphic procedure, a procedure that reifies the reality of the everyday, common-sense lifeworld. However, the concept of intertextuality can be employed without ascribing any intrinsic "reality" to any of its dimensions.

Intertextuality is considered here as a relationship between universes of discourse. Each universe of discourse, through tradition, has developed a universe-specific "set" towards interpretation, towards those interpretive procedures that allow us to manufacture, engage in, and transform respective domains of meaning. This "set" may call for us to suspend or bring forth disbelief or belief, to suppress or call upon the interpretive procedures characteristic of any other universe of discourse. The intertextual nature of universes of discourse enables us to move from one domain to another. These processes are "inter" in the sense of interaction. They do not "stand outside" or "between" their subjects so much as they are emergent in their subjects. The model here is metacommunication, a gesture that is both reflexive and transforming. These processes are mutual (although not necessarily reciprocal) in the sense that the transformation of one domain of meaning will have consequence for other domains of meaning. The ongoingness of tradition—of social process—makes a "finite" province of meaning impossible, for the boundaries of universes of discourse are constantly merging into one another and reemerging as transformed fields of meaning. And with the accumulation of experience with "texts" through tradition, interpretive procedures themselves are modified and transformed. By emphasizing the "textual" I have hoped to emphasize the interpreted, the emergent, the processive, nature of our experience in making meaning.

I have stressed the point that social life itself is a textual phenomenon, a phenomenon emergent in members' interpretive activities. By saying this, I am refusing the privileged position that society has held previously in any cause-effect relationship with other forms of discourse. Society cannot be assumed to be "natural," a base from which all discourse develops as a mirror image, nor can it be assumed to be a priori to other forms of discourse. Just as traditional functionalism developed as an "explanatory" method after a long period of frustration with the problem of origins, so its model of society is one that assumes a coherent presence, a stability lying "behind" social life that fills the epistemological gap caused by the problem of origins.

The model of social process here is one whose locus is the situation and the interpretive acts of members used in defining the parameters and outcomes of situations. The situation is seen as a textual phenomenon because it "comes to be" through interpretive activities. The analogy with what heretofore have been characterized as more formal types of discourse, "texts" in ordinary language's use of the term, is more than metaphorical. The analogy being made here states that just as any oral or written text will come into existence through the interpretive performance of members, so is any social situation contingent upon members' interpretive performance. Furthermore, the range of interpretive procedures used with any text will be constrained, modified, or "loosened up" by members' past experiences with any other form of textuality. Intertextuality is thus a characteristic of our experience throughout social life.

There is no privileged position with regard to interpretive procedures; there is only an assumption of consensus that enables members to go on.[1] And it may be that this consensus is assumed through a pattern of acknowledged misunderstandings. If we agree about what a mistake is, we can begin to agree about what is not a mistake. The force of past experience, its constraints and consensuses, should not be underestimated. Particularly, the hierarchy of relationships making up the statuses of members will help to determine the interpretation of the situation. So long as common sense remains pervasive, uninterrupted, it will have the force of a world view. Goldmann has suggested that

> the distinction between ideologies and world views might be based precisely on the partial—and for that very reason—distorting character of the former and the total character of the latter. At least for medieval and modern society that would allow us to link world views to social classes so long as they still possess an ideal bearing on the totality of the human community; and to link ideologies to all other social groups, and to social classes in decline, when they no longer act except to defend, without much faith or confidence, privileges and acquired positions.[2]

Those aspects of common sense that may be manipulated through nonsense often intersect with the set of aspects of common sense that are in a position to be made suspect. Particularly vulnerable are hierarchical relationships between members; hence the "fall of the mighty" found in much humor. Whatever is available to the manipulations of nonsense is emphasized as the cultural, the learned, the impermanent and transformable. What remains unavailable to nonsense remains as world view, seamless, beyond consciousness and reflexivity. Nonsense operates by means of a split in consciousness, a split characterizing any act of metacommunication. The reflexivity of nonsense breaks open the pervasiveness of common sense. The transformed aspects of common sense are "brought to light," made relative to one another or to other domains of reality. In this way their ideological nature—their position as "mere opinion"—is foregrounded. While realism takes part in the ideology of common sense, attaching itself metonymically and smoothing over the scene of attachment, nonsense bares the ideological nature of common sense, showing common sense's precarious situation—rooted in culture and not in nature. Common sense, which throughout everyday life is assumed to be something natural, given, and universal and thereby characteristic of a pervasive world view, becomes, when juxtaposed through nonsense with alternative conceptions of order, an only partial reality, an ideology.

Nonsense, with its embracing of play and paradox, is a critical activity. To say this, one cannot consider the relationships between types of discourse to be stable across an array of generic forms. Rather, the entire range of genres available to members at any given point of time will constitute a repertoire of interpretive procedures that may be used in accomplishing the text of the particular situation. The range of genres available to such a set of members is a complex system by which those members define the boundaries of experience[3] and structure the reality-generating discourse of social life. The point has been succinctly put by Raymond Williams:

> My own view is that we have been wrong in taking communication as secondary. Many people seem to assume as a matter of course that there is first reality and then, second, communication about it. We degrade art and learning by supposing that they are always second-hand activities; that there is life, and then, afterwards there are these accounts of it. . . . What we call society is not only a network of political and economic arrangements, but also a process of learning and communication.[4]

Nonsense, play, and paradox, as activities that discourse on the nature of discourse, are built into the generic system as methods for innovation and evaluation. These activities offer a critique not only of the texts of common sense, but of the influence of common sense upon other forms of discourse such as proverb, myth, and the prose narratives of realism. As nonsense activities become more and more metacommunicative, their critique becomes directed towards increasingly abstract interpretive procedures. That is, they come to critique the process of interpretation itself. As Bateson suggested in an essay on primitive art, "The fact of conformity or nonconformity (or indeed any other relationship) between parts of a patterned whole may itself be informative as part of some still larger whole."[5]

In this essay, an exploration of the conformity or nonconformity of the procedures used in making fictions will be informative of the relationships between the interpretive procedures characterizing fictions and the interpretive procedures characterizing everyday life. Folklorists have long been concerned with the relationship between fictions and social life, and here I am rephrasing and reevaluating that concern.[6] Previous work has implied that there may exist a unique relationship between *all* fictive forms and *all* social process, but I am suggesting that the work of any given genre will accomplish genre-specific ends. Furthermore, I am suggesting that genres that appear to share the same level of the intertextual construct—genres that stand at the same distance from everyday "reality"—will also share a set of operations by which they employ everyday reality.

From what we know about nonsense—its contingent and paradoxical relationship to common sense, its potential as a critical device—the relationship between types of discourse cannot be assumed to be either reifying or stable, but rather is subject to the purposes and past experience of members. Up until this point I have avoided defining nonsense, choosing to concentrate instead on the nature of common sense and those types of discourse that are "not common sense." While past work on nonsense has focused on what is properly called "nonsense literature," this essay is concerned with *any activity that produces "not sense."* If definitions are "in order," this will have to do. Any further definition is methodologically impossible for two reasons: first, the nature of nonsense will always be contingent upon the nature of its corresponding common sense, and since such common sense is always emergent in social processes (including nonsense activities), the category "nonsense" will never have a stable content; and second, the forms of nonsense will always be determined by the generic system available to the given set of members. Thus riddles may or may not be nonsense, novels may or may not be nonsense, and so on, according to members' ongoing conventions of discourse.

An investigation of particular operations by which nonsense is created is the subject of the next part of this essay. I have chosen five operations or activities used in making nonsense and I have chosen examples of these activities from everyday life and from a wide range of generic forms, including children's folklore, the "nonsense literature" of the nineteenth century, and the "modernist" tradition in literature. My purpose has not been to edify any of these types of discourse, but rather to demonstrate the interpretive procedures their readers engage in, procedures for making nonsense out of common sense. The readers who engage in these interpretive procedures are assumed to share a particular tradition that envelops both oral and written forms. These interpretive procedures are common to members across a variety of genres. I am assuming that those who share interpretive strategies for "true stories" and realism will share interpretive strategies for riddles and metafictions. Again, the focus is on how we go about "making things work," how meaning is assembled from a set of common elements and then disassembled and reassembled.

The idea of a "nonsense tradition" in folklore and literature—a chain of relationships between their respective communities—is easy enough to demonstrate.[7] Nursery rhymes like "The Queen of Hearts," "Tweedledum and Tweedledee," "Humpty Dumpty," "The Lion and the Unicorn," "Here We Go 'Round the Mulberry Bush," and "How Many Miles to Babylon," among others, appear in Lewis Carroll's *Alice in Wonderland, Through the Looking Glass*, and the *Sylvie and Bruno* books. Philippe Soupault, Robert Desnos, Raymond Queneau, and Claude Roy were all interested in traditional children's rhymes, as was James Joyce, who wrote in a letter to Harriet Shaw Weaver on 4 March

1931 that among the texts he was appropriating for *Finnegans Wake* were "dozens of German, French, English and Italian counting out rhymes."[8] Louis Aragon attempted a translation of *The Hunting of the Snark*, and André Breton included Carroll in his 1939 *Anthologie de l'humour noir.* Joyce's debt to Carroll takes up a full chapter in James Atherton's *The Books at the Wake.*[9] Iona and Peter Opie have identified forty-six traditional nursery and street rhymes in *Ulysses*,[10] and Mabel Worthington found sixty-eight nursery rhymes in *Finnegans Wake.*[11] Antonin Artaud tried to translate Carroll's "Jabberwocky," and Nabokov is the Russian translator of *Alice in Wonderland*. In a recent interview, Julio Cortázar said, in answer to the question "What impact has surrealism had on you?":

A decisive and tremendous impact, by way of Antonin Artaud, René Creval and Aragon, not to mention the infinite surrealistic *cronopios avant la lettre* like Lichtenberg, Alfred Jarry, and Lewis Carroll. . . . Federico Garcia Lorca (I am quoting from memory) defined himself as "a wounded pulse that *stalks* things from the other side." . . . That other side of things, those soft clocks in the time of man, those stone clouds of Magritte, those nude girls in the railroad stations of Paul Delvaux—and the Snark, don't forget the Snark that turned in the end to be a Boojum; there you have a synthesis of the attitude that leads me to write within a perspective of total fracturing of what is conventional, what is *fixed*, always looking for certain doors and, above all, certain exits.[12]

These affinities of intertextuality are not surprising, for anyone setting out to transform common sense by means of fictions will have a repertoire of interpretive procedures common to members sharing that domain of "common sense." Where there is a common sense, there will be a common nonsense. But what is of concern here is not external correlations, the correlations of literary history just inventoried. Our concern is with an investigation into the processes of interpretation that are common to a variety of verbal forms. To understand the relationships between varieties of such forms rather than particular instances of the use of such forms, one must ask questions about how interpretation works rather than questions regarding the external history of interpretations. In looking at interpretive procedures I have not been seeking a taxonomy or conclusive set of such procedures. Such a taxonomy would be impossible by virtue of the ongoing nature of common sense and the interpretive procedures that are themselves emergent in common-sense activities. The five nonsense operations I have looked at are all caught up in each other, caught up in a common sense that forces them to merge and emerge at various points in social time. My purpose in focusing upon a particular array of interpretive procedures has been to discover further relationships among dimensions of intertextuality—relationships that appear not only between intertextual levels, but between the interpretive procedures used in creating such relationships themselves.

NOTES

1. David Lewis's work on convention contends that we size up situations and then act in accordance with that sizing up, continuing until something goes wrong and we must reevaluate the situation before we can proceed. What is important is not the particular convention, but the evaluation, the sizing up, the agreement between members that allows the particular convention to proceed, as well as the idea of convention in general. See *Convention: A Philosophical Study* (Cambridge: Harvard University Press, 1969).

2. Lucien Goldmann, *The Human Sciences and Philosophy* (London: Cape Editions, 1973), p. 103.

3. See Dan Ben-Amos, *Folklore Genres* (Austin: University of Texas Press, 1974) for a discussion of the concept of genre and a distinction made between "analytical categories and ethnic genres," and Roger Abrahams, "The Complex Relations of Simple Forms," *Genre* 2 (1969): 104–28.

4. Raymond Williams, *Communications* (Middlesex: Penguin Books, 1962), p. 19.

5. Bateson, *Ecology of Mind*, p. 132.

6. The positions that this concern has taken include the Boasian notion of myth as a mirror for culture and Malinowski's idea that myth serves as a charter for society. Boas's students who developed the culture and personality school of anthropology saw folklore as a mechanism for repression and compensation. William Bascom suggested in "The Four Functions of Folklore," *Journal of American Folklore* 67 (1954): 333–49, that folklore serves the functions of escape, validation, education, and social control. Recent arguments regarding the functions of folklore have been conducted in the pages of the *Journal of American Folklore* by Elliott Oring and Alf Walle: Elliott Oring, "Three Functions of Folklore: Traditional Functionalism as Explanation in Folkloristics," *Journal of American Folklore* 80 (1976): 67–80, and "Notes" by Elliott Oring and Alf Walle in *Journal of American Folklore* 90 (1977): 68–77.

7. See Elizabeth Sewell, *The Field of Nonsense* (London: Chatto and Windus, 1952), for the classic study of nonsense in the works of Carroll and Lear, and her article "Lewis Carroll and T. S. Eliot," in *T. S. Eliot as Nonsense Poets,*" in *T. S. Eliot: A Symposium for His Seventieth Birthday,* ed. Neville Braybrooke (New York: Farrar, Straus, and Cudahy, 1958), pp. 49–56, for a further application of her theory of nonsense. Another, earlier, work dealing with the nonsense of Carroll and Lear is Emile Cammaerts, *The Poetry of Nonsense* (New York: Dutton, 1925). Michael Holquist draws connections between nonsense and modernism in literature in "What Is a Boojum? in *The Child's Part,* ed. Peter Brooks (Boston: Beacon Press, 1969), as does Herbert Gershman, "Children's Rhymes and Modern Poetry," *French Review* 44 (1971): 539–48. Alfred Liede's two-volume work on speech play in oral and written literary forms, *Dichtung als Spiel, Studien zu Unsinnspoesie an de Grenzen der Sprache* (Berlin: Walter de Gruyter, 1963), also draws parallels between folkloric nonsense and literary modernism, particularly German dada. Gilles Deleuze, *Logique du sens* (Paris: Éditions de Minuit, 1969), presents a study of Carroll's nonsense in light of literary theory and Freudian theory.

8. Stuart Gilbert and Richard Ellman, eds., *Letters of James Joyce,* 3 vols. (London: Faber, 1957), 1:302.

9. James Atherton, *The Books at the Wake* (Carbondale: Southern Illinois University Press, 1959), pp. 124–36.

10. In Don Gifford and Robert Seidman, *Notes for Joyce* (New York: Dutton, 1974), p. 543.

11. Mabel Worthington, "Nursery Rhymes in *Finnegans Wake,*" *Journal of American Folklore* 70 (1957): 37–48.

12. "Interview with Julio Cortázar," *Diacritics* 4 (1974): 35–40.

II • making nonsense

3 • reversals and inversions

ORGANIZING EXPERIENCE

In order to discuss the first nonsense operation, the operation of reversals and inversions, we might begin by considering culture as a set of ways to organize experience. In other words, since culture is an outcome of interactions that members see as orderly, rule-governed, productive, we can consider it as isomorphic with the orderly, rule-governed, and productive processes by which it is created. This common-sense coincidence of process and product has long been present as a contradiction in the use of the word *culture* in English. The origin of the word lies in the Latin *cultura*, the tending of natural growth. As Raymond Williams has pointed out, "Culture in all its early uses was a noun of process." It evolved to have three "broad active categories of usage": (1) The independent and abstract noun that describes a general process of intellectual, spiritual, and aesthetic development. This usage originated in the eighteenth century; (2) The independent noun, whether used generally or specifically, which indicates a particular way of life, whether of a people, a period, or a group, a usage originating with Herder and the philosophers of the nineteenth century; and (3) The independent and abstract noun that describes the works and practices of intellectual and especially artistic activities.[1] Thus from the beginning, *culture* has been tied into notions of process, development, hierarchy, and production, and we can see that these terms—characteristic of the use of the term *culture*—have been carried over as the defining characteristics of culture, the thing itself.

Not surprisingly, cultural anthropology has produced models of culture concerned with development and hierarchy, and, more recently, with models of culture as classification. Classification is particularly apt as a model of process and product, for members' versions of the state of things are emergent in classification as a verb, an activity, and the state of things is characterized as a classification, an order brought about by ordering. The idea of culture as classification presents a state of things

57

where there is an apparent isomorphism across several domains of meaning; the order of the world will be mirrored in the order of its various elements. Durkheim's and Mauss's early work, *Primitive Classification,* appearing in 1903, was the first anthropological inquiry into the relationship between social and religious categories and systems of logic. They wrote of "primitive classifications":

First of all, like all sophisticated classifications, they are systems of hierarchized notions. Things are not simply arranged by them in the form of isolated groups, but these groups stand in fixed relationship to each other and together form a single whole. Moreover, these systems, like those of science, have a purely speculative purpose. Their object is not to facilitate action, but to advance understanding, to make intelligible the relations which exist between things.[2]

This early model came packed with an idea of classification as systematic and rule governed, and by the time of structuralism, culture appears in a constellation of concepts—classification, structure, rule-governed behavior—that approximates another structural model, that of language. Edmund Leach has gone so far as to consider culture as mutually understood systems of communication.[3] With this definition, members' reality-generating conversations, their communication of culture, comes to be considered as culture itself. But once culture is seen as an order analogous to the order of communication, a transformational principle is introduced. The order of communication is a shifting and emergent order; the classification process does not work like a clock so much as like a living thing.

Classification as a model for those procedures by which thought, language, and culture both reify and recreate each other was most elegantly explored by Lévi-Strauss. Lévi-Strauss took up the idea of homology implicit in Durkheim's and Mauss's emphasis on "fixed relationships." In *The Savage Mind* he wrote that "analogous logical structures can be constructed by means of different lexical resources. It is not the elements themselves but only the relations between them which are constant."[4] We can consider culture to be not the content of a classification, but the systems of relationships by which the classification is constructed and modified.

As does structural linguistics, structural anthropology sees classification as a system of differences, and thereby a system of similarities. All meaning becomes positional meaning—meaning defined by a relationship to an *other.* From his early work on totemism, Lévi-Strauss argued that the organization of nature is not a consequence of social organization and its particular needs, but rather, that the relationships between species are analogous to the relationships between clan groups.[5] By means of this analogy, animal classifications are used "to think with," as are the metaphorical relations between sex and marriage rules and dietary prohibitions. His point has been taken up in many specific studies in symbolic anthropology. S. J. Tambiah found in his study of Thai classifications that "it is in respect to the universe of land animals that attitudes of affinity and separation, opposition and integration, fuse to produce the complex correspondence of sex rules, house categories and animal distinctions."[6] Similarly, R. Bulmer concluded from his study of zoological taxonomy among the New Guinea Karam that cassowaries, dogs, and pigs stand in special metaphorical relationships to humans analogous to relationships *between* human categories.[7] While orders of experience may be separated through classification, the logical relations between them may retain some degree of constancy, and one system of relationships may thereby be used as a grid upon which another system of relationships can be mapped regardless of specific content.

The connection to the model of intertextuality presented in part 1 becomes apparent—rather than positing a causal relationship between different domains of discourse, our concern is with the ways in which these domains are used to "think with," the types of operations used in moving from one domain to another. "The logic of depiction requires that the whole of logical space be given as soon as one place in it is determined," writes Mary Douglas.[8] We can see cultural classifications as metaphorical in nature. They are not only internally metaphorical in the sense that by means of part/whole relationships different terms share characteristics and thus form overlapping and emergent areas, they are also analogically metaphorical—the relationships between sets of terms share characteristics. An example of an internal metaphor would be:

legs/horse
legs/table

where one *term* is interchangeable with one other term. But in analogical metaphors, it is the *relationship* between each set of terms that is metaphorical, as it is in "Love and marriage, love and marriage, go together like a horse and carriage":

love : marriage : : horse : carriage

The discussion of metaphor in part 1 as an is/is not phenomenon connected with play and paradox was primarily concerned with examples of internal metaphor—short cuts like "busy as a bee" and fresh cuts like "dawn of the rosy fingers" (perhaps already a short cut). With a model of analogical metaphor, we can move to a consideration of the relationships between domains of textuality. The examples from totemic systems that state "bear : deer : hawk : : clan b : clan d : clan h"[9] show a relationship between the text of nature and the text of culture that is isomorphic, "congruent." Similarly, as Jakobson maintained, metonymic relationships increase the effect of the real, the *given* in discourse. For instance, if "bear : clan b" implies all of the above analogy, or if Tolstoy uses "hair on an upper lip" or "a bare shoulder" to refer metonymically to his two types of female characters, there is an increase in the "effect of the real."

This kind of isomorphism is particularly apparent in the structural analysis of myths. For the structuralists, form and content are of the same nature, subject to the same analysis. Lévi-Strauss has suggested that there is not something abstract on the one hand and concrete on the other. Content draws its reality from its structure and what is called form is the structural formation of the local structure forming the content.[10] Dell Hymes provides an example of this interrelationship between form and content in his analysis of a Clackamas Chinook myth, "The Wife Who Goes Out Like a Man." Hymes found that in this myth oppositions in culture are mediated through the structure of the myth.[11] Thus the genres that are isomorphic with the social organization of nature and the social organization of the set of members will vary across sets of members. The native system is, as well, a system of differences between types of discourse defined by their relationship to other levels of organization shared by members. "Significance is always phenomenal," argued Lévi-Strauss in his confrontation with Paul Ricoeur in 1970.[12] The organization of significance in one domain of experience will have import for other domains of experience.

ANOMALY, AMBIGUITY, AND AMBIVALENCE

Thus far in this discussion of culture as classification I have been concerned with intertextual relationships that are complementary and domain reinforcing. But any system of classification comes built with leaks and anomalies. We have only to think of the rule "All rules have exceptions." The problem of a "leak" in the system of rules brings us back to Richard Hilbert's "nonsense experiment." When confronted with gaps in their system of knowledge, members will take refuge in the use of special cases such as exceptions, fate, chance, accident, and nonsense. They will thereby create a condition that is an "impossible context"—that is, a context that can never be contextualized, that can never take place in the "real world" and thus can never contaminate that real world. Edmund Leach has suggested that "language gives us the names to distinguish the things; taboo inhibits the recognition of those parts of the continuum that separate the things."[13] Leach further suggests that for any category p distinguished from an environment $-p$, the overlapping area that is both p and $-p$ will be taboo. The category "p and $-p$" points to the paradoxes of play and metaphor as "new categories" that stand in an is/is not relation to a prior state of affairs. This is one

reason why the metaphorical behavior of nonsense, play, and paradox is removed from everyday life, cut off from its reality-generating
conversations and contexts, and limited to the "never never land," the
contexts of playground, ritual, and fiction.

Taboo can be seen in terms of the states of anomaly, ambiguity, and
ambivalence. The anomalous stands between the categories of an existing classification system; it threatens the integrity of text and context
by being neither one nor the other. The ambiguous is that which cannot
be defined in terms of any given category; it threatens the integrity of
individual categories, being "either this or that or something else." The
ambivalent is that which belongs to more than one domain at a time and
will not fix its identity in any one member of this set of domains; it is
"both this and that." In terms of the intertextual construct, irony brings
in ambivalence, a threat to the hierarchy of interpretations, by talking
through two domains at once. And as fictive texts move more and more
away from the classificatory system of the everyday lifeworld, their
status becomes ambiguous and anomalous—ambiguous because reflexivity puts their generic characteristics in increasing jeopardy, and
anomalous because their contexts become increasingly "impossible." In
her study of pollution and taboo, Mary Douglas wrote: "Dirt was
created by the differentiating activity of the mind, it was a by-product
of the creation of order. All through the process of differentiating its
role was to threaten distinctions made; finally, it returns to its true
indiscriminate character. . . . Formlessness is both the symbol of
beginning and growth and decay."[14]

Like dirt, texts become increasingly "formless" or antiformal as they
move away from a given system of order, for *form* is defined only in
terms of congruence with the existing system of order. Consider the
costume of the clown or fool and its formlessness. As William Willeford
has pointed out, "Charlie Chaplin's baggy trousers and shapeless shoes
have antecedents in the dress of Elizabethan clowns. Lumpishness
suggests chaos registered by consciousness as a mere crude fact; the
audience is confronted with something relatively shapeless, yet material."[15] At the same time, these categories are totally dependent upon
the existing system of order for their anomalous, ambiguous, and/or
ambivalent status. As we have seen in the process whereby metaphors
move from fresh cuts to short cuts, changes in the system of order will
bring about incorporation of anomalous, ambiguous, and ambivalent
categories and the creation of new categories of these types. Thus the
disorder of nonsense may be seen as a not-yet-incorporated form of
order, an order without a context, without a place in the everyday
lifeworld.

One nonsense-making character who has received particular attention
from symbolic anthropology is the trickster, the personification of

ambivalence who appears as raven, crow, and hare in North America; spider, frog, and tortoise in Africa; the rabbit in Afro-American folklore; and the fox in South America. Paul Radin wrote in his classic study of the Winnebago trickster:

> Trickster is at one and the same time creator and destroyer, giver and negator, he who dupes others and who is always duped himself. He wills nothing consciously. At all times he is constrained to behave as he does from impulses over which he has no control. He knows neither good nor evil yet he is responsible for both. He possesses no values, moral or social, is at the mercy of his passions and appetites, yet through his actions all values come into being.[16]

In the Winnebago cycle, trickster tries to go to war alone, makes his right arm fight his left, causes the death of his brother's children by doing everything "strictly forbidden to him"; cohorts with some dancing ducks before attempting to kill them; then talks to his own anus; burns his anus and eats his intestines; loses part of his penis; changes into a woman and marries a chief's son; eats a laxative bulb that fills him with enough gas to scatter a village with his wind; falls into his own excrement; eats some children and their mothers; gets his head caught in an elk's skull; imitates a muskrat, a snipe, a woodpecker, and a polecat; frees the Mississippi of obstacles and causes a waterfall to fall on the land.[17]

These activities of trickster systematically violate the kinds of dietary and marriage rules that in the preceding discussion of analogical metaphor were so important to the isomorphic relationships holding between the organization of nature and the organization of social relationships. The systematic nature of trickster's activities points to his position as a violator of not only specific taboos, but also of the idea of a taboo, the idea of a rule that cannot be violated. Trickster as shapeshifter takes on the form of other species, changes sex, marries and copulates with the same sex and with opposite species, and violates all dietary prohibitions. Furthermore, trickster narratives themselves violate generic rules, being neither profane nor sacred and often appearing in contexts, such as sacred contexts, where they are anomalous, uncategorizable.[18] While trickster embodies a range of negations, he/she also, according to Radin, "is represented as the creator of the world and the establisher of culture."[19] As the embodiment of disparate domains, trickster is analogous to the process of metaphor, the incorporation of opposites into a new configuration. He represents both the breakdown and the emergence of the classifications constituting culture.

PROPER NOTS

The activities of the trickster figure often show the first of a series of operations for turning the common-sense, everyday lifeworld into nonsense—reversals and inversions. The systematic violation of categories and norms of behavior that trickster presents appears as a negation, a reversal, an inversion, of those cultural categories and behavioral norms that make up common sense. If we see culture as a way of classifying and organizing experience, then it holds that each category *p* will not only have an environment -*p* from which it may be distinguished metonymically, but also that many categories will have a "proper" -*p*, an exact inverse in the hierarchy of relations between paradigmatic sets. This is the simplest, most basic type of inversion. Since not every category has a proper not, this gesture first of all involves a reduction of the world into sets with two elements. The varieties of relationships between the two elements are further reduced to two: + or -. The set has a minimum of complexity and a maximum of manipulatability.

The theory of logical types is helpful for an understanding of "proper nots," for it sees categories as arranged according to levels of abstraction: In the set of "not popsicles," for instance, we included "bracelets, nails, hot dogs, and rubber bands." But, to use an example from Bateson, we did not include something like "tomorrow," since using "tomorrow" would involve a jump to another level of logical type. The proper "not floor" would be "a ceiling," just as the proper "not master" would be "a slave." Similarly, right side up/upside down, frontwards/backwards, serve as directions for proper nots. "Proper nots" consist of the reversal or inversion of whole units, and thereby involve the interpreter with all those features that are seen to be significant enough to identify. The proper not is *not* made by saying "This is not this because it has one arm instead of two, or three legs instead of four." Rather, every significant feature is inverted, and thus the proper not depends upon a symmetry built into the classification of things, a symmetry that is perhaps derived from the symmetry of the body. The child's most fundamental experience with inversion is the experience of his or her whole body being dangled upside down, an experience that results in turning the whole world upside down as well.

TAKING THINGS BACK

Reversibility may be a characteristic of our perception of culture in general, and particularly of the idea of culture as communication. While we see the natural world as constant—unchanged by the desires and purposes of human activities except in so far as human activities interrupt or interfere with the natural order—we see culture as constantly in process, transformable, and manipulatable when considered as a process of communication. This point is implied by Lévi-Strauss's statement that one could limit "the expression 'structures of subordination' by opposing it to 'structures of communication'; meaning thereby that there are, in society, two major structural types; structures of communication which are reciprocal and structures of subordination, on the other hand, which are univocal and not reversible."[20] This distinction between reversible and nonreversible structures not only holds against the intertextual division between realism (univocal and nonreversible) and irony/metafiction (multivocal and reversible), it is also symptomatic of a more basic division between fictive and nonfictive events in social life. Nonfictive events are those that happen in social time, that "really did occur" and cannot be "taken back." In contrast, fictive events are framed as reversible events. They can be taken back by saying "This is just a story," or "I was just joking," by asserting their paradoxical is/is not status as events and nonevents. This basic division is evident in games where there is a period that "does not count" and where scores can be reversed back to zero. Here the text of experience virtually can be erased. When experience "really counts," nothing can be done to reverse its ongoingness. The whole domain of "practice," however, gives us another example of a fictive domain, a domain that can be reversed. And from the previous discussion of nonsense and learning, we can see that the reverse—that all fictions are practice domains—may be true as well.

This fundamental distinction between nonfictive and fictive events is further demonstrated in the way we classify pranks and crimes. The interface between pranks and crimes is determined by the reversibility of their effects. Soap can be washed off windows, paint can be sandblasted, windows can be replaced, but scars and death are not held to be reversible. "Hurt" is defined in terms of the body's capabilities to reverse damage. When fraternity members get their heads shaved during "rush," they have confidence that their hair will grow back. It is interesting that when fraternity pranks do result in serious injury or death, it is not the activity "pranks" that is blamed, but the failure in classification. To say "They do not know when to stop" is to say that the fraternity members passed "a point of no return," a point where reversible actions become irreversible because of an error in framing. When people make continued classificatory errors of this type they move from being a prankster to a delinquent, and their participation in social life is forcibly restricted. A reversal of the fraternity illustration of the role of reversible events in the context of social life is the "neck riddle." These riddles narrate events known only to the poser of the riddle, a criminal condemned to death.[21] If the condemned man can tell a riddle that no one can answer, his life will be spared. Carl Withers provides this example:

A man was condemned to be hanged and was riding horseback to the gallows with his hangmen. They offered to spare his life if he could think up a riddle none of them could answer. At the gallows he asked without dismantling:

> Under gravel I do travel
> On oak leaves I do stand
> I ride my pony and never fear
> I hold my bridle in my hand

> (Answer: he had put gravel in his hat and oak leaves in his boot. The answer is the riddler himself) [22]

This type of riddle has the power to reverse its own context, the context of death, to its inverse, the context of life—from seriousness to play—so long as the arbitrary power of the riddler is not tampered with, so long as it is allowed to be framed as a riddle.

While play activities "do not count" and are seen as both atemporal and temporary in status, they also reverse the hierarchy and equilibrium of the common-sense world. In many games there is an outcome that is disequilibrial and reversible. Sutton-Smith has written, "Someone ends up being a winner. One could argue likewise that the intentionality of play is to do things differently; to make a unique response to customary circumstances, and to move events away from their cognitive and affective equilibria." He suggests that the intention of play may be to upset the customary balance of things. [23] Games and play often contrast symmetry and asymmetry. Although this is not true of all games, many times the players begin with equality and end with inequality. There is an implicit arbitrariness in the game status, since the "play" of the game will go back to the beginning state of undifferentiated status before the next play. [24]

Similar states of disequilibrium appear in carnival and rites of inversion proper. Here the mayor is a tramp and the tramp is a mayor, the servant is the master and the master becomes the servant. And in these activities oppositions can become complements and complements become oppositions—a unit can consist of a set of proper nots, or two elements in a contiguous relationship can be transformed into proper nots. Disequilibrium takes the form of segmentation. While unifying rites bring together diverse statuses into equilibrium, the opposite occurs in carnival—closeness is transformed into distance. Kristeva, following Bakhtin's work on Rabelais, has said that carnavalesque discourse is an insult to official discourse—the discourse of law—and that carnavalesque discourse is distinguished by a law that is a transgression, and thereby an antilaw. [25] Thus the work that reversals and negations accomplish is not only a defining against, but a fragmenting, a separating off. When one system transgresses another, it is a splitting and a cutting across. Just as trickster's right hand fought his left, the fool and the clown often appear in pairs that are *split*, in pairs of opposites: Lear and his fool, Don Quixote and Sancho Panza, Don Giovanni and Leporello, Tweedledum and Tweedledee, Shem and Shaun, often exchanging roles, producing a confusion of identity. One has only to think of the popularity of twins in many TV situation comedies, or the confusions of *Finnegans Wake*: "equals of opposites, evolved by a onesame power of nature or of spirit, *iste*, as the sole condition and means of its himundher manifestation and polarised for reunion by the symphysis of their antipathies."[26]

Thus far I have discussed certain aspects of reversals in relation to culture as classification and communication: (1) the symmetrical inversion of proper nots, (2) the hierarchical inversion of relationships, (3) the fragmentation involved in transgressing any system of order. In the remainder of this chapter I consider some specific types of nonsense reversals in fictions: inversions of classes, reversible texts, discourse that denies itself, and the inversion of metaphor.

INVERTING CLASSES

The earliest cartoon is believed to be a "comic strip" papyrus dating from the New Kingdom.[27] The cartoon depicts the breakdown of an old social order—lions are happily playing checkers with gazelles, wolves are protectively watching goats, and a cat is tending a flock of geese. The cartoon reconciles the antinomies lion/gazelle, wolf/goat, cat/geese, by turning "natural enemies" into social allies, and in the case of the first picture, the disequilibrium between the lion and gazelle is transformed into the initial equilibrium characteristic of the game—the impending disequilibrium brought about by the checkers match will be determined by a game order rather than a natural order.

Thomas Wright has said that, among the Egyptians, "The practice having been once introduced of representing men under the character of animals was soon developed into other applications of the same idea, such as that of portraying animals engaged in human occupations or of reversing the position of men and animals so that animals were represented as treating human tyrants in the same manner as they are usually treated by such tyrants."[28] This method of making nonsense, the inversion of animal and human categories, is perhaps the most prevalent of all proper not inversions. Bergson wrote in his essay "Laughter," "Picture to yourself certain characters in a certain situation: if you reverse the situation and invert the roles, you obtain a comic scene."[29] While Bergson was mainly concerned with the comic effect of "something mechanical encrusted on the living," the inversion of human into mechanical categories, his rule of inversion follows just as well with "something living encrusted on the mechanical"—the inversion of mechanical into human categories. Alice, confronted with the Queen's croquet ground where the croquet balls are live hedge hogs and the mallets are live flamingoes and the arches are soldiers bending over on hands and feet, remarks, "You've no idea how confusing it is all the things being alive; for instance, there's the arch I've got to go through next walking about at the other end of the ground—and I should have croqueted the Queen's hedgehog just now, only it ran away when it saw mine coming!"[30]

The inversions of animal and human categories and mechanical and human categories often involve a transformation of the same domains as those that were prominent in the studies of analogic metaphor cited before—animal categories, social categories, dietary categories, and sexual categories. Consider this nonsense rhyme collected by the Opies in their study of *The Lore and Language of Schoolchildren*:

> The sausage is a cunning bird
> With feathers long and wavy;
> It swims about the frying pan
> And makes its nest in gravy.[31]

This example shows a neat inversion in the following manner:

    sausage : frying pan   : :   bird : nest
    bird : frying pan   : :   sausage : nest
    sausage : bird   : :   frying pan : nest

Inversely, the humor of the "How Panurge played a Trick on the Parisian Lady which was not at all to her advantage" chapter of *Gargantua and Pantagruel* turns a human into an animal. By sprinkling the Parisian Lady with "bitch's perfume," Panurge turns her into a literal bitch and she is besieged by male dogs.[32] The inversion here of animal and human categories is particularly radical because it has been done through sexual characteristics.

In his study of nonsense, Emile Cammaerts wrote, "Nonsense steps in gradually, first through the animal story, then through the confusion of all classes and values, finally through the creation of such wild images that they defy classification." He says that nonsense is "a world of topsy-turvydom in which cockle-shells grow in a garden, barbers shave pigs and lions and unicorns are fed on bread and plum cake."[33] The inversions of nonsense work not only by proper nots, as they would if the customer shaved the barber, but by inversions of the terms of a complement—hence the barber shaves a pig, not a man—and other inversions. Carroll's work offers more examples of topsy-turvydom. Father William is sure that standing on his head incessantly will do him no harm, and he also likes to somersault backwards in through the door.[34] The Cheshire Cat gives a definition of madness by inversion:

"You see a dog growls when it's angry and wags its tail when it's pleased. Now I growl when I'm pleased and wag my tail when I'm angry. Therefore, I'm mad."[35]

The inversions of the final dinner party in *Through the Looking Glass*[36] show the use of inversion as a principle to cut across a set of activities. This is the beginning of play with an institutional order, an order affecting a range of behaviors, which we saw above as the inversion of hierarchical relationships in many rites of reversal and game situations. At the Shipley School in Philadelphia, students hold "backwards days" in which a wide range of activities within the institutional order of the school are reversed. On these days everything that is said is taken to mean its opposite—students walk backwards down the halls and systematically do the opposite of all commands and requests of teachers.[37] In many American high schools there are annual class days where students parody the behavior of teachers and football players dress in cheerleaders' costumes and cheerleaders wear football uniforms. Other travesties of this type include students saying the Lord's Prayer backwards in order to "raise the devil," or the inversions typical of the Black Mass.[38] Children take particular delight in nonsense that reverses roles based on size:

> Down in the meadow
> Where the corn cobs grow,
> Flea jumped on the elephant's toe
> Elephant cried, with tears in his eyes,
> Why don't you pick on someone your size?[39]

These inversions of scale are related to the humor of ambiguous boundaries—the humor of giants and dwarfs, stilts and costumes that shrink or enlarge a figure. When such humor depends upon the inversion of categories that stand in a proper not of scale to each other, we can see it as an example of a reversal as well as an example of boundary play.

REVERSIBLE TEXTS

The reversal is a particular threat to hierarchy and direction. If we see everyday life as "getting somewhere," with an implication of progress, the reversal reminds us that what goes up must come down, and that what happens in the domain of culture can often be turned back on itself. Because we see language as something nonmaterial, as something that has no "concrete" effect upon the physical world, it is often a forum for exercises in reversibility. We can see this exercise not only in discourse that is "taken back," but also in several speech play forms that readily demonstrate their ability to turn back on themselves, to proceed ambivalently in either of two directions. The reversals of these texts are "internal" to the text, that is, they involve a reversal of features present in the text. For example, "The goose that stepped into the elevator and got peopled,"[40] is an example of an animal/human inversion that is effected on the linguistic level by the false linguistic analogy of goose : people : : goosed : peopled. Other linguistic inversions can be performed by reversing phonemes:

> Geat but not naudy
> Med the sonkey
> Tainting his pail
> Bly skue[41]

or by reversing morphemes:

> Most people don't know it,
> but actually there isn't a diff
> of bitterance between a
> hipponoceros and a rhinopotamus.[42]

In the mid-nineteenth century, the form of phonemic and morphemic inversion known as *contrapetterie* was popular in France: "Elle fit son prix. Elle prit son fils," "Il le dit a deux fames. Il le fit a deux dames."[43] Playing with these forms involves a reversal of the temporality of speech from the outset. Their cleverness is largely derived from the "foresight," the perception of the text as an integral whole, which precedes performance. They involve a consciousness of the text as *text*, a discourse with boundaries within which one can manipulate its constitutive elements. Conundrums, for example, work with morphemic or lexical inversions by structuring a riddle question whose answer will consist of two symmetrical parts, each half being in some way a linguistic inversion of the other: "What is the difference between an angry circus owner and a Roman hairdresser? One is a raving showman and the other is a shaving Roman." Conundrums turn pairs of "nots" into "proper nots," exact reversals, by moving the status of each member away from the classifications of the everyday world, where they are already improper nots, to the level of linguistic signs, where they can become "proper nots." There are, of course, many differences between an angry circus owner and a Roman hairdresser, but the only differences that count here are linguistic differences.

Each inversion and reversal undercuts the status of the original order, inverting the animal and the human, or the human and the mechanical, or the linguistic sign and what it signifies. Inversions of animal, human, and mechanical categories call status and role relationships into question, and linguistic inversions emphasize the reversible and flexible nature of communication. With the printed page, reversibility becomes available to the entire text as an object—the text can be rearranged in mechanical space in accordance with a variety of orders. Lewis Carroll, who liked to play his music boxes backwards for relaxation, frequently wrote letters back to front, not only in mirror writing, but with the last word first and vice versa so that one had to begin from "the end" and end at "the beginning."[44] One of his *Letters to Child-Friends* reads: "For it made you that *him* been have *must* it see you so: *grandfather* my was, *then* alive was that."[45]

The palindrome is perhaps the most perfect linguistic reversal, equivalent to being able to turn the whole body upside down. The word comes from the Greek, *palindromos*, "running back," and the palindrome is defined as a word, verse, or sentence that reads the same backwards or forwards. The palindrome can work on the lexical level, as in MUM, ANNA, DEED, ANANA, MINIM, MADAM.[46] This is the simplest type of palindrome. A lengthy list of English palindromes appears in the English translation of G. Cabrera Infante's *Three Trapped Tigers*, for the novel's genius of wordplay, Bustrofedon, spends much of his time "unlocking" them. Bustrofedon comes up with "tit, eye, nun, kayak, level, sexes, radar, civic, sos (the most helpful), gag (the funniest), boob"[47] in his list of palindromes, and "live/evil, part/trap, flow/wolf, diaper/repaid, reward/drawer, drab/bard, Dog/God!" in his list of "mirror words."[48] The palindrome can also work on the level of the phrase, as in "Madam I'm Adam," "Able Was I Ere I Saw Elba," and "A Man, A Plan, A Canal, Panama," or on the level of the entire text—Lalanne's *Curiosités littéraires* includes an example of a palindromic poem by the thirteenth century poet Baudoin de Condé:

> Amours est vie glorieuse,
> Tenir fait ordre gracieuse
> Maintenir veult courtoises mours
> Mours courtoises veult maintenir
> Gracieuse ordre fait tenir:
> Glorieuse vie est amours.[49]

Similarly, Bustrofedon longs "for a book written entirely back to front so that the last word became the first and vice versus. And now I know that Bus has taken a trip to the other world, to the opposite, to his negative, to his anti-self, to the other side of the mirror."[50]

Another type of text that uses mechanical space to effect its inversion is "Jesuitical" or "equivocal verse," in which the lines can succeed each other either down or across the page:

I love my country—but the king	Above all men his praise I sing
Destruction to his odious reign	That plague of princes, Thomas Paine
The royal banners are displayed	And may success his standard aid
Defeat and ruin seize the cause	Of France, her liberty and laws[51]

This kind of verse is a graphic display of irony—talking in two contradictory voices at once. Reversals may be seen to be inherently ironic because they produce both a doubling and a contradiction. They are a "doubling back" and have to do with the impossibility of nonsense to go anywhere, to proceed in a straight line towards a "purpose at hand." Consider Monty Python's "Minister of Silly Walks" or Samuel Beckett's Watt, who always prefers to have his back to his destination. Here each motion towards implies a corresponding motion against. With Watt, the net result is movement without direction:

Watt's way of advancing due east, for example, was to turn his bust as far as possible towards the north and at the same time to fling out his right leg as far as possible towards the south, and then to turn his bust as far as possible towards the south and at the same time to fling out his left leg as far as possible towards the north, and then again to turn his bust as far as possible towards the north and to fling out his right leg as far as possible towards the south, and then again to turn his bust as far as possible towards the south and to fling out his left leg as far as possible towards the north, and so on, over and over again, many many times, until he reached his destination and could sit down.[52]

Even Watt's thought becomes increasingly palindromic, reading back to front. "As Watt walked, so now he talked, back to front." On page 164, his inversions begin: "Day of most, night of part, Knott with now." The narrator tells us that "the inversion affected not the order of the sentences, but that of the words only." Then Watt began to invert not the order of the words in the sentence, but the order of the letters in the word. Then he inverted the order of the sentences in the "period," then the words in the sentence together with the order of the sentences in the period, then the letters in the word together with the order of the sentences in the period. Then he began to invert the order of the letters in the word together with that of the words in the sentence, together with that of the sentences in the period, until finally:

in the brief course of the same period, now that of the words in the sentence, now that of the letters in the word, now that of the sentences in the period, now simultaneously that of the words in the sentence and that of the sentences in the period, now simultaneously that of the letters in the word and that of the sentences in the period, and now simultaneously that of the letters in the word and that of the words in the sentence and that of the sentences in the period . . . I recall no examples of this manner.[53]

Watt's movements are the movements of any self-denying and critical operation—the movement of thought caught against itself. The reversibility of discourse is made possible by the reversibility of knowledge itself. Bouvard and Pecuchet discover that while Doctor Morin's *Manual of Hygiene* says that nervous people should avoid tea, Decker prescribed in the seventeenth century that one should drink fifty gallons of the stuff a day to swell the pancreas. "This information shook Morin in their esteem," writes Flaubert.[54] And this is the beginning of Bouvard's and Pecuchet's realization that there can be contradictions in knowledge:

"And from disregard of dates they passed to contempt for facts."[55] The contempt for facts is a contempt for the conditions of knowing that brought about the discourse itself—a contempt for the implicit knowledge underlying the interpretive procedures used in creating "the truth" as well as "reality."

DISCOURSE THAT DENIES ITSELF

The metacommunication necessary for the message "This is play" or "This is a fiction" implicitly carries a denial and a criticism— a denial because of the status of the representation as an activity that is framed as both real and not real, and a criticism because the discourse has been framed, set off, and is examinable from many sides and able to be manipulated. For children, play and fictions hold the fascination of something that is both a lie and not a lie. Thus they are as powerful as a taboo in an anomalous position—a taboo that attracts. Within the rules of fictive discourse, one can "take back" something that is said, since what was said was both said and not said:

> A bottle of pop, a big banana
> We're from southern Louisiana
> That's a lie, that's a fib
> We're from Colorado[56]

Using pairs of opposing terms, children's speech play often pits discourse against itself. Whereas "reversible texts" ambivalently move backwards and forwards, denying any privileged reading, discourse that denies itself systematically proceeds by cancelling itself out. A "narrative" is produced that is self-cancelling, like an equation where everything is voided and the result is 0=0. Here is an example of this type of nonsense:

> Ladies and jellyspoons:
> I come before you
> To stand behind you
> To tell you something
> I know nothing about.
> Last Thursday
> Which was Good Friday
> There will be a mothers' meeting
> For Fathers only.
> Wear your best clothes
> If you haven't any,
> And if you can come,
> Please stay at home.
> Admission is free
> So pay at the door
> Pull up a chair

And sit on the floor.
It makes no difference
Where you sit
The man in the gallery
Is sure to spit.
We thank you for your unkind attention.
The next meeting will be held
At the four corners of the round table.[57]

Such rhymes, too, are ironic, talking in two contradictory voices at the same time. The narrator splits into two contradictory narrators, each denying each other's discourse. The paired oppositions that the narrative presents are states that cannot tolerate each other, yet that in the frame of the discourse are allowed to be and not be at the same time. They are versions of the same paradox by which all fictions are allowed to "exist."

In literature the same device can be exploited, for while the order of reading from left to right across the page captures the temporal order of speech, it can also depict graphically the juxtaposition of opposites. In *Molloy*, the first of Beckett's trilogy of novels, the voice of the character Moran begins, "It is midnight. The rain is beating on the windows. I am calm—all is sleeping."[58] He tells the story of his strange search for Molloy and then his part of the narrative ends, "Then I went back into the house and wrote. It is midnight. The rain is beating on the windows. It was not midnight. It was not raining."[59] Even minor details, which are usually the ammunition of realism, are not to be trusted when Moran speaks. He lets us know, "When I said turkeys and so on, I lied."[60] And when Moran gives information, he is not above taking it away immediately: "What then was the source of Ballyba's prosperity? I'll tell you. No, I'll tell you nothing. Nothing."[61] The effect is a narrative that continually undercuts itself and whose conclusion undercuts everything that has taken place, presumably even the cancellations that the narrative has already internally revealed. *Tristram Shandy* similarly plays with the reader's gullibility: Sterne gives a description of Fontainebleau in chapter 27, then tells the reader that "there are two reasons why you need not talk loud of this to everyone. First, because 'twill make the said nags the harder to be got; and secondly, 'tis not a word of it true."[62] These denials emphasize not only the reversibility of fictive status, but also the position of the fictive narrator as a person who does not have the responsibilities of the narrator of common-sense discourse. The fictive narrator does not have to "stand behind" what he says; he can play trickster, changing the rules of the game, undercutting the reader's assumptions. When Beckett and Sterne deny the reader an absolute knowledge, they are denying a knowledge of the narrative's condition of origin. We are not presented with a text that is rooted metonymically to the everyday lifeworld. Rather, we must accept the fluctuations of a text that is continually self-transforming, that flaunts its detachment from everyday contexts. With literary texts, we are ironically confronted with a "physical" text, but it is a text whose absent author and absent context of origin make it all the more fleeting.

The footnote,[63] like equivocal verse, offers an opportunity for discourse to deny itself visually as well as verbally. As the depiction of a voice splitting itself, the footnote is from the beginning a form of discourse about discourse. Swift takes much advantage of the possibilities of the footnote in his *A Tale of a Tub*. In the fifth edition (1710), he denies the main text of the tale by adding his own footnotes:

This great work was entered upon some years ago, by one of our most eminent members: He began with *The History of Reynard the Fox* but neither lived to . . .

*The author seems here to be mistaken, for I have seen a Latin edition of *Reynard the Fox* above a hundred years old, which I take to be the original; for the rest it has been thought by many people to contain some satirical design on it.[64]

In a further parody of learning in a text that is already a parody of learning, Swift includes notes from William Wotton's *Observations upon the Tale of the Tub* (1705) along with his (Swift's) own footnotes. At one point he makes a double contradiction by having Lambin, a sixteenth-century French scholar, submit a footnote denying Wotton's footnote:

*By his coats which he gave his sons, the garments of the Israelites—W. Wotton.

**An error (with submission) of the learned commentator; for by the coats are meant the doctrine and faith of Christianity, by the wisdom of the Divine Founder fitted to all times, places and circumstances—LAMBIN.[65]

Lambin was, of course, dead long before *A Tale of a Tub* was written. The irony of Swift's footnotes lie in their contradiction of knowledge within a text setting out to demonstrate contradictions in knowledge. Beckett's famous "haemophilia" footnote in *Watt* is another example:

Sam's other married daughter Kate, aged twenty-one years, a fine girl but a bleeder (1)

(1) Haemophilia is, like an enlargement of the prostate, an exclusively male disorder, but not in this work.[66]

A footnote two pages later says that "the figures given here are incorrect. The congruent calculations are therefore doubly erroneous."[67] The footnote in the work of Swift and Beckett is more than a device for supplementing the text, for addressing careless and careful readers "all at once," as footnotes do in nonfictive, "scholarly," texts. In nonfictive texts, the footnote aids the illusion of the real by giving a glimpse of "all that has been left out," all the given information that makes up the true, the real, world. To enter into an agreement with the footnotes of a text is to step further into the text. But in the fictive text, the footnote is often ironic. It stands on the interface between the fiction and reality. To enter into an agreement with the fictive footnote is to stand outside and inside the fiction at the same time. When Beckett and Swift have their footnotes contradict the text, the reader is threatened by a loss of any distinction between the real and the fictive. The assumptions of the reader are split and undercut with every splitting and undercutting of the text. As in the "Ladies and jellyspoons" type of discourse, the process that denies the discourse puts the audience in jeopardy as well.

Discourse that denies itself becomes a matter of structure in Joyce's *Ulysses.* Just as Bouvard and Pecuchet moved from one area of learning to another by a path of contradictions, so *Ulysses,* and later, *Finnegans Wake,* roam from one universe of discourse to another, using a "slash and burn" technique. Joyce wrote to Harriet Shaw Weaver on 20 July 1919:

The word scorching transmitted to me by your associates in reply to my tentative inquiry has a particular significance for my superstitious mind, not so much because of any quality or merit in the writing itself as for the fact that the progress of the book is in fact like the progress of some sandblast. As soon as I mention or include any person in it I hear of his or her death or departure or misfortune: and each successive episode dealing with some province of artistic culture (rhetoric or music or dialectic) leaves behind it a burnt up field. [68]

The idea of a text that never "goes anywhere," that consumes itself with each narrative step, is also illustrated in this traditional rhyme:

> I'll tell you a story
> About old Mother Morey
> And now my story's begun
> I'll tell you another
> About her brother
> And now my story's done [69]

Like *Finnegans Wake* or the game "Mother May I?" this rhyme uses a strategy of hesitation—each step forward can mean a step backwards. And this means that there is always a threat of having to go back to the beginning, a threat that is realized in the last sentence of the *Wake,* which is also the first sentence. Leo Bersani has written of the same phenomenon in Robbe-Grillet's *La Jalousie*: "Each section in *La Jalousie*—ideally, each paragraph, each sentence, each word—is a new beginning. Its relation to what precedes it is ambivalent; it picks up and develops an inspiration in order to destroy the source of inspiration, to reinvent the world in a form which, in turn, will suicidally inspire further inventions." [70] With discourse that denies itself we see an exaggeration of the ability of the fiction to "take back" what it has said. It is a fiction that is caught in a stammer of taking itself back, a self-consciousness that eliminates the possibility of ever being able to say anything definitively.

Thus far, the majority of the examples of literary inversions that I have given have come from the novel, perhaps because the novel, as a genre that has always been concerned with speech, has from the beginning been self-critical. Fielding set upon *Pamela* at once, with *Shamela*, and then with *Joseph Andrews*, the "history" of Pamela's brother. And when Viktor Shklovsky says that "*Tristram Shandy* is the most typical novel of world literature,"[71] it is because the novel systematically lays bare every device the novel had offered up until Sterne's time. But traditionally, literary nonsense, like folkloric nonsense, has been composed in verse or, perhaps more properly, in anti-verse. "The grotesque impression is produced, not by ignoring the general laws of good poetry, but by upsetting them purposely and by making them, so to speak, stand on their heads . . . thought is subservient to rhyme," writes Cammaerts.[72]

Nonsense poetry takes the traditional division between content and form (technique), with its hierarchical weighing of content *over* form, and inverts statuses to present form over content. The nonsense verse of Lear, Carroll, and Morgenstern is not properly *ungrammatical*. Nonsense results from the juxtaposition of incongruities, from the preservation of form at the expense of content. The result is a dispersal of any univocal meaning. Lewis Carroll's *Alice* poems use a set of inversions to change didactic poetry into nonsense poetry: Isaac Watts's "busy bee" is turned into "the little crocodile," Robert Southey's "Father William" is literally turned on his head. The Duchess counsels "Speak roughly to your little boy" in her lullaby to the pig/baby in an inversion of G. W. Langford's "Speak Gently." James M. Sayles's "beautiful star" is turned into "beautiful soup," and the Lobster Quadrille takes on the form of Isaac Watts's moralistic "The Sluggard," only to have a lobster talk and an owl and a panther share a pie in what was once the sluggard's garden.[73] In both the history of the novel and the history of such verse parodies, we can see that the taking over of one text by another is a form of negation, of cancelling out and/or transforming the meaning of the confiscated text. Thus the history of parody is a replica of the reversibility of other structures of communication, of the ability to take back what has been framed as a fiction.

The dadaists and surrealists produced another great body of lyric work that was "grammatical" yet managed to invert the categories and hierarchies of ordinary language and its world, including those of poetry as a genre. Breton wrote that the constraints of art and ordinary language were "the worst of conventions . . . imposing upon us the use of formulas and verbal associations which do not belong to us."[74] Like those narratives that begin and begin again, the surrealist mission was to reinvent the world in every lyric movement. Hugo Ball wrote that the program of dada was to "contradict existing world orders."[75] The surrealists sought to invert the laws of poetry as well as the laws of ordinary language. Traditionally poetry had depended upon inspiration available to a select few and upon taming the subconscious into a logical form. The surrealists offered a poetry of continuous, total inspiration for everybody, the unleashing of the unconscious, and a poetry of process, a poetry that would never be finished, a poetry liberated from the spatial, temporal, and causal constraints of logic.[76] Unlike the nineteenth-century nonsense poets, the dadaists and surrealists were willing to invert the rules of poetic form. The "verse" of the surrealists depended much more upon the logic of talk than upon a logic of rhyme. At the same time, this verse rejected and inverted the logic of talk's ordinary language. Their inversion of lyric discourse thus went one step further than those inversions performed by the nineteenth-century nonsense writers. Dada and surrealism celebrated a poetics of contradiction on the levels of "form" and "content." Tzara wrote in his dada manifesto, "No more manifestoes," declaring, "to be against this manifesto is to be Dadaist . . . in principle I'm against manifestoes, as I am also against principle."[77] And Breton wrote in his 1924 *Manifesto of Surrealism* that the qualities of the surrealist image were: "arbitrariness, seeming contradiction, concealment, the sensational ending weakly, gives to the abstract the mask of the concrete or the opposite, implies the negation of some elementary physical property, provokes laughter."[78] In the same year, he wrote "Soluble Fish," the manifestation of these principles within a narrative of contradiction: "Having caught her in my arms, all rustling, I placed my lips on her throat without a word, what happens next escapes me almost entirely."[79]

THE INVERSION OF METAPHOR

In their contradictory movement, these texts present a critique and a denial of univocal meaning and the ideology of univocal meaning found in common sense. Since this common sense becomes efficient by means of metaphorical short cuts, nonsense often takes as its target such short cuts, and thereby undercuts the "taken for granted" nature of the everyday lifeworld. This is the final inversion that I discuss in this chapter: the metaphorical made literal, what Bergson called "the comic effect obtained whenever we pretend to take literally an expression which was used figuratively or once our attention is fixed on the material aspect of the metaphor."[80] This type of inversion insists upon consistency: the rules of logic, devoid of common-sense content, are presented. Language is continually reduced to a set of parts with a mechanical rule for putting them together. "Skipping the details" and "getting on with the point" are made impossible. Ironically, the effect is often one of abstraction, since tearing down the structure of the discourse into its components makes the structure all the more apparent, if all the more silly. [81]

In folklore, the inversion of the metaphorical and the literal is often enacted by switching frames, specifically by switching from a performance to a "nonperformance" frame. A playful question is switched to the status of a "true" question, and vice versa. The conditions for performance are set up and then taken away at a critical point. Consider "shaggy dog" stories, which play with the ambiguity of joke narratives, narratives that often give no internal sign of being a joke until the punch line. It is the frame that sets up the audience for "a joke." In the shaggy dog story the audience waits interminably for a punchline that turns out not to be a punchline after all. Ultimately, the humor is derived not from an inversion within the narrative itself, but from the frame that says that the joke is and is not a joke at the same time.

Another type of joke relies on the frame of the riddle question to prepare the audience for an enigma, only to make the answer a literal answer, and thereby reframe the question as a literal question. These are riddles like "What did one carrot say to the other carrot?" "Nothing, carrots can't talk," or "What's the name of Pontius Pilate's great-grandmother's straw bonnet maker?" "Nobody knows."[82] Similarly, the wellerism works by creating a context for a metaphorical phrase to be read literally: "I may feel the point, but I don't see the joke," as the sheep said to the butcher. "Good blood will always show itself," said the old lady when she was struck by the redness of her nose.[83] The wellerism takes apart the short cut into its component parts. We could make a wellerism of the example of the metaphorical turned literal offered in part 1: "I think the sun rises and sets on you," said one horizon to another. The humor of the wellerism is compounded by its being a quotation of a quotation. The form "as so and so said" is similar to the form of the invisible quotation marks around proverbs. But while the proverb brings more than one voice to its own discourse, bearing the weight of the voice of tradition in a congruent and forceful "fit" with its own discourse, the wellerism is a voice that splits into two contradictory halves, undercutting both its metaphorical and its literal aspects.

Lewis Carroll makes extended use of this kind of nonsense. In his works meaning is often made material, factual, and consistent at the expense of the understanding that makes up common sense. Jacqueline Flescher has said of Carroll's nonsense that meaning "is in a sense self-contained. In spite of the necessity to *mean*, the power of meaning is reduced to a minimum."[84] The exchange between the White King and Alice in *Through the Looking Glass* is halted by a continual movement from the metaphorical to the literal level:

> "I beg your pardon?" asked Alice.
> "It isn't respectable to beg" said the King.[85]

> "There's nothing like eating hay when you're faint," he remarked to her, as he munched away.
> "I should think throwing cold water over you would be better," Alice suggested, "or some sal-volatile."
> "I didn't say there was nothing *better*," the King replied. "I said there was nothing *like* it."[86]

The confusion with the term "nobody" that follows continues the problem. Sylvie and Bruno have the same troubles with "nobody and somebody,"[87] and even more with the phrase "as busy as the day is long."[88]

An extended literary example of the metaphorical made literal is the "Mr. and Mrs. Campbell" section of Infante's *Three Trapped Tigers*. The chapters are designed along a contradiction: Mr. Campbell narrates an account of an event. Then Mrs. Campbell gives her version, a version that denies many aspects of Mr. Campbell's narrative. Infante includes words that have been crossed out by the narrators in a display that permits the rejected word, the cancellation mark, and the correction to all talk at once: "~~Negro~~ Black," "~~officers of the marines~~ naval officers," "~~Who~~ prostitutes."[89] Thus the contradictions within the text are symptomatic of the larger contradiction going on between the two narratives. Infante further diminishes the univocality of the narratives by running footnotes across the bottoms of the pages in these chapters, footnotes that systematically take apart any "short cuts" that the narrators are making. Here is an example from Mrs. Campbell's narrative:

With the best will in the world Mr. Campbell entangles himself in his own verbal gymnastics—the only kind he is capable of—in trying to make me into a prototype: the only kind; the common female of the species. In other words a mental invalid with the IQ[10] of a simpleton, a cretinous Girl Friday[11], a moronic straight woman[12] . . .

[10] Intelligence Quotient
[11] Literary ref. Mrs. Campbell is addicted to them. See Daniel Defoe's novel *Robinson Crusoe* where there is a character named Friday
[12] Feminization of straight man[90]

The effect is to strip the Campbells' language, to translate what does not need to be translated within an ironic context of a book that is a translation of a book that could not be translated—*Three Trapped Tigers* itself.

A bum approaches Harpo Marx and asks him to spare a dime for a cup of coffee. Harpo reaches into his shirt and pulls out a cup of coffee—this is the metaphorical-turned-literal trick at work in these texts. Gertrude Stein provides a final example of this type of discourse in her "portraits" of painters and her descriptions of everyday objects. Rather than write a description that would move "up" to commonly held assumptions about character and objects, she chooses to break the act of perception into its component parts, and then to define those elements in terms of their relations to each other. Her concern is with difference rather than with the sameness that makes metaphor possible: "All the time that there is use there is use and any time there is a surface there is a surface, and every time there is an exception there is an exception and every time there is a division there is a dividing."[91] Stein's writing is an extreme example of the metaphorical turned literal. It presents what might be more properly called an "antimetaphorical" language in the sense that it rejects the "short cuts" of ordinary language and makes them strange, takes them apart into a new surface that packs its own layers of significance. In this sense her writing presents a critique of metaphor as the only way to move toward abstraction. With Stein's work, particularizing or stripping language of its assumptions turns out to be a movement towards abstraction as well. When the elements of her discourse are taken apart into minimal units of meaning, the effect is "a collection of ones." The discourse is immanently fragmentable, rearrangeable, within a surface that Stein loosely defines as "the object." For the text and object become one— the object is constituted as the text is constituted, by a fragmentation and rearrangement of "seeing."

When the metaphorical is made literal we see that, as was the case with discourse that denies itself, the reader is put into jeopardy. When discourse inverts itself in either of these ways the interpretive assumptions of the reader are inverted as well. The "what anyone knows" common to the everyday lifeworld is undercut, made suspect. The interpretation must begin again and again, fragmenting its assumptions.

In this chapter I have focused upon a set of operations by which nonsense can be made from common sense—the interpretive procedures involved in forming reversals and inversions. The very idea of reversal implies a shared ordering of events, an organization of the world that constitutes the parameters of a culture shared by a given set of members. It is this shared ordering that enables common sense to be taken for granted. Reversals can be performed by exchanging "proper nots," by inverting hierarchical relationships, by reframing in terms of oppositions. Because reversals depend upon a notion of "a prior state of things," they display the same is/is not paradox that is common to play and metaphor —they both affirm and deny an organization of the world with their every gesture. They test the validity of the state of things by turning that state upside down or inside out or back to front. Like any critical operation, they are what they are about, and in employing them we learn the shape and limits of the categories making up culture. Perhaps most importantly, reversals illustrate this rule for fictions: a fiction is reversible. The distinguishing characteristic of the fiction is its reversibility, its status as a form of play that both is and is not in the world, that both counts and does not count.

NOTES

1. See Raymond Williams, *Keywords* (London: Oxford University Press, 1976), pp. 76–80, and idem, *Culture and Society, 1780–1950* (New York: Harper and Row, 1958).
2. Emile Durkheim and Marcel Mauss, *Primitive Classification* (London: Routledge and Kegan Paul, 1963), p. 81.
3. See Edmund Leach, "Magical Hair," *Journal of the Royal Anthropological Institute* 88 (1958): 147–64. It is ironic that language itself is an abstraction, a systematic and rule-governed model, imposed over the flux of actual speech.
4. Claude Lévi-Strauss, *The Savage Mind* (Chicago: University of Chicago Press, 1966), p. 53.
5. Claude Lévi-Strauss, *Totemism*, trans. Rodney Needham (Boston: Beacon Press, 1963).
6. S. J. Tambiah, "Animals Are Good to Think and Good to Prohibit," *Ethnology* 42 (1969): 4–57.
7. R. Bulmer, "Why Is the Cassowary Not a Bird?" *Man* 2 (1962): 5–25. Reprinted in Mary Douglas, *Rules and Meanings* (Middlesex: Penguin Books, 1977), pp. 167–93.
8. Mary Douglas, *Rules and Meanings*, p. 27.
9. Sapir and Crocker, *Social Use of Metaphor*, p. 23.
10. Claude Lévi-Strauss, "L'Analyse morphological des contes russe," *International Journal of Slavic Linguistics and Poetics* 3 (1960): 137.
11. Dell Hymes, "'The Wife Who Goes Out Like a Man': A Reinterpretation of a Clackamas Chinook Myth," in *Structural Analysis of Oral Tradition*, ed. Pierre Maranda and Elli Köngas-Maranda (Philadelphia: University of Pennsylvania Press, 1971), p. 51.
12. Claude Lévi-Strauss and Paul Ricoeur, "A Confrontation," *New Left Review* 62 (1970): 57–74.
13. Edmund Leach, "Anthropological Aspects of Language: Animal Categories and Verbal Abuse," in *Reader in Comparative Religion*, ed. William Lessa and Evon Vogt, 3rd ed. (New York: Harper and Row, 1972), p. 210.
14. Mary Douglas, *Purity and Danger* (New York: Penguin Books, 1966), p. 161.
15. William Willeford, *The Fool and His Scepter: A Study of Clowns and Jesters* (Evanston, Ill.: Northwestern University Press, 1969), p. 16.
16. Paul Radin, *The Trickster* (New York: Schocken Books, 1972), p. xxiii.
17. Ibid., pp. 3–53.
18. See Barbara Babcock-Abrahams, "A Tolerated Margin of Mess: The Trickster and His Tales Reconsidered," *Journal of the Folklore Institute* 11 (1975): 147–86.
19. Radin, *Trickster*, p. 125.
20. Lévi-Strauss and Ricoeur, "Confrontation," p. 65.
21. See Archer Taylor, *English Riddles from Oral Tradition* (Berkeley: University of California Press, 1951).
22. Carl Withers and Sula Benet, *The American Riddle Book* (London: Abelard Schuman, 1954), p. 108.
23. Brian Sutton-Smith, "A Syntax for Play and Games," in *Child's Play*, ed. Herron and Sutton-Smith, p. 300. There is evidence, however, that this is not a

cross-cultural feature of play. K.O.L. Burridge's research on play among the Tangu of New Guinea shows that equilibrium may be the desired outcome of games in a society where cooperation is of primary importance. See "A Tangu Game," in *Play*, ed. Bruner, Jolly, and Sylva, pp. 364–66.

24. Lévi-Strauss, *Savage Mind*, pp. 30–32.

25. Julia Kristeva, *Le Texte du roman* (The Hague: Mouton, 1970), p. 162. See also Mikhail Bakhtin, *Rabelais and His World*, trans. Helene Iswolsky (Cambridge, Mass.: MIT Press, 1968).

26. James Joyce, *Finnegans Wake* (New York: Viking, 1939), p. 92.

27. See Lionel Casson, *Ancient Egypt* (New York: Time Life, 1965) and Thomas Wright, *A History of Caricature and Grotesque in Literature and Art* (1865; reprint ed., New York: Ungar, 1968), pp. 6–8.

28. Wright, *History of Caricature*, pp. 6–7.

29. Henri Bergson, "Laughter," in *Comedy*, ed. Wylie Sypher (Garden City, N.Y.: Anchor Books, 1956), p. 121.

30. Lewis Carroll, *The Complete Works of Lewis Carroll* (New York: Vintage Books, 1976), p. 92.

31. Iona and Peter Opie, *The Lore and Language of Schoolchildren* (London: Oxford University Press, 1959), p. 22.

32. François Rabelais, *The Histories of Gargantua and Pantagruel*, trans. J. M. Cohen (Baltimore: Penguin Books, 1955), pp. 242–44.

33. Cammaerts, *Poetry of Nonsense*, pp. 25–27.

34. Carroll, *Complete Works*, pp. 56–57.

35. Ibid., p. 72.

36. Ibid., p. 264.

37. This account is courtesy of the great lithographer Sam Walker, who was a teacher at the Shipley School from 1975 to 1976.

38. Opie, *Lore and Language*, p. 2. See also H. C. Bolton, *The Counting Out Rhymes of Children* (London: Elliot Stock, 1888), p. 36: "Necromancers of the Middle Ages, pretending to 'raise the evil one,' drew upon the ground mystical geometrical figures—a square, a triangle, a circle—and, placing an old hat in the center, repeated the Lord's Prayer backwards."

39. Lucy Nolton, "Jump Rope Rhymes as Folk Literature," *Journal of American Folklore* 61 (1948): 58.

40. Alan Dundes and Robert Georges, "Some Minor Genres of Obscene Folklore," *Journal of American Folklore* 75 (1962): 221–26.

41. Carl Withers, *A Rocket in My Pocket* (New York: Henry Holt, 1948), p. 196.

42. Duncan Emrich, *The Nonsense Book of Riddles, Rhymes, Tongue Twisters, Puzzles, and Jokes* (New York: Four Winds Press, 1970), p. 219.

43. L. Lalanne, *Curiosités littéraires* (Paris: Paulin, Libraire-Éditeur, 1845), p. 32. See also Liede, "Die literarischen gesellschaftlichen und gelehrten spiele," in *Dichtung als Spiel*, 2: 43–255, and the "drunkard's discourse" in Joseph Hickerson and Alan Dundes, "Mother Goose Vice Verse," *Journal of American Folklore* 75 (1962): 256.

44. John Fisher, *The Magic of Lewis Carroll* (New York: Simon and Schuster, 1973), p. 70.

45. Quoted in Robert Sutherland, *Language and Lewis Carroll* (The Hague: Mouton, 1970), p. 25.

46. See C. C. Bombaugh, "A Palindromic Enigma," in *Facts and Fancies for the Curious from the Harvest Fields of Literature* (Philadelphia: Lippincott, 1905), p. 516. The "enigma's" solution is that the first letters of the first five words spell the last word.

47. G. Cabrera Infante, *Three Trapped Tigers*, trans. from the Cuban by Donald Gardner and Suzanne Jill Levine (New York: Harper and Row, 1971), p. 223.

48. Ibid., p. 224.

49. Lalanne, *Curiosités*, p. 27.

50. Infante, *Three Trapped Tigers*, p. 284.

51. W. T. Dobson, *Literary Frivolities, Fancies, Follies, and Frolics* (London: Chatto and Windus, 1880), p. 143.

52. Samuel Beckett, *Watt* (New York: Grove Press, 1959), p. 30.

53. Beckett, *Watt*, pp. 164–69.

54. Gustave Flaubert, *Bouvard and Pecuchet*, trans. T. W. Earp and G. W. Stonier (New York: New Directions, 1954), pp. 90, 91.

55. Ibid., p. 141.

56. C. H. Ainsworth, "Jump Rope Verses around the United States," *Western Folklore* 20 (1961): 192.

57. Kirshenblatt-Gimblett, ed., *Speech Play*, pp. 108–9.

58. Samuel Beckett, *Three Novels* (New York: Grove Press, 1955), p. 94.

59. Ibid., p. 176.

60. Ibid., p. 128.

61. Ibid., p. 134.

62. Laurence Sterne, *Tristram Shandy*, ed. James Work (Indianapolis: Bobbs Merrill, 1940), pp. 511-12.

63. Footnotes, of course, do not always lie at the foot of the page, but can also appear as notes following chapters, or as notes at ends of books. The marginal gloss can also be used in the fictive text as a denial and a criticism.

64. Jonathan Swift, *A Tale of a Tub*, in *Gulliver's Travels and Other Writings*, ed. Miriam Starkman (New York: Bantam, 1962), p. 315.

65. Ibid., p. 318.

66. Beckett, *Watt*, p. 102.

67. Ibid., p. 104.

68. James Joyce, *Selected Letters*, ed. Richard Ellman (New York: Viking, 1957), p. 241.

69. Benjamin Botkin, *A Treasury of American Folklore* (New York: Crown, 1944), p. 786.

70. Leo Bersani, *Balzac to Beckett: Center and Circumference in French Fiction* (New York: Oxford University Press, 1970), p. 294.

71. Viktor Shklovsky, "A Parodying Novel: Sterne's *Tristram Shandy*," in *Laurence Sterne: A Collection of Critical Essays*, ed. John Traugott (Englewood Cliffs, N.J.: Prentice-Hall, 1968), p. 89.

72. Cammaerts, *Poetry of Nonsense*, p. 40.

73. Florence Milner, "The Poetry of *Alice in Wonderland*," in *Aspects of Alice*, ed. Robert Phillips (New York: Vintage Books, 1971), pp. 245-52.

74. Quoted in Robert Motherwell, *The Dada Painters and Poets: An Anthology* (New York: Viking, 1951), pp. xxvii–xxix.

75. Ibid., p. 51.

76. See Michel Beaujour, "The Game of Poetics," in *Game, Play, Literature*, ed. Ehrmann, pp. 58-67.

77. Tzara quoted in C. Bigsby, *Dada and Surrealism* (London: Methuen, 1972), pp. 4–5.

78. André Breton, *Manifestoes of Surrealism*, trans. Richard Seaver and Helen Lane (Ann Arbor: University of Michigan Press, 1972), p. 38.

79. Ibid., pp. 53–54.

80. Bergson, "Laughter," p. 135.

81. Sewell, *Field of Nonsense*, p. 54.

82. Emrich, *Nonsense Book*, p. 77.

83. From C. G. Loomis, "Wellerisms in California Sources," *Western Folklore* 14 (1955): 229-45, and idem, "Traditional American Wordplay, Wellerisms, or Yankeeisms," *Western Folklore* 8 (1949): 3.

84. Jacqueline Flescher, "The Language of Nonsense in *Alice*," in *Child's Part*, ed. Brooks, p. 137.

85. Carroll, *Complete Works*, p. 224.

86. Ibid., p. 225.

87. Ibid., p. 371.
88. Ibid., p. 370.
89. Infante, *Three Trapped Tigers*, p. 195.
90. Ibid., p. 204.
91. Gertrude Stein, *Selected Writings*, ed. Carl Van Vechten (New York: Vintage Books, 1945), p. 478.

4 · play with boundaries

THE HORIZON OF THE SITUATION

While reversals and inversions are procedures that define relationships between categories, the second type of nonsense operation that I discuss here explores the activity of category making itself—it is play with the boundaries of discourse. In part 1 I presented a model for the interpretive activities of everyday life that saw textuality as a phenomenon emergent in ongoing social interaction. It was suggested that any situation depends upon members coming to share a conception of the horizon of the situation, a conception of what is relevant (appropriate) to the situation in light of this horizon, and an acting with regard to an appropriate outcome of the situation.[1] The "text" of the situation is contingent upon a notion of relevant context, that is, those aspects of intersubjective experience that will figure in forming the horizon of the situation. Context thus involves more than the immediate environment of a situation, for "immediate environment" is itself emergent in and dependent upon interpretive activities transferred from past situations and adaptable to a present conception of "what is going on."

While the meaning of situations is dependent upon a conception of the present, "unique," state of things, such meaning is an adaptation of all prior states of things brought to what is "at hand." Context does not stand guard around the text of the situation, ready to block any leaks in meaning. Rather, it is emergent in the ongoingness of the situation, the "flow" of reality-generating conversation. The boundaries of social discourse are definitive by virtue of the interpretive work that goes on in such discourse. To try to step outside of the universe of such discourse and objectively examine—make conscious—such boundaries is to experience an ever-receding horizon.

Defining the boundary of the situation will thus have a great deal to do with what in experience will be interpreted and what will not be interpreted—with what will be allowed to "exist" or "appear" in the situation and what will remain invisible, white, a blankness. Indeed, it is only by means of such blank spaces that what is interpreted is able to appear. A powerful set of metaphors for this is, of course, the conscious and the unconscious. Consciousness "appears" to us as the given, the interpreted, the intersubjective, unconsciousness as a deep, undifferentiated space. On the interface is the interpretable, the unconscious made conscious. And it is this interface that is the point of reflexivity, risk, and ambiguity in social process. As Bateson has pointed out, there must be a carefully controlled economy between the conscious and the unconscious: "It follows that all organisms must be content with rather little consciousness, and that if consciousness has any useful functions whatever (which has never been demonstrated but is probably true), then *economy* in consciousness will be of first importance. No organism can afford to be conscious of matters with which it could deal at unconscious levels."[2]

While the interpretive activities of everyday, common-sense discourse may be seen to be selective and thus involve an implication of "that which is not said," that which is left unrealized, such selection occurs within the realm of consciousness. What is left unsaid is assumed by members to be apparent, "what everybody knows." In fact, this is precisely why it is safe to allow the unsaid to remain unsaid. "What everybody knows" is arranged hierarchically according to the contingencies of the situation at hand. To make apparent what is unnecessary to the situation, what does not need to be articulated, would be to invert this hierarchy and disintegrate the boundaries of the situation— to disintegrate the very basis of "shared understanding" upon which the situation is constructed. Disaster would result since attention would be dispersed away from any purpose at hand, and the consequent failure to "go on" would undermine all confidence in the viability of the given social construction of reality. This confidence would be further demoralized by a realization that once consciousness is completely made apparent, fulfilled, the unconscious is spent, made manifest, and no longer a resource. Hence the social necessity of having this remain impossible.

The potential for such a disintegration is thereby restrained to domains of the impossible context. Aesthetic activities like play and fictions take place on the interface between the conscious and the unconscious. Art makes manifest aspects of the unconscious by means of skill. "The message of skill of any sort must always be of this kind. The sensations and qualities of skill can never be put into words, and yet the fact of skill is conscious," writes Bateson.[3] But at the same time that skill manifests aspects of the unconscious, it points to the vast potential of the unconscious—its unlimitedness. Because of this pointing towards the unconscious with a conscious gesture, and because of the ambiguous status of art as fiction—its being in and not in the world, its position on the interface of the unconscious and the conscious—the unconscious is never depleted, is never made manifest.

While texts that flaunt their fictive status make such a gesture towards this interface between consciousness and the unconscious, realism becomes more real than real to us by making some aspect of what was left unsaid in the everyday-life situation "said." This "said" is accomplished by means of a metonymy that makes this revealed aspect part of a larger group of shared, though mostly unarticulated, assumptions. It is a "said" that points to a vast and rich domain of the "unsaid." It is through this gesture that realism becomes "truer" than the depicted situation, more real than the reality it represents. The unconscious has been made conscious, but in a movement that heightens and deepens the potential of such unsaid assumptions. In this way, realism always slips into ideology—the gesture of revelation in realism is like a trigger that sets off a metonymic sequence of assumed-to-be-shared values. Realism endows social reality with a fertility and potential that would otherwise be ascribed to the unconscious. It thus gives social life over to nature, placing it in a realm beyond the control of merely human purpose and action.

But as levels of textuality move farther away from realism and towards irony and metafiction, what is "unsaid" becomes more and more articulated, more and more a conscious matter. With the construction of metafictions there is a reflexivity, an articulation of the conditions under which the fiction has come to be, and this movement is one that makes conscious aspects of the unconscious. Not only does the text itself appear as a surface replete with signification, but it also makes conscious aspects of context that would remain unarticulated in everyday life and the fictions of realism. The text thus comes to pack its own context, to carry its own set of interpretive procedures "spelled out" on its surface. This is the movement of nonsense with its impossible context—a context that is unrealizable, that "no one can stand" in everyday life precisely because it is overburdened with consciousness.

Because fictions by definition involve the articulation of a category "the not real" by means of an ambiguous relationship to its proper not, "the real," they are always involved in making conscious aspects of the interpretive procedures by which any textual boundary is constructed. Every frame is about the process of framing, the determination of an outside and an inside, the determination of a text and its context. As fictions become increasingly self-conscious, it is the nature of the frame itself, the relationship between domains, that is focused upon. Thus attention is shifted away from the nature of "the content" of the real or fictive universe and towards the procedures by which those universes are constructed. In the terms of literary criticism, the fictions become excessively "formal"; they become concerned with their own process of manufacture. While we can see realism as making conscious aspects of the unconscious, it also involves the making conscious of what is potentially (although not actually) available to everyday life. There is no movement towards making conscious aspects of the text that would otherwise be left unarticulated. But texts that are metacommunicative involve the making conscious of skill. With increasing reflexivity, they involve a making conscious of the very procedures by which the unconscious is made conscious. With nonsense, skill itself becomes gratuitous and suspect, and is systematically inverted in a movement towards a flaunted, a *skillful*, incompetence—an incompetence that implies competence and the limits of competence with its every gesture.

THE THREAT OF NONSENSE

It becomes apparent that nonsense must of necessity be a kind of taboo behavior. First of all, it involves the constant rearticulation of an anomalous aspect of social life—that is, the capacity of any fiction to be simultaneously p and $-p$. Secondly, as the most radical form of metafiction, it threatens the disintegration of social interaction that would occur if the unconscious was made conscious. It is the realization of the possibility that the discourse of everyday life could become totally conscious of its own procedures: it is the dispersal of attention from a purpose at hand, a halt to the ongoing nature of social discourse, and an extreme movement away from any conception of such discourse as natural. Thus in its concern with states of transition, with the operations taking place between categories more than with the content of the categories themselves, nonsense may be seen as a further anomaly, a marginal or liminal activity in the sense in which this term has been used in studies of ritual. "The coincidence of opposite processes and notions in a single representation characterizes the peculiar unity of the liminal: that which is neither this nor that, and yet is both," wrote Victor Turner.[4] Turner defines *liminality* as the state of being "in betweeen successive participations in social milieux dominated by social structural considerations . . . a sphere or domain of action or thought rather than a social modality."[5] Because nonsense has no everyday-life context, no context "dominated by social structural considerations," and because it is primarily a discourse about discoursing rather than about any "real life" content, its anomalous position may be seen as a liminal one. To engage in nonsense is not only to engage in a state of transition, it is also to engage in an exploration of the nature of transition.

While nonsense is contingent upon the procedures of common sense, as any category is contingent upon its proper not for the definition of the entire range of its significant attributes, nonsense also involves an undermining of the basis of the procedures used in manufacturing common sense. The focus of its attack is members' confidence in a mutual understanding underlying common-sense procedures. Nonsense undermines the idea of "something left unsaid," society's most powerful device for allowing members to believe that they can "stand in each other's shoes." By attempting to say everything, by leaving no aspect of discourse undetermined, nonsense takes control of its own procedures. It bears the threat of the self-generating, self-perpetuating machine.

Making the unsaid "said" is another way for nonsense to make the metaphorical literal, for this gesture is an articulation of the very procedures by which metaphors come to be made. Nonsense often involves a demystification, a stripping, of metaphor of the type that is at work in the writings of Gertrude Stein. If what is profound in metaphor has to do with its resonance to the unconscious, it is nonsense that restores metaphor to consciousness by exposing it as a device, a formal procedure for making new meaning. Again, what is made manifest through nonsense is form, procedure. When nonsense is engaged in reversing the metaphorical and the literal, or the literal and the metaphorical, it is concerned with exploring the procedures by which the two domains are articulated. This is particularly apparent in the reversals of performance levels characterizing many metariddles, metajokes and catch tales. The nonsense operation by which a riddle question is turned into an ordinary discourse question, or a joke into an "unremarkable" true story, is both a transformation from one domain to another and an articulation of the boundary between the two domains. The focus of attention is this boundary between talk and performance, and what is articulated is neither the metaphorical nor the literal meaning of the discourse so much as the shape of the discourse, the procedures by which the boundary is maintained.

In the remainder of this chapter I discuss some specific operations by which nonsense plays with the boundaries of discourse: misdirection, play with a surplus of signification, play with a deficiency of signification, and the manifestation of formal procedures.

MISDIRECTION

The great Baltimore magician, Frank DeOms, used to say of his act, "You see, it's all mis-direction." To play a trick has to do with misdirection, with shifting boundaries, with reframing a universe while the tricked-upon is not looking. Every trick makes us aware of the weaknesses, the leaks, in boundaries that once seemed firm. Consider two types of tricks that Houdini performed. The first were forms of "minor magic" from his early performances. In one of these magic tricks

Houdini would borrow a watch from the audience and then stumble on it, apparently breaking it. The broken watch was a substitute, however, and the borrowed watch would be passed secretly to Bess Houdini, who would place it on the back of a target off stage. Meanwhile, Houdini would apologize profusely and ram the fragments of the broken watch into a pistol. He would then ask Bess to bring him the target. When he shot the pistol, a spring released the borrowed watch, and the watch would then be returned to its owner intact.[6]

In this trick there are two complementary reversals that work as two negatives effecting a positive. A broken watch is inverted into an intact watch by means of what should be a disintegrating procedure, the shooting of a pistol. The pistol functions inversely; it does not shatter, it unites. Analogously, the trick works by splitting the total performance into two parts, into two accounts, one of which hides the other: (1) Houdini breaks a watch, then makes it reappear by shooting the broken parts out of the pistol, and (2) Bess Houdini exchanges a broken watch for the borrowed one, places the borrowed one on the back of the target, and the borrowed watch is released by a spring. The trick works so long as the first narrative is opaque, so long as the second narrative does not infuse its boundaries before closure. The second narrative, like Bess Houdini, must remain officially inauspicious and expendable—invisible yet not invisible throughout the performance.

This is the phenomenon of doubling in the trick—the frame, the activities of the double that form the outer parameter of the event, are hidden until a moment when they appear manifested, revealed, and the trick is fully played. The trick's deception is made apparent, yet not made apparent; it appears as an ominous "unsaid." At the moment of revelation, the opaque narrative is split and its boundaries are diffused. What was unconscious is brought to consciousness as the audience attempts to reconstruct the performance, to say what was left unsaid, this time incorporating the double in order to try to unpack the trick. This idea of a tension between the invisible and the visible presents a further analogy to the liminal phase in ritual, for the subject of passage ritual is, in the liminal period, structurally (if not physically) "invisible." Being in-between categories presents a paradox of reality: "The neophytes are sometimes said to be 'in another place.' They have physical but not social 'reality,' hence they have to be hidden, since it is a paradox, a scandal, to see what ought not to be there."[7] Bess Houdini becomes invisible to the performance because she is the transformation between the two states—the state of fragmentation and the state of joining. Her actions form the invisible outer boundary of the trick, just as the liminal phase of ritual presents an invisible outer boundary of social life, a boundary that is anomalous and forbidden.

The second type of trick that Houdini performed was the escape. The ability to get out of handcuffs, straightjackets, ropes, manacles, cellblocks, and coffins was what made him famous. What is remarkable and compelling about these performances is not a deception made apparent, as it was in the first type of trick. Houdini's escapes depended, rather, upon his own physical dexterity and incredible knowledge of locking devices. His escapes were a demonstration over and over again of a boundary dissolved and dispersed, and his body with its amorphous properties (it was rumored, for example, that he could make his hand smaller than his wrist and that he had trained his toes to be as dexterous as his fingers[8]) becomes an illustration of a text slipping through its frame, reinventing its limits in the same way that trickster changes his shape. The fascination of the trick becomes a fascination with technique, with the formal operations by which the text is made and shattered. The desire that the feats of Houdini invoke is not a desire to know the states of imprisonment and freedom, but to know the operations between these states, to know the point of reversibility and flux. This is the idea of sleight of hand: a skill so far into the realm of artifice that it no longer can be straightforward, no longer can be trusted. It is a performance for performance's sake that will ambivalently undo whatever it has done. There is nothing so noncommon-sensical as sleight of hand.

In children's games, the formation of a boundary is intrinsic to getting in or out of the game. The way to form such a boundary is to make a play gesture, a movement that sends the message "this is play" and marks off the particular space and time that will characterize the game. This movement may take the shape of a mock attack or stunt, by beginning a fiction or by making a ludicrous expression.[9] These performances are ancillary to performance, they are fictions that serve as an inauguration to other fictions. Thereby attention is focused initially upon boundary making, on interpreting the frame that marks off the "playground" from the ground of nonplay discourse. This is especially apparent in the use of counting out rhymes to determine the allocation of roles in a game. As a signal for performance and as performances themselves, counting out rhymes are both fictions and the margins of other fictions. This may be one reason why they, along with tongue twisters and the choruses of lullabies, are often the most "nonsensical" of fictions—that is, their language is farthest removed from the language of everyday life. Their language approaches gibberish, approaches sound without content. Counting out rhymes, tongue twisters, and the choruses of lullabies are what they are about. The rhyme is the instigation of the game, both the interface between reality and the game and the articulation of the interface between reality and the game. A tongue twister does just that (although it is sometimes used as a cure for hiccups, too). And the choruses of lullabies are seen to be a way to directly make a child fall asleep. They not only tell the child to fall asleep, they directly effect his or her falling asleep and are the interface between waking and sleeping, between the real world and the world of dreams.[10] The more hermetic these types of discourse, the more absolute is the split between domains. In counting out rhymes like

> Rumble, rumble in the pot
> One-erzoll, two-erzoll, zickerzoll zan
> Bobtail vinegar, little tal tan;
> Harum squarum virgin marum
> Zinctum, zanctum buck[11]

there is a radical shift away from the discourse of everyday life and towards the discourse of the game. The text of the counting out rhyme is aligned according to the text of the game. The grammar of the verses is not the grammar of everyday talk that preceded them, but the grammar of the game that follows, and is itself given content by the verses. Similarly, Hugo Ball's sound poems such as

> gadjiberi bimba glandridi laula lonni cadori
> gadjaina gramma berida bimbala glandri galassassa laulitalomini
> gadji beri bin glassa glassala laula lonni cadorsi sassala bim
> Gadjama tuffm i zimzalla binban gligia wowolimai bin beri ban[12]

were meant to be not complete texts or products in themselves, but devices for inducing the dada state of mind.

Once the boundary of the game is established, it is kept intact until closure. Breaking the boundary of the game by running off, by throwing down one's bat or racket, or by not paying attention, is poor sportsmanship, just as any return to the "madness" of the real world was a traitorous gesture among the dadaists. There is, however, a type of game that may be seen as a metagame and antigame, since it undercuts the "mutual understanding" that members assume in forming and maintaining the game's boundaries. In children's folklore, these games are often called "black magic," and they effect the same doubling, the same paradox of visibility and invisibility characteristic of Houdini's "minor magic." Here is an example of this game from a turn-of-the-century text, *The Parlor Book of Magic and Drawing Room Entertainments.* This game is called "He Can Do Little Who Can't Do This": "The leader takes a stick in his left hand, thence transfers it to his right and thumps three times on the floor, saying 'he can do little who can't do this.' He then passes on the stick . . . the secret lies in the fact that the stick, when passed on, is first received in the *left* hand and thence transferred to the right before going through the thumping ceremony."[13] In an Arkansas game called "Scissors," several players are seated in a circle. The leader takes a pair of scissors in his hand, crosses his legs unobtrusively and says, "I received them crossed and I pass them uncrossed." As he repeats the words "I pass them uncrossed" he un-crosses his legs and hands the scissors to the player nearest him. The scissors are passed around the circle and the joke is to see how many of the players fail to cross and uncross their legs.[14]

Like the necessary and hidden specter of Bess Houdini in the watch trick, each of these games involves the incorporation of what is assumed to be mere "context" within the text of the performance. The boundaries of the performance are redefined, and the sense of "what everyone knows" about the conventions of context that the audience has brought to the game is shattered by this redrawing of the boundary of the performance. The text asserts its power over context; to be duped by these tricks is to be literally "taken in," for the audience, as the brunt of the joke, becomes a necessary part of the joke. Once every-one knows the "secret" of such games, they are no longer funny. There-fore, such games are always looking for new victims, seizing new territory as well as being about the seizing of such territory. They are similar to the kind of amusement we derive from watching a fly on the face of a politician, a slip sticking out, or someone adding "horns" to someone else by sticking the second and third finger of his hand behind the unwitting victim's head. These are all situations in which the boundary of the text, the body, has been extended, and there is an unequal access to knowing. These tricks again remind us of the necessary incompleteness of our perception of "what is going on," an incompleteness that would threaten disintegration if made complete and that threatens tragedy whenever it is revealed.

SURPLUSES OF SIGNIFICATION

Misdirection within performance depends upon a surplus of signification, the interpretive rule that says that any fictive text is sub-ject to multiple interpretations, and, more generally, there is always more going on than we can know at any given place in time. When the text draws attention to its own boundaries it is questioning the limits put upon the range of its possible interpretations and asserting its own possibilities for multiple meaning. Misdirection is an extension as well as a realignment of meaning. The victim of "He Can Do Little Who Can't Do This" pranks is forced to consider new interpretations, extend-ing the horizon of meaning available to the text.

Stephen Leacock begins one of his nonsense novels, *Gertrude the Governess: or Simple Seventeen*, with a surplus of signification: "It was a wild and stormy night on the West Coast of Scotland. This, however, is immaterial to the present story, as the scene is not laid on the coast of Scotland. For that matter, the weather was just as bad on the East Coast of Ireland."[15] The passage demonstrates the point that the author is free to play on our assumptions as to what "the point" of the text will be, that the author can overload the text with information that the reader will organize along a hierarchical interpretive scheme whether or not the particular scheme is appropriate. We assume that the details of the opening scene are appropriate to the narrative of *Gertrude the Governess,* just as we assumed that coughing, crossing one's legs, or folding one's arms were not to be taken as part of the performance of black magic, or that what Bess Houdini did backstage was not available to the circumference of the performance.

Because a surplus of signification is not only potential, but intrinsic, to any fictive text, the text appears as an enigma, a puzzle from which an interpretation will be worked. In written discourse, there is a distance between author and audience that checks to some degree the arbitrary power of the puzzler. But in face-to-face communication, this power can be taken to full advantage. Thus a wide variety of riddles will manipulate the expectations the audience has regarding interpretive boundaries. Many of these involve a play on words that shifts the boundary of the enigma to another universe of discourse:

There was a house with no doors, windows or any openings except that there was no roof and the walls were too high to climb. Then it started raining, how did he get out?

1. He caught the flu and flew out.
2. He had a bat and ball, so strike once, twice, three times and he was out.[16]

The shift in the first answer is accomplished by the pun with its aural simultaneity. The shift in the second answer works as a written pun as well, since the two uses of "out" are both spelled "o-u-t." Lewis Carroll was a master of these types of puzzles, which are solved through word play. In *Puzzles from Wonderland,* he poses the problem:

Dreaming of apples on a wall
And dreaming often, dear.
I dreamed that, if I counted all,
—How many should appear?[17]

The answer is "ten," and depends upon shifting the parameters of the lexical unit "often" into two separate lexemes. He frequently included such puzzles in his letters to children. In a letter to Agnes Hull, he wrote: "Why is Agnes more learned in insects than most people? Because she is so deep in entomology. Of course you know that 'she' is 'elle'? . . . 'Well' you will say, 'and why is elle so deep in entomology?' Oh Agnes, Agnes, can't you spell? Don't you know that 'l' is the seventh letter of 'entomology'? Almost exactly in the middle of the word, it couldn't be well deeper, (unless it happened to be a *deeper well,* you know)."[18]

This kind of boundary shifting is also common to spelling riddles. These riddles move from a level of orthography in the question to a level of aural discourse in the answer without letting the audience know of the shift. The child will ask, "Can you spell grasshopper?", and the answer is: "G-R-A double leather, repper whopp. Whee O double, leather, repper whopper, Grasshopper." Another example shows what would happen if one could speak writing, if oral discourse could make reference to orthography:

"Spell Mississippi":

Double hump
I
Crooked back
Crooked back
I
Crooked back
Crooked back
I
P
P
I,
Mississippi.[19]

Shifts between aural and written discourse such as these are similar to the kinds of shifts between iconographic signs, graphemes, and other units such as morphemes that are found in the rhebus and the kinds of verses written in autograph books:

YYUR
YYUB
ICUR
YY4 me.

My ♥ ∧ 4 U[20]

These types of riddles can also play with assumptions regarding the nature of knowing and solving problems. In some enigmas, there is an overloading of "technical" information; an abundance of facts and figures is presented that is not necessary to the solution of the problem. This surplus of signification is similar to the "patter" that magicians keep up in order to deflect attention away from the machinations of the trick:

As I was going to St. Ives
I met a man with seven wives
Each wife had seven sacks
Each sack had seven cats
Each cat had seven kittens
Kits, cats, sacks and wives
How many were there going to St. Ives?[21]

The answer is "one," since meeting someone on the road usually means that the person is traveling in the opposite direction. Here the audience is misdirected by the surplus of signification towards assuming that a mathematical puzzle is being presented. The answer, however, is not to be derived from a complicated performance, but rather can be found through "common sense."

Another way to shift parameters is to purposely "miss the point," to set up a situation that will lead the audience to a certain conclusion, as Leacock did in the beginning of his nonsense novel, and then to insert another conclusion, one that in everyday discourse and its hierarchy of values would not be the "relevant" one. Colonel D. Streamer's "Ruthless Rhymes for Heartless Homes" provide examples:

> Making toast at a fireside
> Nurse fell in the grate and died;
> And, what makes it ten times worse
> All the toast was burnt with nurse.

> In the drinking well
> (Which the plumber built her)
> Aunt Eliza fell—
> We must buy a filter.[22]

Nonsense like this points to the essentially undifferentiated nature of information prior to interpretation. Until systems of typification and relevance are brought to the text, it exists only in its physical state. Significance is attributable through the activities of interpretation; it is interpretation that makes the arbitrary nonarbitrary.

The problem of arbitrariness is a problem of causality. We ascribe direction and significance to our interpretations by means of a non-arbitrariness that we see as being socially derived. Although we may believe language to be "arbitrary" in that there is no natural relation between the sign and what it signifies, social life endows language with a nonarbitrariness. The constraints of the situation, of tradition, lend a sense of appropriateness, a sense of "fit," to language in its occasions of use. And the rationalities of common sense will attempt to ascribe such a "fit," to "make sense" out of the state of things, even when confronted with a state that is seemingly senseless. This play between the arbitrary and the nonarbitrary is brought out in the speech play form known as "echo verse." In echo verse what is by nature an arbitrary, yet predictable, answer—the echo—is transformed into a nonarbitrary and not predicted answer. Where we expect repetition without significance, we are surprised by a significance that denies its status as a mere "echo." This echo verse, "Abdul Hamid questioning the echo in the Sultan's palace at Constantinople" includes the following question/answer pairs:

> L'Angleterre?   Mes curiasses?
>   Erre.   Assez.

> Mes Pashas?   Et Suleiman?
>   Achats.   Ment.[23]

Breton was fascinated by the pathology, echolalia, that worked as this type of verse does, but without its congruence. He suggested in his 1924 manifesto that the surrealists make use of it: "Q. How are you? A. You."[24]

The uses of misdirection include the asking of literal questions that are then turned into a trick:

> Do you want me to give you a little red box?
> Yes.
> (Gives him a box on the ear.)[25]

Some trick questions present two alternatives and have two separate answers capable of undercutting the success of either alternative. These are like, "When are you going to stop beating your wife?" Children will ask, "Which would you rather have, a rooster or a pullet?" If the answer is rooster, the questioner will go behind the victim and give him a hoist in the knee. If the answer is pullet, he pulls the victim's nose.[26] These trick questions take care of the short-life-span problem found in black magic, where one eventually runs out of victims. In these doubly prepared questions the audience is always a victim, every exit is barred; the text always spreads its abundance beyond the reader's resources.

Two examples of a surplus of signification in written discourse are the acrostic and the calligram, both of them forms that take on an added dimension through the process of reading the text on the page. Rabelais's bottle may be the perfect calligram, since in writing its form has been made apparent in space, has been filled, and in reading its form is emptied, is dissolved in time as one reads down the page.[27] In the calligram and the acrostic the temporal act of reading is redirected into a spatial act of perception. The spatial revelation will occur only when one redirects one's attention, taking in what was assumed to be irrelevant context—the shape of print on the page, the pattern of the vertical axis of print. With the acrostic, the direction of reading is undermined. One becomes aware of alternative directions of signification on the page. The acrostic can work by means of the initial letter of each line, which was the favored method of much of Lewis Carroll's acrostic verse and Sir John Davies's "Hymns to Astrae," all twenty-six of which spell out "Elizabeth Regina," or it can work in other directions. Poe, for example, invented a valentine for Frances Sargent Osgood in which the first letter of her name was the first letter of the first line, the second letter of her name, the second letter of the second line, and so on.[28]

The calligram and the acrostic, like Houdini's watch trick and the enigmatic riddles, present texts that are split, doubled. The double comments upon, corrects, and reframes the first text—the text of temporal reading—until the moment of closure, where the reader must reconstruct and realign his interpretation to take account of the gestalt produced by both texts. In calligrams like Rabelais's bottle or the mouse's "Long and sad tail/tale" in *Alice*, the poem transforms the content into a form made manifest.[29] The shape of language on the page, like the posture that the body assumes during the performance of black magic, becomes intrinsic to the text itself, and the reader is further pushed towards looking for significance in accordance with new hierarchies of relevance and wider contextual boundaries.

Isaac D'Israeli believed that contorting the boundaries of the text was correlative to contorting the boundaries of nature: "It was at this period, when words or verse were tortured into such fantastic forms, that the trees in gardens were twisted or sheared into obelisks and giants, peacocks or flower pots."[30] Just as nonsense can refuse to let print run its lines, it can also refuse to let nature take its course. The nonsense operation of misdirection not only deflects attention from content to form in games, riddles, and the written page, it also will often rewrite natural categories, transforming them into fictions with multiple and discontinuous boundaries. This is the movement accomplished in Lear's "Nonsense botany," where such specimens as the "Barkia Howlaloudia" (a stem with dog's faces, their mouths wide from howling), the "Jinglia Tinkettlia" (with tea kettle blossoms), and the "Bottlephorkia Spoonifolia" (with spoons for leaves, a bottle for a stem, and forks for petals) grow.[31] Robert Wood's *How to Tell the Birds from the Flowers* is similarly a set of visual puns based upon verbal puns, where "A Sparrow and Asparagus," "The Blue Mountain Lory and the Blue Morning Glory," "The Roc and the Shamrock," assume identical forms.[32] The verbal text thereby takes over the visual text, making it conform to verbal parameters. This is the opposite of the calligram, where the verbal text, like a fluid, is poured into the vessel of a representational text. In these examples of nonsensical botany, the natural world is made to conform to the discourse. In contrast, any form of realism will attempt to make discourse conform to the natural world.

Another way to use a surplus of signification to bring about misdirection is to construct a text in which the information presented on the page hides the aural content of the text. This can be done by using gibberish to hide the aural content, as it does in the children's song "Marzeetotes an' Dozeetotes an' Liddlelamzeetivee. 'An' a kiddle etiveetoo, wouldn't you?" (Mares eat oats and does eat oats and little lambs eat ivy, and a kid will eat ivy, too, wouldn't you?). The same trick is performed by the imperfect homonyms of this narrative, "Anser on Griddle": "(Ridden end anguish languish honor vacate shun.) Ones pun term, dare lift inner ladle court etch honor itch offer lodge, dock florist, too chilled wren under pair ants. Dear parens culled ham Anser on Griddle, cuss onus oh bore, inner alter ah gull . . . "[33] Another way to effect this is to present a false contrast in languages. What looks like a foreign language on the page turns out to be English when the visual content is pronounced with the "proper foreign accent." Luis Van Rooten's "Mots d'heures: gousses, rames"[34] is an entire volume of Mother Goose rhymes written this way in "French." Similarly, *Macmillan's Magazine* printed in February of 1872 a letter from a Mr. Thomas Chatterton, who announced that during a seance a Hermann von Schwindel had told him that Lewis Carroll's "Jabberwocky" was taken from "Der Jammerwoch," a German ballad. Mr. Chatterton announced that the original version in German began:

> Es brillig war. Die Schlichte Toven
> Wirrten und wimmelten in Waben;
> Und aller-mumsige Burggoven
> Die mohmen Rath' ausgraben[35]

Joyce often plays this trick in *Finnegans Wake*. For example, this passage where he writes in "Gaelic": "mhuith peisth mhuise as fearra bheura muirre hriosmas,"[36] that is, "with best wishes for a very merry Christmas."

In many of these texts the idea of a "surplus of signification" has to do with the several universes of discourse present in any given act of communication: with oral forms the boundary of the text is often extended to include the position and gestures of the body or aspects of the environment as coterminous to the discourse proper; with written forms the potential for boundary shifting opens up to include the sound of reading with all the potential gaps between "saying out loud" and "seeing on the page." The shape of language on the page, the physical dimension of print, becomes important to the discourse. The idea of "ornament" in discourse, the extension of discourse for art's sake, the use of "unnecessary" details, becomes another aspect of the making conscious that distinguishes art from everyday life. Whatever other functions it serves, such as misdirection or concealing information, ornament always serves to mark off ordinary discourse from extraordinary discourse, to tend towards a message "This is art."

It is not surprising that those texts that turn themselves inside out, revealing their machinery, often draw attention to their own use of ornament, to the pattern of digression and elaboration in the text. *A Tale of a Tub*, for example, consists mostly of digressions. In his "Digression in Praise of Digressions," Swift says: "The society of writers would quickly be reduced to a very inconsiderable number, if men were put upon making books, with the fatal confinement of delivering nothing beyond what is to the purpose."[37] Sterne writes in *Tristram Shandy* of the "moral impossibility" of telling a straightforward history. The writer will have "views and prospects to himself perpetually soliciting his eye . . . he will moreover have various

> Accounts to reconcile:
> Anecdotes to pick up:
> Inscriptions to make out:
> Stories to weave in:
> Traditions to sift:
> Personages to call upon:
> Panegyricks to paste up at his door:

He suggests that "a good quantity of heterogenous matter be inserted, to keep up that just balance betwixt wisdom and folly, without which a book would not hold together a single year."[38]

The problem of ornament is, again, the problem of defining the boundaries of the fictive text. Realism attempts to recoup the measurements of everyday discourse, the limits with which that discourse determines what must necessarily be said and what should be left unsaid and thereby assumed. But with texts that flaunt their fictiveness, the matter of the dimensions of discourse becomes problematic. This is a problem of description as well, for anything set off to be depicted threatens an unlimited amount of significance. With realism, a balance of significance and insignificance is sought after, a balance borrowed from common sense. But in fictions concerned with their own process of composition, the idea of dimensions becomes *apparent*. Here, exaggeration and miniaturization are foregrounded as techniques. Consider Uncle Toby's miniature fort in *Tristram Shandy*,[39] where the accumulation of details increases until the miniature becomes larger than life. Each miniature emphasizes the point that a surplus of signification will not be diminished by a reduction in the material being discussed by the discourse. A reduction in physical scale will not result in a reduction of descriptive scale. On the contrary, the manipulation of the physical dimension of the described object can extend the limits of significance beyond the "median" provided by everyday discourse. In addition, the manipulation of the physical dimension of print itself will not result in a corresponding reduction or exaggeration of significance. This is the experiment worked in moving print into a smaller and smaller physical space, as in nineteenth-century "watchcase" verses where poems were written in increasingly receding circles on a small piece of paper that would fit inside a watchcase.[40] Similar manuscripts were designed to fit into nutshells of the kind Swift mentions as "an Iliad in a nutshell" in *A Tale of a Tub*.[41] Peter Bales, an Elizabethan writing master, tells in Harleian MS 536 of "a rare piece of work brought to pass by him—the whole Bible contained in a large

English walnut no bigger than a hen's egg, as many leaves in the book as in the Bible and as much on the page."[42] These curiosities of literature present ways to test the parameters of the text, to juxtapose discourse against its physical dimension, attempting to reach the point where its physical dimension can no longer bear it. The content is no longer what matters—these curiosities are a gesture towards pure form, but a gesture that also points to a disjunction between the physical world and the world of discourse.

The miniature always tends towards exaggeration—it is a selection of detail that magnifies detail in the same movement by which it reduces detail. The gesture of filling the page out to its corners that characterizes the discourse of *Finnegans Wake* is a gesture that emphasizes the microcosmic aspect of the text—the text as an exaggeration of significance within a restricted physical space. Similarly, Raymond Roussel has shown that a miniaturization of a depicted landscape does not diminish the task of description. His poem "La Vue" (1904) is a work of 2,000 lines describing a seaside prospect engraved on a lens set into a penholder. The same volume includes poems of 1,000 lines each, "Le Concert" and "La Source." "Le Concert" describes the heading of a sheet of hotel writing paper, showing the hotel itself, an omnibus standing in front of it, the lake beyond, and the public gardens with a bandstand. "La Source" takes as its subject the label of a bottle of mineral water showing the spring that is the bottle's source and a girl in a peasant costume serving customers the same mineral water.[43] These works of Roussel demonstrate that a reduction in the physical dimension of the object depicted can in fact increase the dimension of significance. The text has the capacity to "blow up," magnify, and exaggerate the dimensions of the discourse of everyday life, for even in realism the task of the text is a task of representing a language that has already imperfectly mapped itself upon the parameters of a conventional world. Roussel's experiments with detail, like those of Robbe-Grillet in *La Jalousie*, present an infinitely receding horizon of description.

In folklore, forms of hyperbole such as tall tales and Jonathanisms provide ways to test the limits of everyday categories, especially the categorization of the body. Jonathanisms like "There was a man in Boston who was so large when a babe that it was impossible to name him all at once"[44] are nonsensical because they imply an impossible context and because they also challenge the limits of a range of boundaries borrowed from everyday life. When Alice begins to shrink from imbibing the liquid in the bottle that says "Drink me," she wonders what the limits of her miniaturization will be, "for it might end, you know," said Alice to herself, "in my going out altogether, like a candle. I wonder what I should be like then?"[45] Eating the cake that makes her grow taller, she resolves that she will have to send a carrier to put on her shoes and stockings for her. The rabbit's fan makes her shrink again and another "Drink me" bottle, this time in the rabbit's house, continues her transformations. Like the body of Houdini, Alice's body becomes amorphous. She both loses and explores her sense of identity.

In everyday life our size is determined by measurement to context, to those things in the surrounding environment. Size is a matter of differential identity, of "measuring up" or "measuring down" in relation to some other. But in nonsense, size becomes determined by those things inside the boundary of the text—thereby demonstrating the paradox of any internal measurement. This is the tendency of the "whopper"-telling session to pile hyperbole upon hyperbole, for measurement becomes a matter of alignment internal to the mode of discourse once an absolute break to the "real world" is effected. As Sterne says in *Tristram Shandy*, "A dwarf who brings a standard along with him to measure his own size—take my word—is a dwarf in more articles than one."[46]

The "Cyclops" chapter of *Ulysses* is an extravaganza of speech engaged in what Joyce called the technique of "gigantism," the blowing up of attitudes and language into unbelievable postures. While "the Citizen" presiding over the assemblage at Barney Kiernan's is the dominant figure of the chapter, it is language itself that is the correlative to Polyphemus; it is language that appears *monstrous*. It was the language of 1904 bourgeois everyday society that Joyce took to make gigantic and preposterous. He parodies legal, parliamentary, medical, and scientific jargon and the styles of all that class's fictions—the Gaelic revival style, the classical revival style, the Gothic revival style, and the theosophical style, the style of dialogue in sentimental novels, the style of nursery books, the Apostles' Creed, and the Old Testament. Most of all, he parodies the language of popular journalism, a language always striving towards a surplus of signification: a newspaper's feature story of a large-scale social event, with its catalogue of socially prominent participants; a newspaper's plug for a theatrical program; "minutes" of a meeting written for a newspaper; sports journalism; legal journalism; art journalism; church news; a newspaper account of the departure of a foreign visitor; a newspaper account of a natural disaster. The language comes to speak the characters. The chapter becomes a display of the social organization of significance—information is arranged hierarchically and "blown up" to significance in accordance with the categories of discourse. Ironically, the "overloading" of language with significance approaches the limits of language. The point where the discourse bursts with significance is the point of pure ornament and opacity. This is also the confrontation of Pantagruel with the Limousin "who murdered the

French language,"[47] a language of pure style, a language that has flown from the restrictions of signification, that no longer feels compelled to *mean*.

Exaggeration and miniaturization with their surplus of signification and amorphous properties are characteristic of all in-between states, all states of being other-than-in-the-proper-place. This becomes especially apparent during the liminal phase in ritual, where initiates are exposed to ritual symbols that are condensed and thereby exaggerated. Such symbols involve "the condensation of many meanings in a single form, economy of reference, predominately emotional or oretic quality, and associational links with regions of the unconscious."[48] Turner concluded from his study of Ndembu ritual, where ritual masks portray certain natural and cultural features as disproportionately large or small, that "to enlarge or diminish or discolor in this way is a primordial mode of abstraction. The outstandingly exaggerated feature is made into an object of reflection."[49] He concluded that the grotesqueness and monstrosity of liminal sacra should be aimed not so much at frightening the initiates as "at making them vividly and rapidly aware of what may be called the 'factors' of their culture."[50] When one attempts to define cultural categories in terms of position, in terms of relationships between categories, there is always a movement towards testing the limits of those categories, for in defining a boundary, one learns something about what lies on the other side of it. This presents another analogy to the role art plays in establishing an economy between the conscious and the unconscious—the use of "gigantism" as a technique tests the balance of that economy, the point where "making conscious," where a surplus of signification and the presentation of skill, slips back into the unconscious, the inarticulate, again.

DEFICIENCIES OF SIGNIFICATION

Conversely, the boundary of the text can be made ambiguous by a deficiency of signification, by gaps or tears in the performance, or by a refusal to close the frame around the text. Such a splitting is implicit in the idea of metacommunication—the capacity of the text to "break frame," to leak from one universe of discourse to another. For example, the narrator of *Three Trapped Tigers*, under a heading "Some Revelations," presents four blank pages to the reader.[51] The pages serve as a sign of the composability of the discourse. They beckon to the writerly reader the way the blank pages at the end of cookbooks invite revisions of the text, or the way the map in "The Hunting of the Snark" works:

> Other maps are such shapes, with their islands and capes!
> But we've got our brave captain to thank'

(So the crew would protest) 'that he's brought *us* the best—
A perfect and absolute blank.[52]

Sterne does the same thing in *Tristram Shandy*, when he tells the reader
to write his own description of Widow Wadman, "as unlike your wife
as your conscience will let you," giving the reader ample physical
space in the text to do so.[53]

Among curiosities of literature the most ready example of a puzzle
formed by a deficiency of signification is the lipogram, a composition
from which the writer has rejected all words containing a certain letter
or letters. The earliest lipogram is believed to be a "Hymn to Ceres and
the Centaurs," written by the Greek poet Lasus in 550 B.C., a lipogram
that omitted all *s*'s. Nestor composed an Iliad in which each of twenty-
four songs rejected any words containing a consecutive letter of the
alphabet.[54] The most famous set of lipograms is probably Lope de
Vega's five novels, each of which omit a different vowel.[55] The
lipogram, like black magic or the riddles containing a surplus of
signification, depends upon the audience's tendency to assume gestalts.
The audience is not aware that the composition is a lipogram until the
composition is reframed as such and given the status of "a trick." The
lipogram involves a play with the presence and absence of letters in the
text, and with a pattern that is thereby both invisible (not present) and
visible (apparent by its absence). In black magic negative space is made
positive—that which should not count is made to count—and in the
lipogram, too, negative space is made significant, but in a gesture
of deficiency and negativity, for the significance is absent to the scene
of interpretation. The reader is confronted with a significance that is
not available, that has been made absent. This pattern is therefore
analogous to what I called the "second narrative" of Houdini's watch
trick—a narrative that is apparent upon closure as a trick, but that is
still unavailable to the audience. What is significant in Lope de Vega's
five novels is what is missing, not what is present. What is significant is
a form made apparent, just as what is significant in the magic act is what
remains hidden, secret, and unrevealed—the trick, the mechanics of
form. Like a home where the mechanical and the tool-like remain hidden
in basements and workrooms, or between the walls of the house, the
realistic text operates behind television cabinets and radiator covers.
The text of ambiguous boundaries presents a glimpse of machinery
made tantalizing.

Another tactic that written discourse can take to play with a
deficiency of signification is to present an ambiguity by an absence of
punctuation. Without punctuation, the words on the page form an
undifferentiated mass. Punctuation slices through the text, marking
off a set of territories. Here is an example of this type of word play

that places the "punctuation" of line endings at odds with the missing punctuation:

> Every lady in the land
> Has twenty nails on each hand
> Five and twenty on hands and feet
> This is true without deceit.
>
> (Every lady in the land
> Has twenty nails. On each hand
> five, and twenty on hands and feet.
> This is true without deceit.) [56]

Again, once the missing element is restored, once technique is made manifest, the puzzle, the "magic," is solved.

Using a deficiency of signification to indicate a false gestalt is probably the most common operation of children's scatological humor. For example, "What starts with F and ends in uck?" "Firetruck." [57] Children often use the imperative of rhyme to make the audience "fill in the blank" and switch to another rhyme with another, nonscatological meaning. Baltimore children have several rhymes that work like the punctuation puzzles above—what the audience assumes to be the end of the line is really the beginning of the next phrase. The audience is given a false gestalt that is scatological, while the performer's gestalt remains indirect and "clean":

> Lulu had a steamboat
> The steamboat had a bell
> Lulu went to heaven
> The steamboat went to
> Hello, operator, give me number nine
> If you disconnect me,
> I'll kick you in the
> Behind the refrigerator
> lies a broken glass
> Lulu fell down
> And broke her big fat
> Ask me no more questions,
> I'll tell you no more lies,
> That's what Lulu told me
> Just before she died. [58]

A collection of *Censored Mother Goose Rhymes* published in New York in the 1920s achieves the same effect as the rhymes from folklore when it gives significance to terms by making them absent:

> Jack and Jill went up the hill
> To _____:
> Jack fell down and broke his _____,
> And Jill came tumbling after. [59]

The collection illustrates the point that making a category ambiguous, absent, and taboo endows it with an attraction that those categories that are conscious, that are "everyday," cannot achieve. It also emphasizes the attractive power of those categories that present a tension between boundaries, a tension of presence and absence with the latter's implication of the vast signifying resources of the unconscious. As the sinologist Stephen Albert in Borges's story "The Garden of the Forking Paths" has said, "The rules of the game forbid the use of the word itself. To eliminate the word completely, to refer to it by means of inept phrases or obvious paraphrases, is perhaps the best way of drawing attention to it."[60]

As in the previous examples of a deficiency of signification, the use of this technique of "not saying something" in literature often takes the form of a gap, a weakness in the text, that emphasizes both the limits and the force of the performer's power over the audience. Swift makes use of this technique in *A Tale of a Tub*, including several "Hiatus's in MS," flaws in the manuscript, with notes like: "Here is pretended a defect in the manuscript, and this is very frequent with our author, either when he thinks he cannot say anything worth reading, or when he has no mind to enter on the subject, or when it is a matter of little moment, or perhaps to amuse his reader (whereof he is frequently very fond), or lastly, with some satirical intention."[61] In both *Tristram Shandy* and *Three Trapped Tigers*, a death in the narrative is accompanied by black pages in the text—pages meant to signify "nothing," which thereby present the paradox of "signifying nothing." Infante's use of this technique is especially effective, since the black pages are not numbered and thereby "do not count." They are simultaneously there and not there. Like the fiction itself, they both exist and do not exist. Sterne omits chapter 24 of book 4, yet he makes reference to it in chapter 25. It is thus present, but invisible, there and not there; we cannot read it as we can read the other chapters, yet we can read *about* it in the following chapter. And if chapter 25 is about chapter 24, its own integrity as a chapter is broken and split.

With Beckett's work, the flaws in the manuscript become a matter of willed and unwilled incompetence. In *Molloy*, Moran says, "Oh, the stories I could tell you, if I were easy. What a rabble in my head, what a galaxy of moribunds. Murphy, Watt, Yerk, Mercier and all the others. I would never have believed that—yes, I believe it willingly. Stories, stories, I have not been able to tell them. I shall not be able to tell this one."[62] In *Malone Dies*, Malone says, "Ah yes. I have my little pastimes and they," and a blank space follows. Then Malone says, "What a misfortune, the pencil must have slipped from my fingers, for I have only just succeeded in recovering it after 48 hours of intermittent efforts. . . . I have spent two unforgettable days of which nothing will ever be known."[63] *Watt* is sprinkled with question marks implying some deficiency in the text, and also includes a "hiatus in MS."[64] Each such hiatus, each flaw or gap, emphasizes the fundamental inability of the text to recoup the world and at the same time reminds the reader that the interpretive procedures that can be brought to the text stand in the same relation to the text as the relation that the text bears to the world—a flaw in the text will result in a flaw in interpretation. The text's limits in signifying "reality" are passed along to the reader/ audience.

MANIFESTING THE IMPLICIT

Black magic effects a transformation of the text's boundaries by extending a significance to gestures that is equal to the significance of language. Thus the rule of everyday discourse that sees the gesture as supplementing, augmenting, language is inverted. The language becomes a servant to the gesture, which is the true focus of the trick. "Content" becomes secondary to "form." The gesture is the shape the language assumes in space. Similarly, the transformation of parameters in literature is effected by including elements of the environment that would ordinarily be invisible, secondary, and supplementing—the shape of language on the page in the case of calligrams, the pattern of elements not included in the text in lipograms and some scatological verse, and the hiatuses in the manuscripts of some literary texts. Incorporating the physical "reality" of the text into the fictive frame, making the frame part of "the picture," is another way to accomplish this transformation of text and context.

To do this is to make reality less real and the fictive more real, a movement accomplished in one stroke because of the relationship between the two domains. This is the technique of much of the *Sylvie and Bruno* books, where the author's literary imaginings come first, and "actual fact" follows. Carroll asserts that ideas come to him "like an effect without a cause." The narrator writes: "'So, either I've been dreaming about Sylvie,' I said to myself, 'and this is reality. Or else I've really been with Sylvie, and this is a dream! Is life itself a dream, I wonder?'"[65] This is also how the *objet trouvé*, the found work of art, is made. The boundary of the text is extended into an appropriate context just as it was in black magic. When Alice says "Stupid things" within the range of the jurors at the trial of the Knave of Hearts, the jurors write down "Stupid things" on their slates.[66] The objet trouvé does not increase the reality of the work of art so much as it points to the artful and accomplished quality of reality. Duchamp's urinal and Andy Warhol's Campbell cans have the effect of making the world a strange and powerful articulation of the interface between the unconscious and the conscious. The world is reframed with the gesture that reframes the "ready-made."

Robbe-Grillet has suggested that the order of the contemporary novel "has the great advantage of calling attention to its own artificiality, of pointing to its mask with its finger, instead of hiding behind the appearance of something natural, an essence, an ideological trap. It is artifice itself which appears on the scene in the novel."[67] Artifice, of course, is a device just as realism is a device. Certain "natural" conventions become employed over and over again in the assertion of artifice, and when these devices become "short cuts" rather than "fresh cuts" they have already made the traitorous passage to the side of the natural. All of these devices for making artifice have in common a technique of splitting, a breaking up of the "seam" of the text, a reflexive gesture towards the boundaries of the text, an intrusion of another, contradictory (and therefore ironic) voice.

I have discussed the use of footnotes to present a voice in contradiction to the voice of the text. The use of footnotes and margins in the fictive text presents several inversions. Footnotes in the nonfictive text take the voice of a learned and rigorous *other*; in fictive texts they present an implicit denial of the status of the text. The voice of the fictive footnote is either superfluous or clowning, or an authoritarian and pretentious voice, stretched through "gigantism" to the point of silliness. The rapid shifting of the voice in power, the voice that is to be trusted, has the effect of a dispersal and scattering of the text and thereby a dispersal and scattering of the real.

Consider the interplay of the voices of Pope and Swift in *The Dunciad: The Dunciad* written by Pope, dedicated to Swift; Swift under the pseudonym of Martin Scriblerus writing an introduction to the text and several facetious footnotes; Pope writing some of his own notes, sometimes by parodying the voices of other authors, as in Book the IV, Line 194, "(Through Christ Church long kept prudishly away)," which has a note saying "This line is doubtless spurious and foisted on by the impertinence of the editor; and accordingly we have put it between hooks." Pope thereby parodies the practice of Dr. Richard Bentley, who, in his edition of Milton, bracketed any lines he believed to be "spurious" for his own reasons.

Nabokov is another master of the ironic inclusion of the physical accouterments of the text within the text. Like the accolades of *The Dunciad*, the paperback edition of Nabokov's novel *Ada* includes a testimonial from Van Veen, one of the book's two main characters, among those from the *New York Times* and the *New York Review of Books*. The irony of Van's testimonial is compounded by the role he plays in the text as simultaneously a character in and an author of that very text. *Lolita* begins with a foreword written by one John Ray, a friend of Humbert Humbert's lawyer, Clarence Choate Clark. Ray tells the reader, who has not yet begun *Lolita*, the fate of all the characters in the book from the point at which Nabokov/Humbert's narrative ends. He suggests that the "actual crime" may be looked up by the inquisitive in the daily papers for September 1952. His conclusion, "*Lolita* should make all of us—parents, social workers, educators—apply ourselves with still greater vigilance and vision to the task of bringing up a better generation in a safer world,"[68] can be placed alongside the examples of a gigantistic style found at Barney Kiernan's, a style so typical of everyday life it becomes fictive, a short cut made into a fresh cut. At the conclusion to the narrated events of the book, Nabokov appears in his own voice with an essay, "On a Book Entitled Lolita," writing: "After doing my impersonation of suave John Ray, the character in *Lolita* who pens the foreword, my comments coming straight from me may strike one—may strike me, in fact, as an impersonation of Vladimir Nabokov talking about his own books."[69] *Lolita* thereby effects the same kind of manipulations of frame, the moving of the boundary between the two universes of discourse—reality and fiction—in a perpetual shifting. The "impersonations" of Nabokov here are illustrative of the phenomenon of the infinite mask—the mask that, when stripped off, covers another mask, which covers another mask, and so on to infinity.

Pale Fire may be seen as the most extreme gesture towards scattering the text into its physical surroundings, for the "story" of *Pale Fire*— the story of Kinbote's journey from Zembla to America, his relationship to John Shade and the writing of "Pale Fire," the poem—is absent from the physical text, and "the text" consists of all the accouterments of textuality: a foreword, whose dimensions include everything prior to and following the text, but not the text itself; a manuscript written by Shade; a commentary by Kinbote meant to supplement the manuscript, but which "in fact" presents a set of systematic contradictions to the manuscript; and an index by Kinbote that is a supplement to the commentary, but not to the manuscript. The "story" of *Pale Fire* is written between the lines, is discernible through a pattern of contradictions revealed by the split in the narrative voice. Nabokov has constructed a story as lipogram, and the absence becomes scatological, becomes an aspect of Kinbote's veiled sexuality. By calling his text *Pale Fire*, Nabokov further moves out to context, for this title implies the possibility of another critic, another Kinbote, taking up the Nabokov text and reconstructing it with foreword, commentary, and index ad infinitum. *Pale Fire*, like any magic trick, is all *technique*—it is about the manufacture of textual parameters, about the limits of interpretive procedures as much as it is about anything else.

Notes in the fictive text become obligatory, they tear the reader away from any center of attention, and, in novels like *Pale Fire*, the accouterments of textuality become the text. Michel Butor has suggested that the marginal sentence, phrase, or word "is like an ink spot which soaks in, which spreads, and which will be counteracted, contained, by the spreading of the next spot. The word thus functions like a color. The names of colors and all words which designate the quality of a surface or a space will have an especially remarkable power to permeate the page."[70] This diffusion and spreading is demonstrated in book 2 of *Finnegans Wake* in the nightletter written by H. C. Earwicker's three children, Kevin, Jerry, and Isabel, with Kevin's (Shaun's) voice on the right, Jerry's (Shem's) voice on the left, and Isabel's voice in the footnotes. The three voices speak in three distinct styles. Shem's voice appears as an ironic aside, full of bursts of word play ("Swing the banjo, batams, bounce the baller's blown to fook") in italic lower-case letters, while Shaun's voice presents in Roman upper-case letters glosses that resemble the titles of learned treatises ("PROB-POSSIBLE PROLEGO-MENA TO IDEAREAL HISTORY"). Halfway through the letter, the boys switch voices and typefaces. Isabel's voice is printed in a smaller version of the text's typeface, and her language resembles a child's version of adult speech, "When we play dress grownup at alla ludo poker you'll be happnessised to feel how fetching I can look in clingarounds."[71] The effect is a visual cacophony of voices; the reader's attention is continually diverted to the edges of the page. The text appears as something in-between and absent, something the reader only glimpses out of the corner of his eye. The children's text develops a style of "scrupulous meanness," meaning brought about by a shattering of meaning. Similarly, the notes to *The Waste Land* set up a pattern of resistances to meaning. Interpretation takes place in a restricted field, as it did in Kinbote's version of "Pale Fire." The capacity of *The Wasteland* to inspire multiple interpretations is shut down by the limited system of correspondences available in the notes. It is as if Joyce endorsed *The Skeleton Key to Finnegans Wake* and had it appended to the definitive edition.

With the fictions of Borges, the boundaries of the text become even more ambiguous. Borges writes "real" footnotes to "real" reviews of imaginary books, thereby calling into question the status of those footnotes and reviews. "The composition of vast books is a laborious and impoverishing extravagance," writes Borges. "To go on for five hundred pages developing an idea whose perfect oral exposition is possible in a few minutes! A better course of procedure is to pretend that those books already exist, and then to offer a résumé, a commentary."[72] He addresses the problem of the integrity of the text in "Pierre Menard, Author of Don Quixote." If a map is of natural size, which is map and which is object? Pierre Menard, writing/rewriting *Don Quixote*, comes to write the effect of reading. The boundary of the text exists at the limits of its readings, and yet, with each reading, the text is dissolved and another text emerges. In another story, "An Examination of the Work of Herbert Quain," Quain says, "I do not belong to Art, but merely to the history of art." Quain, invented by Borges, has invented a story that insinuates two arguments, and the reader, "led astray by vanity, thinks he has invented them." Borges writes, "I was ingenious enough to extract from the third, 'The Rose of Yesterday,' my story of 'The Circular Ruins.'"[73] Thus Borges has invented a character who invents his own readers, who think that they have invented the story. And among these duped readers is Borges, who has invented out of this invention his own story, "The Circular Ruins," a story that is absent to "An Examination of the Work of Herbert Quain," but that is in turn about a man who meets a man he has dreamed only to realized that he himself has been dreamed by that very man.

In each fiction where the author becomes a character and the sense of reading and writing become implicated in the text, the boundary between fiction and reality—between text and context—is dissolved and reformed, and the interpreted, the fictive, nature of reality is emphasized. In Flann O'Brien's *At Swim-Two-Birds*, the author of the novel, Dermott Trellis, is put to trial by his characters for injustices he has done to them. In Borges's story, "Theme of the Traitor and Hero," a traitor is allowed to rewrite his destiny according to a set of fictive destinies, so that his death will be a hero's death and cancel the damage to the cause he has betrayed. There is also Claude Mauriac, speaking in his own voice at the end of *L'Agrandissement,* saying, "This book is the story of a gentleman who is wondering how he will write a novel that I have already written," or the characters at the end of Nabokov's *The Gift* or Garcia Marquez's *One Hundred Years of Solitude,* who begin to write the novel they have just appeared in. John Barth writes in his story "Title":

Story of our lives. The last word in fiction, in fact. I chose the first person narrative viewpoint in order to reflect interest from the peculiarities of the technique (such as the normally unbearable self-consciousness, the abstraction and the blank) to the nature and situation of the narrator and his companion, despite the obvious possibility that the narrator and his companion might be mistaken for the narrator and his companion. Occupational hazard.[74]

Fictions like these play with the boundary between character and author (Nabokov's Ada and Van, O'Brien's Dermott Trellis, Barth slipping in and out of his fictions), between author and reader (Sterne's lady reader, Joyce writing "wipe your glosses with what you know"), and between reader and character (the fictions of Borges, for example, where destinies are fulfilled through fictions).

In all these operations by which boundaries are manipulated—

misdirection, a surplus or deficiency of signification, the incorporation of formal procedures—there is an increasing consciousness of the origin and nature of interpretation. These texts are concerned with instructions for their own reading. As they become increasingly self-conscious, they are like do-it-yourself kits, replete with ingredients for a world and instructions for its manufacture. In this sense they are always more or less than a text and never simply "a text"—they are a sum of their readings, yet a possibility beyond their readings. They flaunt the amorphous and liminal nature of the fictive position, and their boundaries—their margins, notes, and gestures—become a metaphor for the escape and capture of identity and meaning. They point to the problem of "identity," that common-sense gesture by which the world is fixed, held permanent, if only for a moment. These texts that dissolve at their own borders and reappear with new boundaries over and over again may be symptomatic of another paradox of classification—the problem of distinguishing the life within the body from the body that carries it in and through the world.[75]

NOTES

1. See the section of chapter 1 called "The Sense of Common Sense."
2. Bateson, *Ecology of Mind*, p. 143.
3. Ibid., p. 138.
4. Victor Turner, *The Forest of Symbols* (Ithaca, N.Y.: Cornell University Press, 1967), p. 99.
5. Turner, *Dramas, Fields, and Metaphors*, p. 52.
6. Harold Kellock, *Houdini: His Life Story, from the Recollections and Documents of Beatrice Houdini* (New York: Blue Ribbon Books, 1928), pp. 126–27.
7. Turner, *Forest of Symbols*, pp. 95, 98.
8. Kellock, *Houdini*, p. 3–4.
9. Brian Sutton-Smith, "Boundaries," in *Child's Play*, ed. Herron and Sutton-Smith, p. 104.
10. The choruses of lullabies may also play a role in the development of other performance competences. Alan Lomax and Edith Crowell Trager have suggested that vowel preferences may be implanted by mothers in their children via lullabies during infancy, and that these patterns help to shape the development of adult folk song. See "Phonotactique du chant populaire," *L'Homme* 4 (1964): 5.
11. Bolton, *Counting Out Rhymes*, p. 3.
12. See Hans Richter, *Dada: Art and Anti-Art* (New York: McGraw Hill, 1965), p. 42.
13. Signor Blitz, ed., *The Parlor Book of Magic and Drawing Room Entertainments* (New York: Hurst, 1889), p. 40.
14. Paul Brewster, *American Nonsinging Games* (Norman: University of Oklahoma Press, 1953), p. 124. See also the Indiana game called "Poker," p. 124.
15. Stephen Butler Leacock, *Nonsense Novels* (New York: Dodd Mead, 1929), p. 21.
16. Archer Taylor, "Wellerisms and Riddles," *Western Folklore* 19 (1960): 56. Joyce uses a variation of this pun in his "Vladimir Dixon" letter of protest appended to *Our Exagmination Round His Factification for Incamination of Works in Progress*, ed. Beckett et al. (New York: New Directions, 1972), p. 193: "In

gutter dispear I am taking my pen toilet you know that, being leyde up in bad with the prevailent distempter I opened the window and in flew Enza."

17. Carroll, *Complete Works*, p. 819.

18. Letter to Agnes Hull in *A Selection from the Letters of Lewis Carroll to His Child-Friends*, ed. Evelyn Hatch (London: Macmillan, 1933) pp. 139–40.

19. Paul Brewster, "Spelling Riddles from the Ozarks," *Southern Folklore Quarterly* 8 (1944): 301–3. The resemblance of E. E. Cummings's "Grasshopper" poem to this example would make it also a suitable answer to the spelling riddle, "Spell Grasshopper."

20. Withers, *A Rocket in My Pocket*, pp. 94, 162.

21. Sabine Baring-Gould, *A Book of Nursery Songs and Rhymes* (London: Methuen, 1895), p. 143.

22. Colonel D. Streamer, *Ruthless Rhymes for Heartless Homes* (Boston: R. H. Russell, 1901).

23. W. T. Dobson, *Poetical Ingenuities and Eccentricities* (London: Chatto and Windus, 1882), p. 231.

24. Breton, *Manifestoes*, p. 34.

25. Botkin, *Treasury of American Folklore*, p. 776.

26. See Opie, *Lore and Language*, p. 71. Mathematical puzzles of this type include: Four *te* cups on a table. One broke. How many were left? (Three tea cups or 39 indeterminate cups.)

27. Rabelais, *Gargantua and Pantagruel*, p. 703. Christian Morgenstern's calligram "The Funnels" also flows towards the direction of reading. See "Die Trichter," *Galgenlieder/The Gallows Songs*, trans. Max Knight (Berkeley: University of California Press, 1966), pp. 32–33. See also many of the examples of *vers figures* given by Lalanne in his *Curiosités littéraires*, many of which are bottles, flagons, and glasses (p. 16).

28. Dobson, *Poetical Ingenuities*, pp. 198–203.

29. A nineteenth-century reader's note in *The Journal of American Folklore* ("The Black Cat" and "The Wild Fowl," *Journal of American Folklore* 10 [1897]: 322–24) gives two examples of narratives that adults told to children involving the drawing of elements of the story as the narrative proceeds, for example:

T stands for Tommy T
Tommy built walls to his house V

until all these lines form a final figure, the black cat or the wild fowl, which appears at the story's climax. The game of "Hangman" works the same way, the form of the hangman emerging through the process of the game. But in the two narratives discussed here, there is an attempt to link the content of the narrative with the content of the figure and to narrative time; the revelation of the figure occurs as the narrative unfolds. The stories are like calligrams for oral discourse, the form unfolds through the telling, just as the form unfolds through the writing in the calligram.

30. Isaac D'Israeli, *Curiosities of Literature*, 3 vols. (London: Routledge, Warnes, and Routledge, 1880), 1: 295.

31. Edward Lear, *The Complete Nonsense Book*, ed. Lady Strachey (New York: Dodd Mead, 1912), pp. 199–211.

32. Robert Wood, *How to Tell the Birds from the Flowers: A Revised Manual of Flornithology for Beginners* (New York: Duffield, 1917).

33. Gene Gluesing (mimeograph), "Anser on Griddle," The Annenberg School, University of Pennsylvania, Philadelphia, 1976.

34. Luis Van Rooten, *Mots d'heures: gousses, rames* (London: Angus and Robertson, 1968).

35. Quoted in Langford Reed, *A Book of Nonsense Verse* (New York: Putnam, 1926), p. 48.

36. Joyce, *Wake*, p. 91. See also A. M. Nitramof, "The French Originals of English Nursery Rhymes" ("Allons à dada à Bains-Brie à la Croix"), in Cammaerts, *Poetry of Nonsense*, pp. 79–81. Similarly, there is the language invented by

Jonathan Swift and Thomas Sheridan called "Latino-Anglicus": "De armis ter de an" = "Dear Mister Dean." See Vivian Mercier, *The Irish Comic Tradition* (London: Oxford University Press, 1962), pp. 231-32.

37. Swift, *Tale of a Tub*, p. 357.

38. Sterne, *Tristram Shandy*, p. 37.

39. Ibid., p. 614.

40. Dobson, *Poetical Ingenuities*, p. 232.

41. Swift, *Tale of a Tub*, p. 356.

42. Dobson, *Literary Frivolities*, p. 12.

43. These works by Roussel are discussed by Vivian Mercier in *The New Novel from Queneau to Pinget* (New York: Farrar, Straus, Giroux, 1971), pp. 20-21, and by John Ashbery, "On Raymond Roussel," in Raymond Roussel, *How I Wrote Certain of My Books*, trans. Trevor Winkfield (New York: Sun, 1977), p. 51. For an analysis of Roussel's techniques see Michel Foucault, *Raymond Roussel* (Paris: Gallimard, 1963).

44. C. G. Loomis, "Jonathanisms: American Epigrammatic Hyperbole," *Western Folklore* 6 (1947): 214.

45. Carroll, *Complete Works*, p. 23.

46. Sterne, *Tristram Shandy*, p. 316.

47. Rabelais, *Gargantua and Pantagruel*, pp. 183-85.

48. Turner, *Forest of Symbols*, p. 29.

49. Ibid., p. 103.

50. Ibid., p. 105.

51. Infante, *Three Trapped Tigers*, pp. 280-83.

52. Carroll, *Complete Works*, p. 761.

53. Sterne, *Tristram Shandy*, pp. 470-71.

54. Lalanne, *Curiosités*, pp. 29-30.

55. Dobson, *Poetical Ingenuities*, p. 220, and idem, *Literary Frivolities*, pp. 58-68.

56. Dobson, *Literary Frivolities*, p. 249. See also Emrich, *Nonsense Book*, p. 65: "I saw a fishpond all on fire."

57. David Winslow, "An Annotated Collection of Children's Lore," *Keystone Folklore Quarterly* 11 (1966): 172.

58. Collected at Rutland Elementary School, Baltimore, Maryland, May 1976. For other examples, see E. B. Browne, "Southern California Jump Rope Rhymes: A Study in Variants," *Western Folklore* 14 (1955): 18.

59. Kendall Banning, *Censored Mother Goose Rhymes* (New York: privately printed, 1926).

60. Jorge Luis Borges, *Ficciones*, ed. Anthony Kerrigan (New York: Grove Press, 1962), pp. 99-100.

61. Swift, *Tale of a Tub*, p. 313.

62. Beckett, *Three Novels*, p. 137.

63. Ibid., p. 222.

64. Beckett, *Watt*, p. 238.

65. Carroll, *Complete Works*, p. 296.

66. Ibid., p. 115.

67. Alain Robbe-Grillet, "Order and Disorder in Film and Fiction," *Critical Inquiry* 4 (1977): 5.

68. Vladimir Nabokov, *Lolita* (New York: Putnam, 1955), p. 8.

69. Ibid., p. 313.

70. Butor, *Inventory*, p. 51.

71. Joyce, *Wake*, pp. 260-308.

72. Borges, *Ficciones*, p. 15.

73. Ibid., p. 78.

74. John Barth, *Lost in the Funhouse* (New York: Bantam, 1969), pp. 106-7.

75. This problem is suggested in Bateson's metalogue with his daughter, "Why Do Things Have Outlines?" in *Ecology of Mind*, pp. 27-37. Bateson asks his daughter how she could draw the outline of a flock of sheep or of a conversation.

The problem becomes whether relationships and living things have outlines. Sutton-Smith concludes in his essay entitled "Boundaries" (*Child's Play*, ed. Herron and Sutton-Smith, p. 105) that "what begins as a study of ecology may be impossible to pursue without a parallel study of the psychic structures that exist concordantly within the individual players."

5 · play with infinity

The manipulation of boundaries, performed in time as well as in space, may also involve a play with the possibility of infinity. Just as play with the boundaries of discourse events involves a transformation of members' expectations regarding the horizon of the situation, so play with infinity involves a transformation of another aspect of members' expectations—their sense of events as characterized by distinguishable beginnings and endings. Reality-generating conversations are endowed by members with historical boundaries. These boundaries depend upon a shared sense of what counts and does not count—a sense of discrete events that can be arranged in a temporal order, one after the other. And this implies both a causal order, events causing other events, and a hierarchical order, events contingent upon the import of other events. The discreteness of events depends upon a temporal as well as a spatial sense of closure, and each sense implicates, is *relative to*, the other.

This essay began with a discussion of etymology and here we return to it. Etymology becomes the prototype for the attempt to distinguish "objectively" the boundaries of any language event. Every attempt to define a word dissolves into the occasions of its use, and any attempt to define the occasions of its use dissolves into a set of common-sense procedures that are themselves emergent through "occasions of use." Here again is the ever-receding horizon, the infinite regress characteristic of "explaining explanations." This is the etymological situation of Alice, who learns from the White Knight that the name of a song is called "Haddock's Eyes," the name is really "The Aged Aged Man," the song is called "Ways and Means," and the song really is "A-Sitting on a Gate."[1] The language event is thus caught in a historical regress. What the song "really is" becomes only one of its possible aspects through its history of use. The "object" comes to be through a succession of situations.

The problem of etymology is part of a larger problem regarding time and its correlative, the notion of temporal order. In his lectures on "Lived Experiences of Time," Husserl contended that there is a set of "laws of time" that are self-evident. He included among these laws the following:

1. That the fixed temporal order is that of an infinite two dimensional series
2. That two different times can never be conjoint
3. That their relation is a non-simultaneous one;
4. That there is transitivity, that to every time belongs an earlier and later, and so on.[2]

These laws of time "stand behind" everyday-life situations. The two-dimensional infinite series becomes, like the unconscious, a place of possibility. Events in everyday life are determined by a measuring, a lining-up against this intersubjective sense of time. Time becomes one of those phenomena that Schutz called "selected systems of reference,"[3] phenomena that in themselves become prototypes of order. To coordinate social events with an intersubjective, ordered system of time is to lend a sense of order and precision to the events themselves.

Time in the everyday lifeworld thus depends upon a sense of "time in the abstract" that is historical (serial and linear) and infinite, stretching beyond experienced time in "both directions." Here is a paradox in the common sense of time, for while members see events as discrete, having discernible beginnings and endings, they see time itself as infinite, beyond any knowable origin or end. Thus everyday events are measured along a dimension that is itself impossible to measure. Time in the abstract sense may give everyday life a model of order and possibility, but it does not provide a model for temporal boundary making. Intersubjective time is often seen thereby in tension with ongoing, infinite time. Human events do not partake of this infinity; rather, they are characterized by temporal limits. This is how intersubjective time allows for what Schutz called "a coordination of different individual plan systems."[4] Time in the common-sense world is used for the coordination of "purposes at hand," the coordination of our accomplishments, plans, and goals. Thus time can be "achieved," given closure, in the everyday lifeworld. Paradoxically, events are seen to "count" by "taking up time," by being "given time," while such quantities are necessarily reductions of an infinite "amount" and therefore not reductions in any abstract sense of duration. But these quantities *are* reductions in an intersubjective, everyday duration whose quantity is limited; they are coterminous with the body's experience of the lifeworld. For a fiction to close its boundary "realistically" is often to close it in accordance with the shape of closure in the everyday life-world: the day, the season, the year, the lifetime.[5]

As fictions move away from realism and the temporality of the everyday lifeworld, the paradoxical specter of infinite time emerges with its problems of origin and ending. Realism is characterized by the beginnings and endings of an hour, a day, a week, a year, or a lifetime rather than the beginnings and endings of the universe of time itself. Apocalyptic and utopian fictions appear at the second level of inter-textuality presented in part 1—the level of myth and science fiction. They are concerned with a temporality that is not "here and now," and it is the separated-off nature of this temporality that is more im-portant than the specific direction it takes. Michael Holquist has written of utopias:

Golden ages are set in the past; More's utopia exists contemporaneously with More's England; Looking Backward and most anti-utopias are set in the future. What is distinctive about all these utopian times, however, is their subsuming quality of arbitrariness. Utopian time is more utterly a convention than is even our artificial clock time. Thus it is in a sense misleading to speak of past, present or future in utopia.[6]

Once fictions break away from the kind of metonymy found in realism, their temporal order is parallel to, or askew with, the temporal order of everyday life. There is no continuity of time once there is no conti-nuity of domain, and the direction and purpose of temporality becomes specific to the particular domain at hand. As Holquist suggests, a move-ment away from the temporality of everyday life will increase the effect of the arbitrary, the cultural, and the fictive nature of the idea of temporal order.

PLAY TIME

Once the world of everyday life and realism is cut off from the fiction, there is a concurrent movement toward play time. With an articulation of operations characteristic of play, the abstract temporal order is made apparent, is flaunted. At the point of free play, the removal of hierarchical order and privileged signification, there is a gesture towards infinity, where the origin and end of things disappear. Derrida has written of the movement of decentering structure:

This movement was that in which language invaded the universal problematic; that in which, in the absence of a center or origin, everything became discourse—provided we can agree on this word—that is to say, when everything became a system where the central signified, the original or transcendental signified, is never absolutely present outside a system of differences. The absence of the tran-scendental signified extends the domain and the interplay of signification ad infinitum.[7]

The movement of play, the making apparent of operations, the inversion of hierarchy, and removal of privileged signification, becomes a movement, like etymology, of infinite regress. Like any form of ostensive metacommunication, play implicates itself—is caught up in a reflexive and infinite gesture. Its every utterance undercuts itself and gives us movement without direction, temporality without order.

Thus there is a temporal movement to the paradox of metacommunication. Complementing this, there is a temporal paradox to any metacommunicative gesture, for while metacommunication is involved in the articulation of boundaries of space and time, those boundaries surround something that both "is and is not" able to partake in the space and time of the everyday lifeworld. Play time occurs yet does not occur; it is outside the temporality of the lifeworld, yet it has definite temporal parameters that can be measured in terms of that lifeworld. However, the hermeticism of the play world makes such measurement useless. Like time in utopias, time in play may be limited to any specific "amount" and at the same time implicate the infinity of the abstract time system. The player, both in and out of the world, partakes of a duration that is measurable yet measureless. Within the parameters of the play world, infinity is *realized*. This has to do with the Epimenides paradox, for any paradox of self-reference like the Epimenides or play paradox becomes a paradox of infinite regress.[8] They present a condition that cannot be verified internally, since there is no measuring rod for infinity. And they cannot be verified externally, since they only refer to themselves. As Rosalie Colie has pointed out, such paradoxes begin an infinite action, not an infinite progress.[9] They are examples of perpetual motion set off without hope of direction or privilege.

The idea of play as a directionless activity is pervasive, lying at the heart of the establishment of play's inverse—the activities of work. One of work's most prevalent characteristics is its productiveness, its closure-made-manifest. Conversely, the production of nothingness, a quality mirrored in the very status of play, comes to be characteristic of all play activities. Nonsense makes nonsense and is thus in this sense a closed and self-generating field. While the work of the discourse of everyday life is a set of purposes at hand, the work of nonsense is reflection and self-perpetuation. Nonsense is "good for nothing." It closes itself off to reference, to utility. "Well, well, weld iron rods into abstract patterns, say, and you've still got real iron, but arrange words into abstract patterns and you've got nonsense," writes John Barth in his story "Title."[10] And, as the reflexivity of this particular story demonstrates, when you're "good for nothing," you aren't in a hurry to get anywhere—the journey becomes the destination.

This is the quality of play noted in most definitions: it is an activity where means become more important than ends. Huizinga wrote:

"Play is a voluntary activity or occupation exercised within certain fixed limits of time and space, according to rules freely accepted but absolutely binding, having its aim in itself and accompanied by a feeling of tension, joy, and the consciousness that it is 'different' from 'ordinary life.' "[11] Play is an intrinsically rewarding activity. It is done "for play's sake." It takes up time and space, has discernible external boundaries, and yet endows the player with a consciousness of timelessness, with an experience outside the everyday lifeworld that partakes of infinity. The connection with other varieties of "other worlds" becomes apparent in Eugen Fink's ontology of play:

> Play is not for the sake of a "final goal" and cannot be marred by profound uncertainty as to the correctness of our conception of happiness. In contrast with the restless dynamism, the obscure ambiguity and the relentless futurism of our life, play is characterized by calm, timeless "presence" and autonomous, self-sufficient meaning—play resembles an oasis of happiness that we happen upon in the desert of our Tantalus-like seeking and pursuit of happiness.[12]

REPETITION AND QUOTATION

Infinity comes imbued with timelessness. It appears as the measurement that cannot be measured, a boundary that is never arrived at, that is perpetually deferred and yet always potential. It is like those other possibilities—the literal potential of the metaphorical and the possibility of simultaneity—that are deferred in everyday life and made apparent in nonsense. Consider an aspect of the reversibility of fictions: If actions can be undone, made "not to count," they also can be done again and again—they bear an intrinsic possibility of repetition. Yet repetition presents the same is/is not paradox characteristic of the status of play, fictions, and infinity. Repetition is possible only in domains other than the domain of everyday life, for in the domain of "reality" it must exist and not exist. We can say "it happened again," holding that all elements of the "it" and the "happened" were *the same*, yet the event has taken part in the ongoingness of time and space and thus is never the same event. The only conclusion is that repetition is itself an event, a "third event," which is limited to the domain of fictions. Because context is always ongoing in social life, repetition can never "take place"; for it to "take place" is for it to take up new quantities of space and time that make it no longer a repetition.

Repetition can only take place in a domain where context is folded into text, where the text can control all variations in context by presenting an illusion of timelessness. Like reversibility, repetition is both a fiction and a fundamental aspect of fictions. Ironically, repetition, whose nature is seen as ongoing, can only achieve this quality of ongoingness by "swallowing" the ongoing quality of context, by holding context *still*. Here again is the threat of the self-generating, self-perpetuating machine. The machine's threat is the disregard of context, an ongoingness despite the conditions of reality, the "blindness" characteristic of the "mechanical application" of any rule. Rule becomes a form of repetition, for it is what is invariant through time and space, what is applied in spite of ongoingness. And here is the fiction of rule-governed behavior, a notion of human action in spite of history, action that can only appear within, or by the aid of, fictions.

Infinity and repetition implicate each other, and both are marks of the movement towards form for form's sake that was characteristic of the procedure of misdirection. Elizabeth Sewell has written of nonsense: "The sum total is unimportant—it is the composition of it that matters, for this is to be the composition of the universe of nonsense, a collection of ones which can be summed together into a whole but which can always fall back into separate ones again."[13] Nonsense thereby illustrates a myth of the origin of numbers. Lacan, following Frege, has said:

> I propose that you consider the real numerical genesis of two. It is necessary that this two constitute the first integer which is not yet born as a number before the two appears. You have made this possible because the *two* is here to grant existence to the first *one*: put *two* in the place of *one*, and consequently in the place of *two* you see *three* appear. What we have here is something which I can call the *mark*. You already have something which is marked or something which is not marked. It is with the first mark that we have the status of the thing.[14]

Just as in inversion a class could be defined and delimited by its proper not, so by means of repetition, the integer—the object—is made to appear. What is repeated is what *is*, a parameter defined in spite of time. Once two can stand in the place of one—can be exchanged in a reversal of temporality—three is possible. Repetition endows the object with self-generation and self-perpetuation. "The first repetition is the only one necessary to explain the genesis of the number," writes Lacan, "and only one repetition is necessary to constitute the status of the subject."[15]

If repetition in fictions is an aid to our sense of closure, giving us a sense of return to a beginning, it is because repetition is always involved in giving integrity to what is repeated. It is the second mark, a mark of sameness or difference, that endows the first mark with being and that begins the possibility of infinity, of a temporality outside of the temporal constraints of everyday life that is the possibility of the fiction itself. This becomes apparent in fictions like the plays of Robert Wilson, where repetition establishes a code from which any variation can be marked.[16] The difference is "a real difference," it "counts," and thus it reifies the boundaries of the code being manufactured, the pattern of the repetition and the difference that is a movement to another pattern. Richard Foreman uses repetition in a similar way:

> My plays, therefore postulate, form a PARADISE
> where the "allowed" mental move is the move to
> undercut all impulses, to self-block, to strategically
> change the subject, so that a desired emotion
> is produced—
> that emotion invoking of the feeling of
> the infinite
> the infinite in each grain of sand
> the infinite (and open) in the small cell of
>   each "moment" of my plays (since each
>   cell is an item "x" that generates
>   its own multitude of non or anti "x's."[17]

The establishment of boundary and difference through repetition is at the center of any movement toward textuality. All verbal play as the representation of an utterance is bound up in the possibility of quotation—a repetition of discourse, a detachment of discourse from its context of origin. Quotation is a method of making texts, a way to give integrity to discourse and to focus interpretive procedures within a set of parameters defined by what is internal to the quotation "marks." Quotation involves an infinite regress and an infinite resource. The discourse, once repeated, is given existence and detachability independent of a context of origin. Its origin dissolves into an etymological infinity, while its detachability gives it self-generation. By means of quotation, discourse comes to speak through us.

Yet all discourse is quotation—all discourse speaks us, has been spoken before. Discourse removed from its context of origin takes with it the aspect of the sentence that Benveniste has called "the infinity of use." Discourse that pretends towards an absence of quotation, an absence of convention, is a myth of the type "frameless activity." It is the convention of the conventionless—speaking from the heart, from nature, from a privileged place of signification. This is part of the hierarchy implicit in quotation's economy. Quotation from domains beyond the experience of the participants, beyond immediate context, has the force of an extended spatial and temporal boundary, a "for all times and for all places" force. To say "they say," "you know how it is," or "we all know that," to use proverbs, fables, and gossip, is to allow past experience to speak through present experience with an "integrity" and a "detachment"—an "objectivity." Like talking with the heart or with nature behind you, the focus is on the message, away from the particular circumstances of origin.

But to focus on the quotation *mark* is to focus on the form of meaning, the mechanical aspect of the discourse, the slot being filled. Here quotation is marked, tainted, made speculative. As I. A. Richards noted in *How to Read a Page*, quotation marks show the limits of what is quoted. They can imply that the words within them are in some way open to question or that what is quoted is "nonsense" or that there is no such thing as the thing they profess to name. They can say the *so-called*, or that we are talking about the word itself as distinguished from its meaning.[18] Like any frame, quotation marks define and delimit the status of what is enclosed. Particularly, they separate their content from the real and the natural. A unicorn is more believable than "a unicorn," the real and the natural more real and natural than "the real" and "the natural." Quotation marks are marks of convention, marks of interpretation. Like any convention, they can work in either of two directions—they can mark the discourse as more real than real, as ideology, as truth beyond any particular historical context, or they can mark the discourse as "merely conventional," as a fiction among fictions.

It is the second of these directions, marking the discourse as the conventional, that is taken by nonsense. Nonsense uses quotation to play with infinity, to point to the self-generating capabilities of quotation and other forms of repetition, to point to how things work, the operations of form. This type of play with quotation, which might be called "nesting," is the first of four operations that nonsense uses to play with infinity: nesting, circularity, serializing, and play with infinite causality.

NESTING

In folkloric forms, nesting is a phenomenon that can move "in" or "out" towards infinity. Nesting can be found at work in those objects called Chinese boxes: a box, doll, or set of baskets that contains within it another box, doll, or set of baskets, and within that box, doll, or set of baskets, lies another box, doll, or set of baskets, and so on. The possibility, if not the actuality, of infinity is thus presented. A German counting out rhyme used in games like hide and seek provides a literal example of nesting:

> In mein Grossvaters Garten stand ein Baum.
> In dem Baume lag eine Nest,
> In dem Neste lag ein Ei,
> In dem Eie lag ein Brief,
> In dem Briefe stand's geschrieben
> Wer auf hundert kommt muss Kriegen,
> 10, 20, 30, 40, 50, 60, 70, 80, 90, 100[19]

Nesting can also be done by fictions that repeat themselves using a set of infinitely receding quotation marks: "It was a dark and stormy night, and the captain said to the crew, 'Crew, tell me a story.' And the crew said, 'It was a dark and stormy night, and the captain said to the crew. . . .'" Another way to perform nesting is to start from the smallest box and move outward into infinite space, as children sometimes do on envelopes:

Kennedy Road
Airville
Pennsylvania
East Coast
United States
North America
Western Hemisphere
The World
The Solar System
The Galaxy
The Universe

Nesting as quotation, as story within story and discourse within discourse, may be seen as an exploration of the nature of textuality and the possibilities of allusion. A relationship between texts is not only hypothesized, it is inevitable. Nesting flaunts the interdependence of discourse; every text bears within itself an infinity of prior and potential texts as well as the idea that its own text can be repeated. This apparition of texts within texts finds a graphic demonstration in the children's song called "The Billboard Song." The singer narrates a preface that tells of how wind and rain blew away parts of a billboard so that one could read the layers of messages beneath:

Come smoke a coca cola,
Drink catsup cigarettes
See Lillian Brussels wrestle
With a box of castanets.

Pork and beans will meet tonight
And have a finished fight
Chauncey de Pew will lecture on
Sopolio tonight

Bay rum is good for horses
It is the best in town
Castoria cures the measles
If you pay five dollars down

Teeth extracted without pain
At the cost of half a dime
Overcoats are selling now
A little out of time
Do me a favor—drop dead[20]

The song, like the billboard discourse it represents, is a surface inscribed by an infinity of overlapping, mutually implicating layers of textuality.

The infinity of this network of allusions is implied by the song's "arbitrary" ending, an ending effected by borrowing closure from the everyday lifeworld. With any text, allusion may point to the everyday world, to the "truisms" of past experience, or to other texts. With the last type of pointing, speculation arises. The text comes to flaunt its fictive frame and is no longer under obligation to make sense by pointing consistently to one domain. Like the billboard song, it reveals layers of textuality beneath which there is nothing but an apparition, a skeleton, of form.

Perhaps no one has explored the possibilities of nesting in literature so much as John Barth has in his metafictions. Barth begins his story collection *Lost in the Funhouse* with a do-it-yourself kit for a Moebius strip that says continuously "Once upon a time there/was a story that began." Like any Moebius strip, the discourse becomes a surface where inside and outside continually reverse positions, where there is an impossibility to the statuses of inside and outside. This collection contains a long tale called "Menelaiad" that tells the story of Menelaus telling to himself the story of Telemachus's visit, when Menelaus told Telemachus the story of how he slept with Helen for the first time in eight years and told *her* the story of his encounter with Proteus, when he told Proteus the story of his meeting with Eidothea, when he told Eidothea the story of the last days of Troy, at which time he recounted to Helen the story of the days before his marriage and of his marriage to her. Each new narrative situation demands a story that takes Menelaus farther and farther back in time. And at some point, he becomes Proteus and Proteus becomes him and together they become an infinite voice that is "the absurd unending possibility of love."[21] Barth has extended the possibilities of tale within tale so extensively that the story becomes the surface of a voice whose identity is never definitive, but rather is caught up in the multiplicity of texts that constitute the voice itself.

In "Dunyazadiad," the first part of Barth's *Chimera*, the narrative voice is the voice of Dunyazade, Scheherazade's sister and double, and Barth himself appears as their "genie." Dunyazade tells the reader that Barth and Scheherazade "speculated endlessly on such questions as whether a story might imaginably be framed from inside, as it were, so that the usual relations between container and contained would be reversed and paradoxically reversible."[22] The tales of *Chimera* not only implicate each other by means of allusion—they implicate all of Barth's work and all of fiction as well. They are about making fictions, about the fictions and the fictiveness of fictions. A clue is given in the chorus of "Dunyazadiad": "The key to the treasure is the treasure." But the center of the unfolding of text within text, an unfolding that necessarily has no center, is a passage in "Bellerophoniad" in which Bellerophon (who is modeling his fiction on the fiction of Perseus, who models his fiction on the paradigm of "the hero" throughout all fictions) finds in a bottle a note from Jerome Bray, a character from another of Barth's novels, *Giles Goat Boy*. Bray tells of trying to write a novel called *Notes:*

> It will represent nothing beyond itself, having no content except its own form, no subject but its own processes. Language itself it will perhaps eschew (in favor of what it is not clear). On the other hand, at its "Phi-point" (point six one eight et cetera of the total length, as the navel is of the total height of human women) there is to occur a single anecdote, a perfect model of a text-within-a-text, a microcosm or paradigm of the work as a whole: not . . . the "Key to the Treasure" story, but . . . a history of the Greek mythic hero Bellerophon: his attempt to fly on Pegasus to Olympus like Apollo's crew to the moon; his sting, his free downfall to Earth like ditto's to the U.S.S. Hornet; his wandering alone in the marsh, far from the paths of men, devouring his own Reset.[23]

From this point, the fate of Bellerophon is not the fiction of a mythic hero, but that of an ordinary mortal, Bellerophon's brother and double, Deliades. Just as Deliades has lived as Bellerophon, slayer of Bellerus, so the last part of *Chimera*, the serpent's tale, has turned out to be truly a serpent swallowing its own tail, a mythic hero fiction turned into its double and "reset," cancelling itself out to infinity. It ends with an interruption that is the interruption that begins the "Dunyazadiad": "At this point I interrupted my sister as usual to say . . ." and so the "Bellerophoniad" is not the last story of the three-part series, but the central story, the story in a story over which Barth and Scheherazade commiserate in the "Dunyazadiad." It is the end that always turns out to be a middle, and thereby moves to infinity.

Infinity becomes a possibility as soon as allusion turns reflexive: not just a text referring to itself and its own frame, but also a text exploring the nature of textuality. These are the fictions of infinity written by Borges. The "Library of Babel" that Borges invents is "a sphere whose consummate center is any hexagon, and whose circumference is inaccessible."[24] By examining examples of variations with unlimited repetition, a librarian "of genius" discovers the fundamental law of the library—that all possible combinations of the 20 orthographic symbols are included in the library and that there are no two identical books in the library. The Library of Babel includes everything: "the minute history of the future," "a version of each book in all languages," "the interpolations of every book in all books."[25] The library is symptomatic of the infinite composability of texts, the infinity of allusion "in both directions." In the search for a book that is the cipher and perfect compendium of all the rest, someone suggests a method that is exactly Frege's theory of the origin of numbers: "In order to locate Book B, first consult Book C and so on *ad infinitum*. . . ."[26] The conclusion to the story suggests an interpretation of the paradox of infinity as a parameter of timelessness: "I dare insinuate the following solution to this ancient problem: *The Library is limitless and periodic*. If an eternal voyager were to traverse it in any direction, he would find after many centuries, that the same volumes are repeated in the same disorder (which, repeated, would constitute an order; order itself). My solitude rejoices in this elegant hope."[27] Other proposals for infinity suggested by Borges include: "a single volume consisting of an infinite number of infinitely thin pages, each apparent leaf of the book dividing into other analogous leaves and the inconceivable central leaf having no reverse"; or a volume whose last page would be the same as the first and so have the possibility of continuing indefinitely; and a fiction that bifurcates in time, not in space, where a character faced with alternatives chooses simultaneously all of them.[28]

In all these varieties of play with infinity, the text dissolves into its allusions. There is no center to the text since there are no boundaries from which to measure it. The text dissolving in this way is the text of *Don Quixote* under the pen of Pierre Menard. This repetition shows the Quixote beginning a process of infinite self-generation. Plagiarism becomes a crime of literature because it flaunts a deficiency of signification. Like the absences in scatological discourse, there is William Morris's contention that all stories have been written; everything has been filled in, and fictions must of necessity be what Joyce called in the *Wake* "the last word in stolen telling." And a deficiency of signification is rapidly turned into a surplus of signification, adding too much of another discourse to the discourse at hand. All play is involved in plagiarism because all discourse speaks through us as social discourse. Like the Library of Babel, play has an infinite number of elements with which to make infinite use. Plagiarism preserves the status of fictions. If we were to admit that there is no plagiarism, we would be admitting that true repetition is an impossibility in the flux of space and time—an admission that cancels out the fictive domain.

The text turning into its allusions is also what happens in *Bouvard and Pecuchet*. Flaubert's notes for the unfinished novel show the Menardian ending he intended: "A good idea cherished secretly by each of them. They hide it from one another. From time to time they smile when it occurs to them, then at last they communicate it simultaneously; To copy as in the old days. . . . They set to work."[29] Barth has called such fictions "the literature of exhaustion," a literature that has exhausted its resources and so must begin over and over again at the scene of its own boundaries in an infinite regress. The task that Bouvard and Pecuchet set before themselves is to be copying clerks to the world. Swift makes fun of such a project in *A Tale of a Tub* when he writes: "I have been for some years preparing materials towards a Panegyric upon the World: to which I intended to add a second part, entitled A Modest Defence of the Proceedings of the Rabble in all Ages. Both of these I had thought to publish by way of an appendix to the following treatise; but finding my common-place book fill much slower than I had reason to expect, I have chosen to defer them to another occasion."[30] Such fictions point to the absurdity of the idea of a "true and complete" description, for a description that proceeded naturally, without recourse to typifications or hierarchies of relevance, would ultimately recoup the object, would dissolve into the object itself: a map the size of its territory.

This is the point where reflexivity and absurdity merge, where the text "knows too much" about itself and can no longer proceed without splitting. One way to do this is by means of a double. There is Wallas, the detective hero of Robbe-Grillet's *The Erasers* who becomes the murderer he has been seeking, Dostoevskij's Golyadkin dissolving into an infinity of Golyadkins, or the parodist of Nabokov's *Pnin* who eventually turns into the victim of his parodies. This is the threat to the writer, making his own character "over," over and over again, and the reader, who is "what he reads." Moran says in *Molloy*, "The fact was there were three, no four Molloys. He that inhabited me, my caricature of same, Gaber's and the man of flesh and blood somewhere awaiting me. . . . There were others too, of course. But let us leave it at that, if you don't mind, the party is big enough."[31]

As soon as "point of view" becomes split, an infinity of points of view is implied. The text itself can be subject to this kind of splitting as Nabokov well illustrates in *Pale Fire* and *Lolita*, where the accouterments and allusions of textuality produce a text in infinite regress from its story, its point of closure and desire. This is the effect of Humbert Humbert saying in *Lolita*, "Parody of a hotel corridor. Parody of silence and death."[32] At the conclusion to his "Commentary" in *Pale Fire*, Kinbote muses: "I may pander to the simple tastes of theatrical critics and cook up a stage play, an old-fashioned melodrama with three principles: a lunatic who intends to kill an imaginary king, another lunatic who imagines himself to be that king, and a distinguished old poet who stumbles by chance into the line of fire and perishes in the clash between the two figments."[33] The absent reading of *Pale Fire* extends infinitely through an infinite universe. It is the madness of Kinbote that has reduced that universe into a set of elements whose infinite combinations will always result in a version of his fiction.

Three Trapped Tigers splits into two texts and two languages, and the English half comes to mourn the betrayal that has caused the splitting: "And I went back to where I was sleeping dreamiendo soñing of the sea lions on page a hundred and one in the Spannish varsion: Morsas, re-Morsas, Sea morsels. Tradittori."[34] The text comes to betray itself.

It can no longer support the illusion of integrity. When this happens, the text is displaying the paradox characteristic of all play with mirrors, all doubling and repetition. The mirror both confirms and questions identity in a single stroke. When one looks into a mirror, there is a splitting of subject and object, watcher and watched. One can look at one's self as an object, from more than one point of view, as others do. Yet there is also the terrifying possibility that the repetition will go on, that the splitting will occur in reverse and the self will break off towards infinity. And even more frightening is the possibility that all one will see in the mirror is another mirror, a doubling of reflexivity that cancels into nothingness.

In nesting is thereby revealed a fundamental problem of the notion of framing and metacommunication—the problem of "what is within the frame?" Chinese boxes contain within them other boxes. They are contentless. There is "nothing there." They are an illustration of the problem of logical types and the paradox it bears of container and contained, form as content and content as form. There is no privileged place for content. All frames, all metacommunication, take the exhausting path of an infinite regress. The infinite set of messages about messages, texts within texts, that was presented in the model of intertextuality destroys the notion of "content" independent of framing. Content appears as another occasion for interpretation, a character whose passage must be taken up in the next story, a double who splits into an infinity of doubles, who dissolves into the boundary of his being.

CIRCULARITY

Circularity is a second type of play with infinity. Circularity and nesting both provide methods for extending discourse by means of what Viktor Shklovsky called "closed form," that is, beginning and ending on the same motif, while "inside," other stories can be told. Tzvetan Todorov has pointed out that the phenomena of closed form and open form in discourse represent the "rigorous projection" of two fundamental syntactic figures used in the combination of two propositions between them—subordination and coordination.[35]

Our organization of nature gives us several paradigms for circularity— the months of the year, the seasons, the seven colors of the rainbow. To name such series is to experience a final element that rejoins the first, to experience a continual return. Circularity is implicit in the reversibility and repetition of play. When means are the object rather than "ends," when one's goal is precisely to never arrive anywhere, the circle emerges as the form of this activity. Thus to begin a game is often to join hands and "get into a circle," "to form a circle" whose boundaries will be continually broken and rejoined. To form the circle is to be implicated in it, to be caught up in it. The problem is to get in or out, on or off. The problem is a problem of mastery, of stopping infinity arbitrarily. One way to control the circle is to take a turn, to set up an arbitrary stoprule that will define and delimit the circle and impose a sense of linearity upon it. When the circle is controlled by turn taking, it is given a mechanism to stop.

This may be the operation behind the rule "everyone must take a turn" in everyday conversation. Conversations without turn taking are "absurd"; they never get anywhere, they are filibusters, prisoners of infinity. For turn taking to be reality generating, it must stay "on the track," must officially disregard form and stick to content, to the gist of the purpose at hand. It depends upon a collusion formed by the participants. The surrealists were well aware of this procedure of turn taking and took advantage of it to effect disorder. Breton wrote in the 1924 manifesto: "The forms of Surrealist language adapt themselves best to dialogue. . . . My attention, prey to an entreaty which it cannot in all decency reject, treats the opposing thought as an enemy; in ordinary conversation, it 'takes it up' almost always on the words, the figures of speech, it employs; it puts me in a position to turn it to good advantage in my reply by distorting them."[36] In nonsense, turn taking never gets anywhere; the turn is a continual *re*turn to a beginning. Each "ending" is marked as the beginning of another round or another game. In children's folklore there are many examples of circular discourse. Most often they work like Breton's surrealist project— as a dialogue that is sabotaged, that is meant never to go anywhere, an endless conversation. This can be done through interrogative routines like this riddle: "Pete and Repeat were walking down the street. Suddenly Pete went away. Who was left?" or through endless dialogues:

> That's tough.
> What's tough?
> Life.
> What's life?
> A magazine.
> Where do you get it?
> Newsstand.
> How much?
> Fifteen cents.
> I've only a dime.
> That's tough.
> What's tough?[37]

Dialogues like this work against the questioner; he is caught in a circle controlled by the first speaker. The dialogues have the form of a routine, however, and imply a performance involving a collusion between participants, in which case it is the audience that is duped. Such dialogues often have the power of a chant—a repetition whose object is a transformation to another plane of being. Their ostensive content is taken over by a repetition that is pure form, until what the performances are about is what they do. This becomes apparent in marching chants as simple as "left, right, left, right" and as complicated as:

> Left! Right! I left my wife and twenty-
> four children alone in the kitchen
> without any gingerbread. Did I do
> right? Oh, by jingo, I had a good job
> but I left my wife and twenty-four
> children alone in the kitchen
> without any gingerbread. Did I do right?[38]

Like the rhyme, the march is a march without any particular direction, a march for the sake of marching. Here the endless repetition of the circle is what enables the endless linearity of the march. The chant is repeated to dizziness or exhaustion. It is a way of getting to the altered state of consciousness that is play itself. The voice in John Barth's story "Echo" says, "A cure for self-absorption is saturation: telling the story over as though it were another's until like a much-repeated word, it loses sense."[39] Here is an example of another children's chant, which on every level is about its own repetition:

> I know a man named Michael Finnegan—
> He wears whiskers on his chinnegan.
> Along came a wind and blew them in again;
> Poor old Michael Finnegan, begin again[40]

Beginning again and again in a repetition impervious to historical constraints is at the heart of slapstick—a clown who, knocked down time after time, bounces back in a reversibility that cannot be marred Robert Desnos, the great surrealist poet, declared in an article called "Mack Sennett, Libérateur du Cinéma" that slapstick is "in short, only the most disconcerting form of lyricism."[41] Slapstick is lyric because it is paratactic; it presents an infinite action that never arrives, never gets anywhere. Think of Chaplin in *Limelight* as a concert violinist with Keaton at the piano: each time Chaplin begins to play, his leg shrivels into the leg of his pants. He pulls down his leg, but as soon as he begins to play, the same thing happens again.

With Gertrude Stein, beginning again and again becomes a conscious tenet of poetics. In her essay "Composition as Explanation" she writes, "Beginning again and again explaining composition and time is a natural thing. It is understood by this time that everything is the same except composition and time, composition and the time of the composition and the time in the composition."[42] She explains that in *The Making of*

Americans, "There was a groping for using everything and there was a groping for a continuous present and there was an inevitable beginning of beginning again and again and again."[43] Hence her concern with generations, with the "same" events occurring over and over through a time that thereby is imbued with timelessness. This is the beginning of those thousand pages: "Once an angry man dragged his father along the ground through his own orchard. 'Stop!' cried the groaning old man at last, 'Stop! I did not drag my father beyond this tree.'"[44]

Just as in nesting a story dissolves into an infinity of enclosed stories, so in circularity a story can dissolve into an infinity of digressions and returns. Closed form is closed only at the perimeters, at the site of framing. The absent center, the bottom that has "fallen out" of the discourse, remains threatened by infinity. This is how Barth's story "Lost in the Funhouse" works. Each narrative gesture, each attempt at a narrative event, is interrupted by a digression, an infinite regress of explanation regarding the act of storytelling itself. When, after many pages, the narrator finds that he has gotten "nowhere" he writes, "We should be much farther along than we are; something has gone wrong; not much of this preliminary rambling seems relevant. Yet everyone begins in the same place; how is it that most go along without difficulty but a few lose their way?"[45] The boundaries of the Funhouse are constant—the door leading out is beside the door leading in. Or are they the same door? Within the Funhouse lies an exhausting possibility of infinity, of closed form. Borges's labyrinths and the Funhouse present metaphors of the absent center, a place that can only be reached by exhausting all possible pathways. And yet the center is merely a frame, a space. The center becomes more and more unreachable with each step towards it. Like the circle, the labyrinth and the Funhouse take up and transform their readers. We cannot be both in and out, off and on. We are at stake in their game.

This type of game is intrinsically a game of bad faith, a game that takes as its task the undercutting of assumptions. If the fiction here is a do-it-yourself kit, it is often one with misleading directions—directions that will not allow the reader to arrive anywhere, to "accomplish" something. This happens in the index to *Pale Fire* where the entry under *Word Golf* says "S's predilection for it 819; see Lass"[46] and the entry for *Lass* says "see Mass" and the entry for *Mass* says "see Male" and the entry for *Male* says "see Word Golf." The same trick is used by Julio Cortázar in *Hopscotch*. *Hopscotch* presents "two books," two plans for reading. One can read it according to the order of the pages in the book as printed, or one can read it by means of an alternative order, which Cortázar presents at the "Conclusion" to the first order. The first "book" is read up to chapter 56. The second book begins at chapter 73 and traverses the book, including all of the first reading, except for chapter 55. The alternative reading "ends" in chapter 131, which says at *its* end that the reader should go to chapter 58, which says at *its* end that the reader should go back to 131, and so on to eternity. The reader is caught up in the circle, not allowed outside of it unless the text is rejected "out of hand." Ironically, chapter 55 stands as the absent center, an unreachable oasis ending: "they slid towards each other as if to fall into themselves, into the common earth where words and caresses and mouths enfolded them as a circumference does a circle, those tranquilizing metaphors, that old sadness satisfied with going back to being the same as always, with continuing, keeping afloat against wind and tide, call and fall."[47]

As a final example of literary circularity, there are those aforementioned fictions like Gabriel Garcia Marquez's *One Hundred Years of Solitude* and Nabokov's *The Gift* that "end" with a character taking up a pen to write the book he has just appeared in. It is by means of the circle that the fiction is thus closed off as a surface, and text and context are folded into each other. Here the circle implicates the field between author and text, and the reader is to some degree left outside the game. In texts like Barth's *Chimera* or *Finnegans Wake*, where the last sentence is completed by the first sentence, the reader is caught up in the game, and the author stands outside the circle, controlling the machinery of circularity.

Circularity is the shape of play, an activity centered in itself that is both repeatable and reversible. One can continue in the circle in the same direction or turn and go the other way around. In either case, the same boundary is inscribed again and again. Yet it only can be the same boundary so long as one does not step out of or off of the circle and traverse it with the linearity of everyday time. The circle confronts us not only in the form of a paradox, but with the form of all paradoxes—a quality of limitedness and limitlessness "all at once."

SERIALIZING

Circularity and nesting can be seen as two methods for extending discourse through "closed form." Two ways of extending discourse by means of open form serve as concluding examples of play with infinity. They are the uses of unlimited series and causal chains.

Todorov links open form with coordination, a way of extending by addition. Addition is "integral" to the uses of series precisely because it is what enables us to repeat. To be able to place things in series, things from any universe of discourse, is possible because of the sameness of the integer. One elephant and one window are both "one," as are one cabbage and one king. And because one, two, three, four . . . is a given, it is possible to have one, an elephant; two, a window; three, a cabbage; and four, a king. And because the series of integers is part of an abstract sense of time as partaking in infinity, anything that can be added or subtracted can also partake of infinity. And when the focus is placed on the counting, on the "form" and not on the "thing"—not on the everyday-life classification of content—the play with infinity tends to nonsense, for the focus has turned to pure form and the self-perpetuation of counting for counting's sake.

While the seasons, the months, and the days of the year provide us with paradigms of circular infinity, numbers provide us with paradigms of linear infinity. When one counts for counting's sake, the classifications and hierarchies of the everyday lifeworld are flattened into a line of infinite possibility. As Anna Balakian has said in an essay on surrealism, "The infinite is the plane of reality in which combinations that we might call absurd in the normal order of things, or logically impossible are accepted as possible."[48]

There are several ways in which nonsense can use numerical series to play with infinity. One is to go on counting beyond the limits of everyday reality. When children use numbers for divination in jump rope rhymes by counting "How many kisses will I receive?" or "How many children will I receive?" the counting is determined not by the everyday constraints upon kissing and child bearing, but by the number of jumps the child can make before missing, a number that can threaten infinity and always threatens exhaustion. This jump rope rhyme ends with the same use of numbers:

> Hello, hello, hello, sir,
> Can you come out and play, sir?
> No sir, Why sir?
> Because I've got a cold, sir.
> Where'd you get the cold, sir?
> At the North Pole, sir.
> What were you doing there, sir?
> Catching a polar bear, sir.
> How many did you catch, sir?
> 1, sir, 2, sir, 3, sir, 4, sir, etc.

In these examples, counting is aligned against an element—kisses, children, and polar bears—and proceeds by means of a performer and audience agreement that there can be an infinite number of kisses, children, and polar bears in the universe of fiction. Another way to use numbers to threaten infinity is to align the world to the counting. A classic example is the number rhyme:

> one, two, buckle my shoe
> three, four, shut the door
> five, six, pick up sticks
> seven, eight, lay them straight

nine, ten, a good fat hen
eleven, twelve, who will delve
thirteen, fourteen, draw the curtain
fifteen, sixteen, maids in the kitchen
seventeen, eighteen, who is waiting
nineteen, twenty, my stomach's empty[49]

Rhymes like this, the "This old man, he played one"-type, threaten an endlessness by counting outward. While this type of rhyme is endless by an infinity of numbers, a rhyme that "counts down" threatens endlessness by exhaustion, as is the case in drinking songs like "ninety-nine bottles of beer on the wall, ninety-nine bottles of beer. You take one down and pass it around, ninety-eight bottles of beer on the wall. . . ." This song makes use of exhaustion on the level of content as well, for the inevitable slurring of words that results as one approaches the last bottle of beer represents the slurring that would occur if one actually had swallowed ninety-nine bottles of beer, rather than "ninety-nine bottles of beer."

Aligning the world to the counting will always threaten endlessness so long as it is agreed that anything can be placed under the domain of the number; so long as one elephant and one window are still *one*. This is the principle underlying any example of numerical composition. For instance, the *Iliad* and the *Odyssey* were divided by Alexandrian philologists into twenty-four books because that was the number of letters in the Greek alphabet.[50] Curtius gives several examples of compositions aligned according to the number thirty-three, the number of years in Christ's life: Dante's epistle to Can Grande has thirty-three sections, Villon names the name of Christ in stanzas three and thirty-three of his *Testament*, Nicholas of Cusa provided in his will that thirty-three old men be maintained in a hospital established by himself.[51] Because there can be thirty-three of anything in the world, the world itself can be fictionalized into a manifestation of the number thirty-three, or any other number. Bergson noted the comic possibilities inherent in "pure counting" without resort to common-sense hierarchies in his essay on "Laughter": "Just as M. Perrichon is getting into the railway carriage, he makes certain of not forgetting any of his parcels: Four, five, six, my wife seven, my daughter eight, and myself nine."[52]

M. Perrichon's counting brings us to the nonsense of the list—the possibility that one can make a vertical arrangement of anything. The list can threaten infinity by repetition (closed form), as it does in divination series like "Who will I marry? Rich man, poor man, beggar man, thief, doctor, lawyer, Indian chief" or "What will I live in? Mansion, ranch, farm, church, school, trailer, prison, camp."[53] Or it can threaten infinity by open form, by the addition of an unrestricted number of elements. Any list that ends in *etc.* threatens infinity in this way. The list, when written, inverts the order of reading, for the dynamic of reading is horizontal, taking the eye from left to right and offering closure along this horizontal axis. The list is vertical; it runs against this dynamic. Like the acrostic or calligram, it provides content in the space of the printed text that before was insignificant, was "merely form." The antihierarchical and anticausal nature of the list is especially apparent in the printed list, for while the list has a top and bottom, a higher and a lower, there is no subordination in this. Elements are added one to another without a significance to their order. Whether "complete" or "incomplete," the list that is not "ordered" or "motivated" presents elements in equal status. Those at the top are no more important than those at the bottom.

When the elements of the list have equal status, they can work like those numerical compositions that align the world to themselves. The list threatens an exhaustiveness that is lyric, that offers an interchangeability of elements across a horizontal temporal axis. Williams includes in *Paterson* an exchange between an interviewer and himself in which the interviewer suggests that one of Williams's poems "sounds just like a fashionable grocery list!" "It is a fashionable grocery list," answered Williams.[54] Williams made the lyric situation dissolve into a list of its constituent elements. G. Cabrera Infante has explored the same kinds of fictive possibilities in his short story "Revelations of a List Maker." He writes that he is "planning to write a masterwork, no less, which will consist of nothing but a list. So far

> (
> 7:15 p.m.
> Closerie des Sapins
> Kraainem
> Brussels
> Belgium
> Western Europe
> Eurasia
> Earth
> The Solar System
> The Milky Way
> The Universe
>)

certain limitations—the infinite range of my theme, the inexhaustibility of the arrangement, and the difficulty of listing the characters, to mention only the novelistic restraints—stand in the way of my enumerative abilities.

The story becomes, obviously, a metalist, a list about the limits and possibilities of list making. Infante writes that "listing listings," for example:

> lists
> indexes
> rolls
> minutes

catalogues
tables
outlines
inventories
almanacs
assessments
censuses
checklists

and genealogical trees for which one cannot see the woods of Biblical generations—
simply by putting them one after another—is a pleasure that goes far beyond the
bounds of mere collecting to transport the imagination to digital delight and ex-
haustive ecstasy.[55]

Not only Biblical genealogies work this way, so does the catalogue as a
literary form. Consider the fantastic genealogies of Gargantua and Pantagruel, and the names of H. C. Earwicker and Anna Livia Plurabelle's
"untitled mamafesta."[56] In such texts, where the narrative horizontal is
continually scattered and rejoined in a kind of epic catalogue, the text
becomes a game of lists. The book itself, with its numbered pages, one
after the other, becomes a kind of counting, a form holding a world of
possibilities. The list threatens the exhaustion of any inventory, and—
when used for its own sake—it threatens the exhaustion of an inventory
of everything. *Ulysses*, constructed by timetables and registers, maps
and all the other "litterature" that appeared in Dublin on 16 June 1904,
may be seen as an inventory and compendium of the Dublin universe.
On a less grand scale there is Beckett's Malone on his deathbed, using
the inventory to "kill time." He says, "I want, when the great day
comes, to be in a position to enounce clearly, without addition or omis-
sion, all that its interminable prelude had brought me and left me in the
way of chattels personal. I presume it is an obsession."[57] And, amid the
story of Macmann, "Quick, quick, my possessions. Quiet, quiet, twice,
I have time, lots of time, as usual."[58] Similarly, Watt realizes that he
himself is little more than an element in a list and that everything has
the potential to become a list: "Here today and gone tomorrow, a term
in a series, like the series of Mr. Knott's dogs, or the series of Mr. Knott's
men or like the centuries that fall from the pod of eternity." In order
to get some rest he thinks "of the possible relations between such series
as these, the series of dogs, the series of men, the series of pictures, to
mention only these series."[59]

Counting sheep before sleep is done for the sake of the counting and
the sleep that ensues. One can count whatever one wants to count.
Counting towards an inventory of the world works like this, too—like a
chant or a neck riddle, switching the counter to another universe of
being. The use of series becomes another method for exploring the
possibilities of text making. The oral or written "inscription" of each
integer becomes the establishment of textual boundaries and the

system of integers becomes a statement about the relationships between those boundaries, the space between them. The number system, self-perpetuating and infinite, provides a model for the "arbitrary" composability of all fictions.

INFINITE CAUSALITY

If we think of the list as occuring in time as well as in space, we begin to imply a causal relationship between the events of the list that is arbitrary and nonsensical. Robbe-Grillet has pointed out the following rule of everyday life and realism: "Causality and chronology are really the same thing in traditional narrative. The succession of facts, the narrative concatenation as is said today, is based entirely on a system of causalities: what follows phenomenon A is a phenomenon B, the consequence of the first; thus, the chain of events in the novel. The very order of traditional narrative will be causality and temporality as causality."[60] Within the parameters of any "real" event, there is causality and a necessary contingency. The "effect" of the event offers closure until the next event. One only has to think of parents who always ask "OK, who hit who first?", or for that matter, of the child who says "He started it." One thing follows the other as if it had to. To admit to a nature of the world that would be otherwise would be to admit to a leak in the nonarbitrary connectability of events.

Nonsense does not undermine the idea of causality so much as it undermines the sense of contingency and necessariness underlying the everyday sense of causality. In nonsense, anything can cause anything else and everything causes everything else. Nonsense illustrates Mary Douglas's statement that once one point is determined, "the whole of logical space" is determined. In the discourse of nonsense, causality is everywhere in all directions, and is as arbitrary as the list. When "anything can happen," anything can happen in any order. The possibilities extend beyond the causal inversions of characters manipulating writers or the Red Queen's "Sentence first, verdict afterward," or the Unicorn telling Alice, "You don't know how to manage looking glass cakes. . . . Hand it round first and cut it afterwards." Carroll wrote in his *Game of Logic* that "it isn't of the slightest consequence to us, as Logicians, whether our premises are true or false; all *we* have to make out is whether they lead logically to the conclusion so that, if *they* were true, it would be true also."[61]

The nonsense of endless causality exploits this feature of sequential logic—that once you grant the existence of the premise, you grant a sequence of following statements, each of which implies its own consequent statements. The sequential series thus acts like the numerical series—a contingent statement (2) gives status to an enabling statement

(1), and they generate a series that can produce an infinite number of following statements (3, 4, . . .). This is how tag works—you grant an "it" role and from then on the game can proceed by an infinite chain of "its." All games of tag threaten infinity and end in exhaustion.

One of the most common forms of nonsense causality is concatenation or chain verse, in which the last word or phrase of a line is used for the beginning of the next line.[62] This form is common to both oral and written tradition and threatens infinity by its obvious quality of self-perpetuation. "The House That Jack Built" and "Chad Gadya" provide familiar examples. In the late-nineteenth century, American newspapers sometimes ran cumulative verses—one newspaper would give a few lines and other papers would follow with more verses. The chain only ended when the newspapermen got tired of writing verses.[63] Concatenation or chain verses obviously present a crisis of closure. Here phonology determines causality:

> Deed'n deed'n double deed,
> I sowed my garden full of seed.
> When the seed began to grow,
> Like a garden full of snow;
> When the snow began to melt,
> Like a garden full of hemp;
> When the hemp began to peel,
> Like a garden full of steel;
> When the steel began to rust,
> Like a garden full of dust;
> When the dust began to fly,
> Like an eagle in the sky;
> When the sky began to roar,
> Like a lion at my door;
> When the door began to crack,
> Like a hickory at my back;
> When my back began to smart,
> Like a penknife at my heart;
> When my heart began to bleed.
> 'Deed indeed. I was dead indeed.[64]

The quiz show in *Finnegans Wake* uses this technique in answer to question "8. And how war your maggies? Answer: They war loving, they love laughing, they laugh weeping, they weep smelling, they smell smiling, they smile hating, they hate thinking, they think feeling, they feel tempting, they tempt daring, they dare waiting, they wait taking, they take thanking, they thank seeking. . . ."[65] The "mocking bird" chain song ("Papa's gonna buy me a mockingbird, and if that mocking bird don't sing, Papa's gonna buy me a diamond ring, and if that diamond ring don't shine . . .") often ends in an abrupt physical "cut": Papa's going to whip me until I sweat,[66] or, in an example from Baltimore, "Papa's gonna whip my black behind." This is like the abrupt

"Drop dead" ending to "The Billboard Song." The only way to end the causal chain is to add an arbitrary stop rule. Another way to close the causal chain arbitrarily is to add a chorus that is detachable, like the ending of this concatenation rhyme:

> I found a silver spoon
> I gave it to my mother
> To buy a little brother
> The brother was too cross
> I sold him for a horse
> The horse wouldn't go
> I sold it for a dollar
> The dollar wouldn't pass
> I stuck it in the grass
> The grass wouldn't grow
> I stuck it in the snow
> The snow wouldn't melt
> I stuck it in my belt
> The belt wouldn't buckle
> I put it in my knuckle
> My knuckle wouldn't bend
> Peanuts, peanuts, five cents a pack!
> Wrapt it in paper with a string around.[67]

The concatenation can also be ended by adding a jump rope verse that calls for closure by counting, like "I like coffee, I like tea/How many boys are stuck on me?"[68] In these verses, repeating or rhyming or punning an element is enough to keep going. Repetition and rhyming and punning become legitimate forces of causality.

All of these examples have been of "open" forms; the links in the chain are added one after another. Infinite causality can also be effected through closed form, where the beginning and ending are "set" and the chains unfold infinitely between them like a "shaggy dog" story, a story in which the narrative events ramble on without direction and purpose, away from as much as towards an ending. Closed form is found in riddles that use nonsensical causal chains like: "Why are fire engines red?"

> Two and two is four
> Three times four is twelve
> Twelve inches in a ruler
> Queen Mary was a ruler
> Queen Mary ruled the sea
> There are fish in the sea
> The fish have fins
> The Finns fought the Russians
> The Russians are Red
> Fire engines are always rushin'
> That's why fire engines are red.

The children's retort to the insult, "You're a drip," works the same way:

A drip is a drop
A drop is rain
Rain is nature
And nature is beautiful
Thanks for the compliment[69]

A causality that is infinite is also characteristic of all picaresque fictions—fictions that consist of a string of adventures tied to each other not by causality so much as by their happening to the hero one after the other, "come what may." The picaresque's path is one of a continually delayed arrival. The objective of the picaresque journey is the journey itself. Like John Barth's "key to the treasure" that is the treasure, or the infinity of a shaggy dog story, a snipe or a snark hunt— the ending will be postponed, deferred and anticlimactic, illustrating Breton's principle of surrealism, "the sensational, ending weakly." The point is not to finish, but to sustain the journey; the "wild goose chase" is about the chase and not about the goose.

Edward Lear's nonsense picaresque, for example, "The Adventures of Mr. Lear, the Polly, and the Pusseybite on Their Way to the Ritertitle Mountains," narrates a set of events that are both reversible and infinitely rearrangeable. "Mr. Lear and the Polly and the Pusseybite incidentally fell over an unexpected cataract, and are dashed to atoms . . . The two venerable Jebusites fasten the remains of Mr. Lear, the Polly and the Pusseybite together, but fail to reconstruct them perfectly as three individuals." Then "Mr. Lear and the Pusseybite and the Pollycat and the two Jebusites and the Jerusalem Artichokes and the Octagonal Oyster Clippers all tumble into a deep hole and are never seen or distinguished or heard of never more afterwards."[70] The adventures of this ever-increasing set of characters is infinitely composable, events can be tagged on so long as the strength of writer and audience holds out. Death and near-death will not stand in the way of the reversibility of Mr. Lear, the Polly, and the Pusseybite, or the characters of most cumulative tales.

The preface to the 1929 reprint of the first surrealist manifesto lauds "the imagination which alone *causes* real things." This was the kind of causal persistence—an insistence upon the arbitrary—that delighted Breton, who wrote: "I believe in the pure Surrealist joy of the man who, forewarned that all others before him have failed, refuses to admit defeat, sets off from whatever point he chooses, along any other path save a reasonable one, and arrives wherever he can."[71] With other writers, the chain of arbitrariness is maintained at the expense of the stability of grammar, nouns, and punctuation. Gertrude Stein suggested in her lectures that "we must get rid of nouns, for objects are never stable." This was also the direction of Marinetti's war on punctuation, *parole in libérta*, the abolition of punctuation, the adverb, and the adjective, and the rejection of syntax. According to Marinetti's new orthodoxy, the verb had to be used in the infinitive and every substantive had to have its double.[72] The idea presented in this manifesto of surrealism, "Steinism," and *parole in libérta* is to create a discourse of infinite perpetuation, a discourse that is both insular and inviolable and, at the same time, able to accommodate everything in the world to the infinite motion of its machinations.

The nonsense of infinite causality is infinite not only at its "end," its end of composability, it also presents a type of etymological infinity at its other end, its beginning. In any fiction that is self-perpetuating, or any fiction that is self-generating, the causality of "authorship" becomes erased. The fiction comes to write the world. There is no place to point to in answer to the question "Who is writing/talking?" other than "the writing/talking is writing/talking." In this sense, a method of infinite causality is being used whenever nonsense effaces the boundary between author and reader, reader and character, or author and character. The picaresque hero is always the victim of his own fictions, is always written by his fictions. And the author of the fiction thereby turns out to be the world, the context of the fiction that envelops the "official" author, hero, and reader. The picaresque hero goes through a world that is already written. This is Quixote meeting people who have already read *Don Quixote*, or the facility with which Pierre Menard can also write the novel. It is no "accident" that Edward Lear includes Mr. Lear among the three heroes of his nonsense picaresque, or perhaps more appropriately, it is an accident like all other forms of nonsense causality.

The infinity of the mistake, of the perpetual blunder, the false step that is self-perpetuating, becomes an aspect of nonsense causality. This jump rope rhyme provides an example of this technique:

> I went upstairs to make my bed;
> I made a mistake and I bumped my head.
> I went downstairs to milk my cow;
> I made a mistake and milked the sow.
> I went in the kitchen to bake a pie;
> I made a mistake and baked a fly.[73]

The mistakes of the first rhyme are infinitely add-able. They produce an ever-receding horizon away from closure, "one step forward, one step backward." The principle of selection is not one of commonsense actions following one another. Nor is it the "proper not" of each action that fills the slot of "the mistake." Rather, out of the vast domain of "nots" that stand opposite to the proper common-sense procedure, the jump rope performer will select an action according to a principle of rhyme. And rhyme, like phonology or punning, does not easily offer closure in terms of a common-sense idea of causality.

All of these forms of play with infinity—nesting, circularity, the series, and the causal chain—are ways of showing the infinite connectability of all things and the arbitrariness of most connections—the mechanics of the composability that is textuality. The problems of "where to begin" and "where to end" are placed in a paradoxical context of timelessness that is the fictive universe itself. The voice of Beckett's "Unnamable" says "the search for the means to put an end to things, an end to speech, is what enables discourse to continue. . . . I know no more questions and they keep pouring out of my mouth. I think I know what it is, it's to prevent the discourse from coming to an end. . . . The essential is never to arrive anywhere, never to be anywhere."[74] Nonsense, whose proper domain, subject, and form are "nothing," promises the infinity of nothingness, for nothing is a quality without an extrinsic boundary or measurement. Nothing can always beget more or less nothing. It is self-generating and self-perpetuating. Thus "The Unnamable" "can't go on" and goes on, and Swift could write: "I am now trying an experiment very frequent among Modern authors; which is to write upon Nothing: when the subject is utterly exhausted, let the pen still move on; by some called the ghost of Wit, delighted to walk after the death of its body."[75]

In nonsense, closure can only be imposed upon infinity by an arbitrary stop rule, a rule that says "Enough" in a metafictive voice. If these nonsense activities show the absence and arbitrariness of all beginnings and endings, they always show the absence and arbitrariness of all middles as well. With this method of making nonsense, the center —the place of privileged signification—drops out and all that is left is a voice infinitely tracing itself into an infinite domain.

NOTES

1. Carroll, *Complete Works*, p. 244.
2. Husserl, "Lived Experiences of Time," in *Rules and Meanings*, p. 74.
3. Schutz, *Collected Papers*, 1:301.
4. Ibid., p. 222.
5. See Barbara Herrnstein Smith, *Poetic Closure* (Chicago: University of Chicago Press, 1968), p. 129.
6. Michael Holquist, "How to Play Utopia," in *Game, Play, Literature*, ed. Ehrmann, p. 112.
7. Jacques Derrida, "Structure, Sign, and Play," in *The Structuralist Controversy*, ed. Richard Macksey and Eugene Donato (Baltimore: The Johns Hopkins University Press, 1972), p. 249.
8. Colie, *Paradoxica Epidemica*, p. 360.
9. Ibid., p. 519.
10. Barth, *Lost in the Funhouse*, p. 109.
11. Huizinga, *Homo Ludens*, p. 28.

144 / MAKING NONSENSE

12. Eugen Fink, "The Oasis of Happiness: Toward an Ontology of Play," in *Game, Play, Literature*, ed. Ehrmann, p. 21.

13. Sewell, *Field of Nonsense*, p. 54.

14. Jacques Lacan, "Of Structure as an Inmixing of an Otherness Prerequisite to Any Subject Whatever," in *Structuralist Controversy*, ed. Macksey and Donato, p. 191. Gilles Deleuze discusses Frege's theory of numbers in relation to Lewis Carroll's nonsense in *Logique du Sens*, p. 42.

15. Lacan, "Of Structure as an Inmixing," p. 191.

16. For a discussion of Wilson's work in relation to problems of order and disorder in sign systems, see Robbe-Grillet, "Order and Disorder," p. 15.

17. Program from the Richard Foreman/Kate Mannheim production, "Blvd. de Paris (I've got the shakes)" (New York, 1977).

18. I. A. Richards, *How to Read a Page* (New York: Norton, 1942), p. 66.

19. H. C. Bolton, "More Counting Out Rhymes," *Journal of American Folklore* 10 (1897): 318-19.

20. Florence Maryott, "Nebraska Counting Out Rhymes," *Southern Folklore Quarterly* 1 (1936):58, 59.

21. Barth, *Lost in the Funhouse*, p. 162.

22. John Barth, *Chimera* (Greenwich, Conn.: Fawcett, 1972), p. 32.

23. Ibid., p. 266.

24. Borges, *Ficciones*, p. 80.

25. Ibid., p. 83.

26. Ibid., p. 85.

27. Ibid., pp. 87, 88.

28. See "Notes" to "The Library of Babel," and "The Garden of the Forking Paths," in Borges, *Ficciones*, p. 97.

29. Flaubert, *Bouvard and Pecuchet*, pp. 347-48.

30. Swift, *Tale of a Tub*, p. 308.

31. Beckett, *Three Novels*, p. 115.

32. Nabokov, *Lolita*, p. 121.

33. Vladimir Nabokov, *Pale Fire* (New York: Putnam, 1962), p. 212.

34. Infante, *Three Trapped Tigers*, p. 481.

35. Tzvetan Todorov, *The Poetics of Prose*, trans. Richard Howard (Ithaca, N.Y.: Cornell University Press, 1977), p. 21.

36. Breton, *Manifestoes*, p. 34.

37. Withers, *A Rocket in My Pocket*, p. 133.

38. Ibid.

39. Barth, *Lost in the Funhouse*, p. 95.

40. Withers, *A Rocket in My Pocket*, p. 68.

41. See J. H. Matthews, *Surrealism and Film* (Ann Arbor: University of Michigan Press, 1971), p. 36.

42. Stein, *Selected Writings*, p. 516.

43. Ibid., p. 548.

44. Ibid., p. 261.

45. Barth, *Lost in the Funhouse*, p. 75.

46. There is, of course, no page numbered 819 in "Pale Fire" or *Pale Fire*.

47. Julio Cortázar, *Hopscotch* (New York: Avon, 1975), p. 338.

48. Anna Balakian, *Surrealism: Road to the Absolute* (New York: Noonday, 1959), p. 11.

49. Sabine Baring-Gould, *Book of Nursery Songs and Rhymes*, p. 142.

50. Ernst Robert Curtius, *European Literature and the Latin Middle Ages* (New York: Harper and Row, 1953), p. 502.

51. Ibid., p. 505.

52. Bergson, "Laughter," p. 101.

53. Winslow, "An Annotated Collection," p. 154. See also J. O. Heck, "Folk Poetry and Folk Criticism," *Journal of American Folklore* 40 (1927): 1-77, who gives examples of counting "How many hats, flowers, rooms, windows, horses,

carriages, beds, chairs, tables, stoves and dishes" and the series "What kind of dress? (silk, satin, calico, rags)" and "What kind of house? (brick, stone, marble, frame)."

54. William Carlos Williams, *Paterson* (New York: New Directions, 1963), pp. 224-25.

55. G. Cabrera Infante, "Revelations of a List Maker," *New Yorker*, 19 September 1977, pp. 32-35.

56. Consider the lists of games in Rabelais, *Gargantua and Pantagruel*, p. 126, and Joyce, *Wake*, pp. 83-85, for examples of the cataloguelike nature of these two works.

57. Beckett, *Three Novels*, p. 196.

58. Ibid., p. 246.

59. Beckett, *Watt*, p. 136.

60. Robbe-Grillet, "Order and Disorder," p. 5.

61. Quoted in Kathleen Blake, *Play, Games, and Sport: The Literary Works of Lewis Carroll* (Ithaca, N.Y.: Cornell University Press, 1974), p. 70.

62. See Dobson, *Poetical Ingenuities*, p. 53.

63. For example, the *Boston Globe* ran a verse that began:

An Arab came to the river side
With a donkey bearing an obelisk:
But he would not try to ford the tide
For he had too good an *

and invited other papers to add verses. See Dobson, *Poetical Ingenuities*, pp. 166-67.

64. W. H. Babcock, "Games of Washington Children," *American Anthropologist* 1 (1888): 273.

65. Joyce, *Wake*, p. 142.

66. Nolton, "Jump Rope Rhymes," p. 54.

67. Heck, "Folk Poetry and Folk Criticism," p. 30.

68. Paul Brewster, "Rope Skipping Rhymes," *Southern Folklore Quarterly* 3 (1939): 177.

69. We can easily switch this into the riddle, "Why is 'you're a drip' a compliment?"

70. A page is missing, unfortunately, from the original of this picaresque. See Edward Lear, *Teapots and Quails and Other New Nonsense*, ed. Angus Davidson (Cambridge: Harvard University Press, 1953), pp. 51-54.

71. Breton, *Manifestoes*, p. 46.

72. See Bigsby, *Dada and Surrealism*, p. 27.

73. Nolton, "Jump Rope Rhymes," p. 58. See also the game, "Trials, Troubles, and Tribulations," in W. W. Newell, *Games and Songs of American Children* (1903; reprint ed., New York: Dover, 1963), p. 102: "All participating are blindfolded, and, joining hands, march forward singing 'Here we go through the Jewish nation, Trials, troubles and tribulations.' The marching continues until the players bring against a door or cause a general downfall by tripping on some obstacle."

74. Beckett, *Three Novels*, pp. 299, 307, 338.

75. Swift, *Tale of Tub*, p. 393.

6 · the uses of simultaneity

MARKING SIMULTANEITY

In the last chapter I began with four "self-evident laws of time" and discussed their relationship to the sense of time characterizing everyday life. This was a relationship that contrasted the self-evident law of infinity ("the fixed temporal order is that of an infinite two-dimensional series") with the importance of closure in common sense and realism. In this chapter I discuss the use of simultaneity in making nonsense out of common sense. Simultaneity, as a nonsense method, stands in direct contradiction to the remaining three laws of Husserl's "lived experiences of time": (2) That different times can never be cojoint; (3) That their relation is a nonsimultaneous one; and (4) That there is transitivity, that to every time belongs an earlier and later. Simultaneity defies both an abstract sense of time and a common sense of time. While infinity flaunts a discrepancy *between* rule and practice, showing the difference between our abstract sense of infinite time and our everyday sense of time having closure, simultaneity flaunts a problem in both rule and practice—the impossibility of time being in more than one place at once.

Simultaneity carries a paradox like the paradox of nothingness, fictions, play, and metaphor. It is defined as the quality of existing, happening, occurring at the same time in more than one space; the quality of being coexistent in time while being contiguous in space. It is thus a characteristic of activities, a phenomenon that, in coming to define itself, must split. Simultaneity is neither here nor there, but the reconciliation of a paradoxical contradiction between hereness and thereness. It is like the paradox of nothingness, for it cancels itself out—to say that two events are simultaneous is to dissolve those events into each other in time while they cannot be dissolved in space, and therefore to deny the possibility of simultaneity by saying "two events." It is like the paradox of fictions and play, for it presents a phenomenon that both is and is not, that must comment on its own coming to be in

146

order to be. It is a paradox like metaphor since it has to do with the interaction of events and is emergent in that interaction as a third, fourth, or nth integer event. In this sense, simultaneity can be seen as a metaphor of time, for it involves a metaphorical nexus of two or more temporal categories, a nexus that in itself is a new category, more than the sum of its constituent parts. But such a metaphor is nonsensical, for it is left without a possible context. A possible context would be a nexus *in space and time*, but such a nexus would result, not in simultaneity, but in identity.

Simultaneity is utopian in the sense that it is a time of timelessness, a time without a context. Our attention can be "drawn" to one event, or to another event, but we cannot experience both of these events at the same time because we can be in only one place at a time. We can only experience their simultaneity. We can know that those events occurred at the same time and thereby experience simultaneity as a third event. Simultaneity becomes, like the unicorn or the snark, an imaginary beast, a phenomenon that is known only through abstraction, through an unrealizable possibility. Simultaneity is a nonsense phenomenon, a phenomenon estranged from common sense. It can only be experienced through the creation of multiple domains. At the same time, it is an aspect of the very idea of multiple domains. What is remarkable about simultaneity is convergence, and not what is converged. Therefore simultaneity works as other nonsense operations do, bringing attention to form, to method, to the ways in which experience is organized rather than to the "content" of the organization in any particular time and space.

Everyday life is characterized by what Schutz called a "tension" in consciousness. This is a tension of attention to a purpose at hand, a tension by which action and work are accomplished. The working self is experienced as a total self, a self that is wholly involved in bringing about a project of action through bodily movements.[1] And the working self brings about its projected state of affairs through direction, through a time and space that, as intersubjective phenomena, are definitive and irreversible. Hence the importance of focusing, of bringing attention "to the point." Often the eye of realism in literature or film, moving from one object in a room or landscape to another, brings each object to the attention of the reader/audience, creating a notion of a surrounding, an appropriate context, in which a character first appears. The realistic eye is centered, focused, in the literal and metaphorical sense, and an illusion of opacity and sharpness is created. The realistic eye is narrative—one event follows another, is contingent upon the event that has passed before it and causes the event that follows it. It is an eye that moves primarily in time, an eye with a past and a future. As the White Queen says in *Through the Looking Glass*, "The rule is, jam tomorrow and jam yesterday—but never jam *today*."

When attention is split, there is a movement towards nonsense. An aside in a play, a caricature in which heads and bodies are interchangeable, the attempt to rub your head and pat your stomach, or pat your head and rub your stomach at the same time, the sideshow—these are all movements that diverge a focus, that interrupt the direction of attention and subvert the hierarchies of relevance characterizing such focusing and attention. We "don't know where to look." As in the case of scatological verse, we are confronted with both a surplus and a deficiency of signification. We cannot "turn" to a conclusion. Rather, we are left with an infinity of divergences by which an ending is deferred. All of these examples—the aside, the caricature, the simultaneous action, the sideshow—have the status of a "feat." Tzara wrote in his "no more manifestoes" manifesto, "I write this manifesto to show that people can perform contrary actions together while taking a fresh gulp of air."[2]

This accomplishment presents an extraordinary exception to the kind of perception we bring to events in the everyday lifeworld. Children recognize this extraordinariness in a set of rituals performed on the occasion of any coincidence. If two children say the same thing at the same time, the ritual that ensues will insure the appropriate obligations and precautions to be associated with the event. The Opies recorded several of these rituals. In Monmouthshire children link the little fingers of their right hands and wish, and their wish will come true. The idea that a letter will follow an instance of simultaneity is common to several areas of Britain. In Swansea, girls count the number of letters in the word or words that were spoken simultaneously, and by going through the alphabet to that point, they find the initial of the person from whom the letter can be expected.[3] In America, children sometimes shout "Jinks," then begin to count to ten, and the first person to get to ten shouts "Owe me a coke." American children also engage in colloquies: after saying the same word at the same time, two children, without speaking, link "pinkies" and the first child says "Needles," the second replies, "Pins," continuing:

Triplets	Twins
When a man marries	His troubles begin.
When a man dies	His troubles end.
What goes up the chimney?	Smoke
What comes down the chimney?	Santa Claus[4]

Colloquies like this work in the same way as the "obliques" of Rabelais, those complex enumerations by which horizontal and vertical structures are collapsed into each other, characterizing the dialogues of

Pantagruel and Panurge as they do in chapter 38 of book 3, "How Pantagruel and Panurge Proclaimed the Virtues of Triboulet."[5] The oblique is two voices coterminous in one space, and it is always about simultaneity. Triboulet is at one time both columns of characteristics, just as the children's obliques are responses to the simultaneity that has occasioned their use. But the voices that spoke all at once and at the same time in simultaneity are now split back into two distinct voices, two distinct columns. Instead of converging within the same space, the voice of the oblique diverges within the same space.

The rituals of simultaneity performed by children are the beginning of an attempt to use simultaneity to flaunt a fiction, a performance. They are purposeful contrivances. And contrivance, like Fate, Chance, and Accident, is something out of the control of common sense, something unbelievable, something that could not happen. The deus ex machina is a machine of reversibility and improbability, a machine that transforms the temporal order of events into a surface, a drawing board, on which many possibilities are coterminous. When we say that a narrative is "too contrived," we are saying that it shows too much simultaneity, too much coincidence, that too much has been allowed to converge within the space of the fiction. When something does not "ring true," it is because it approaches the perfection of pure form. We say that the author is "playing God," that the fiction has pretense to a form beyond our everyday sense of knowing. An omniscient narrator speaks from the vantage point of an eternity that is simultaneous. He can see everything at once. Once the omniscient voice appears and comments upon its vision, there is a movement towards the paradox of metacommunication. In true stories, omniscience is taken for granted, "played down." The teller is concerned with putting himself in the audience's shoes and having the audience put themselves in his shoes, and so events are narrated as they would be experienced in everyday life, one after another. This is how narratives of fright like ghost stories work—the audience is never allowed to know more at any given time than the victim knows. Once we have moved to the horror film technique of showing the monster or the murderer waiting behind the door, we have moved to irony and tragedy with their split voices, "If only I had known."

Managing simultaneity in a true story is always a clumsy matter. One must make use of "meanwhile, back at the ranch"-type devices. Simultaneity is a flaw in the flow of the true narrative, it moves the narrative from linearity into an unfolding space, and admits that there is signification beyond the range of narrated events, that our knowledge of "what is going on" is necessarily incomplete. But while simultaneity is an impediment to the true story, it is, as the children's rituals celebrate, the stuff of which fantastic stories are made. It is the defining characteristic of that consummate *event*, the coincidence—a cutting across of time over space that is remarkable, anecdotal, noteworthy.

As soon as a fiction makes a gesture of self-reference, simultaneity moves in. Any metacommunicative gesture is involved in making a statement of simultaneity, since it points to two coexistent events whose existence is a mutual contradiction. The simultaneity of meta-communication is what allows its participants to entertain a possibility of multiple universes of meaning. This is the possibility, indeed, the necessity, of living in more than one universe of discourse within the space and time of one's life. And this is also the impulse behind the nonsensical movement away from univocality in time and space and towards the multiplicity of simultaneity. This is Carlyle's wish for "space-annihilating and time-annihilating hats."[6] Borges edited an Argentine edition of *Sartor Resartus*, writing in a preliminary note:

Each book is an ideal orb, but we are usually pleased that its author, in the space of a few lines, confounds it with reality, with the universe. We are delighted that the protagonists of the second part of *Don Quixote* have read the first part, just as we have. It delights us that Aeneas, wandering through the streets of Carthage, looks at sculptures of the Trojan War on the facade of a temple and also sees, among so many mournful images, his own effigy. It delights us that on the six hundred and second night of the 1001 nights the queen Shaharazad refers to the story which serves as the preface to all the others, with the risk of arriving once again at the night in which she relates it, and so on into infinity.[7]

The detachability of fictions, their transference from a context of origin to other contexts, endows them with a simultaneous existence, an existence in more than one domain at a time. The fiction exists outside of and across the time and space of the everyday-life world.

NARRATIVE SPACE

Simultaneity in nonsense may be seen first of all as this kind of collapsing of time, as a war on time that achieves what Gertrude Stein called in "Composition as Explanation" a "continuous present," a moving of the temporal dimension of the fiction into a kind of narra-tive space where things happen "all at once." This is especially apparent in the modern novel, where there is a deliberate transformation of inter-subjective, standard time, into a time particular to the fiction. The influence of other genres breaks open the line of standard time in such works. Consider Joyce's use of polyphonic music in *Ulysses*, or Beckett's *Watt*, remembering "three frogs creaking Krak! Krek! and Krik! At one, nine, seventeen, twenty-five, etc. and at one, six, eleven, sixteen etc. and at one, four, seven, ten, etc., respectively."[8]

Specifically, the use of simultaneity in prose has achieved a disruption of conventional narrative temporality. This narrative temporality involves consecutive, causal events culminating in a climax that is followed by a denouement. The triangle not only gives a horizontal order to temporality; it provides a hierarchical weighing of temporality as well. This hierarchical order implies that temporal order is a causal order, that events increase in significance through time, and that the event reaches a saturation point (climax) yet does not stop abruptly. Closure is symmetrical, events closing the narrative have a comparable significance value to those events that began the narrative. And while the quality of the denouement has the same significance as the beginning events, the quantity is reduced, for these final events lie in the overwhelming shadow of the climax.

While this model can be seen as particular to narrative events in Western fiction, it is also a model for defining the parameters of events in everyday life. It is the shape of the true story; it is also the shape of conventional historical truth. The conjunction of temporality and causality, the accumulation of significance in the direction of past to future, are all characteristic of the temporal conventions of the everyday lifeworld. Therefore, any fiction that seeks to disrupt the temporality of realism will move the shape of events into the reversible and shifting boundaries characteristic of simultaneity. Sterne was an early master of this kind of departure from the temporal conventions of narrative. In the sixth volume of *Tristram Shandy*, he draws a set of diagrams of meandering lines to describe the progress of the first five books of the novel.[9] He says that he is mending his ways and will soon be able to proceed in a line as straight as one drawn with "a writing master's ruler (borrowed for that purpose) turning neither to the right or to the left."[10] Yet he asks "how it has come to pass, that your men of wit and genius have all along confounded this line with the line of GRAVITATION."[11]

John Barth uses the same technique in his story "Lost in the Funhouse," making the very topic of temporal order into a digression, a movement off the temporal line and into an infinite space. While Ambrose is lost in the funhouse, the narrator says:

The action of conventional dramatic narrative may be represented by a diagram called Freitag's Triangle:

A ⟋ B ⟍ C

or more accurately by a variant of that diagram

A—B ⟋ C ⟍ D

in which AB represents the exposition, B the introduction of conflict, BC the "rising action," complication or development of the conflict, C the climax, or turn of the action, CD the denouement, or resolution of the conflict. . . . This can't go on much longer. It can go on forever. He died telling stories to himself in the dark.[12]

The effect is a story that never gets to the point, that is continually deferred. The digression offers a simultaneity that is both on and off the page, that begins to move into the spaces between the linearity of print itself. Reading becomes a matter of departure and return, of picking up and putting down a narrative thread that is knotted, split, and broken.

In his essay on *Tristram Shandy*, Shklovsky pointed out that Homer never depicts simultaneous actions. Even when according to the course of events two actions have to occur simultaneously, Homer depicts them as following one another. But Sterne, Cervantes, and Shakespeare all celebrated the narrative device of the subplot, and Sterne went so far as to point to and parody the subplot and the intrusion of new material into the narrative.[13] The printed text allows a degree of discontinuity that would become unmanageable if embedded in oral discourse. The book as book allows one to see more than one word at a time. Out of the corner of the eye another page is always visible. One can both read and reread out of sequence, and past and future thus become "copresent." Hugh Kenner has suggested that the development of the book as book, and specifically the development of the footnote, is a step in the direction of discontinuity, of "organizing blocks of discourse simultaneously in space, rather than consecutively in time."[14] The reader of Joyce, Beckett, Cortázar, Nabokov, Borges, or Swift does not explore the causal relations obtaining between events in a sequence so much as he wanders between lines, along margins, exploring a discontinuous surface of language unfolding in space. Similarly, the surrealists' fascination with film was a fascination with free association, with unexpected visual juxtapositions and the ability to arrange concrete images in an order at odds with that of conventional spatial and temporal reality.[15]

The printed narrative provides a model for the relativity, the interdependence, of space and time; it is temporality unfolding in space. Long before relativity theory, C. L. Dodgson had suggested "A New Theory of Parallels" in his *Curiosa Mathematica*. Edmund Wilson has added, "And is there not a touch of Einstein in the scenes in which the Red Queen has to keep running in order to stay in the same place and in which the White Queen gives a scream of pain before she has pricked her finger?"[16] The program that Robbe-Grillet outlined in *For a New Novel* was as well a program for denying the everyday sense of time, for inventing a temporality that was abstract and ideal. He wrote that *La Jalousie* was constructed so that any attempt to reconstruct its temporality according to an external chronology would lead to an impasse, a set of contradictions: "Here space destroys time and time sabotages space. Description makes no headway, contradicts itself, turns in circles. Moment denies continuity."[17] This is also how the oblique narrative of John Barth's "Lost in the Funhouse" works. Each narrative movement is accompanied by a double, a voice that moves in space rather than in time, whose concern is metafictive. The double systematically cancels out the narrative voice at each step. The story is a replication of the contradictions between movement and directions in the children's game, "Mother May I?" The mother's voice, outside the action of the game, can and does transform the action into the tracing and retracing of a space.

MULTIPLE WORLDS

For time and space to be denied there must be a suspension of the everyday lifeworld, of participation in what Schutz called the "epoché" of the natural attitude. Butor has written, "Just as every organization of durations within a narrative or a musical composition—recurrences, recapitulations, superimpositions and so on—can exist only as a result of suspension of customary time in reading or listening, so every spatial relation which is maintained by the characters or by the adventures described to me can reach me only through the intermediary of a distance which I determine in relation to the place around me."[18] Thus one must begin to partake in a domain of otherness that, like the chant, brings one to something like another plane of being. With one repetition, with the two that starts off one and everything after two, time is moved into simultaneous worlds, a new domain becomes possible. Borges asked in *Labyrinths*, "Is not one single repeated term sufficient to break down and confuse the series of time?"[19]

The dadaists and surrealists were especially interested in using simultaneity as a technique to produce nonsense, to reach a state of being that was a contradiction to what Ball had termed "existing world orders." The 6 February 1916 opening of the Cabaret Voltaire featured recitations of simultaneous poetry designed by Tzara, Huelsenbeck, and Janco to create a "nonsensical but sonorous effect." The poetry consisted of the simultaneous reading of three unrelated texts in three different languages, and it became the most popular activity of Zurich Dada.[20] Huelsenbeck wrote that simultaneous poems like "L'Admiral cherche une maison à louer" were reenactments of "a sense of the merry-go-round of things, demonstrating the Dadaist's conviction that life does not consist of logical and sequential events but of a bewildering and disordered simultaneity."[21] Where polyphonic music had presented a model of harmonic simultaneity, the dadaists presented a simultaneity at war with itself. Following Marinetti, they created a "music" that would portray a jangled nerve of sound. They called this *bruitisme*, a cacophony of drums, machines, and voices that sought to provoke the public into a recognition of ex-tralogical world views, to "convey a sense of the multiplicity of simultaneous experience which was the essence of life" through sound.[22]

The surrealists, too, delighted in fate, chance, hazard, and accident. All of the events occuring within these domains were celebrated as evidence of a fundamental and mystical disorder of the world. In his *Le Paysan de Paris*, Louis Aragon looked for the marvelous in daily chance meetings and chance events. Breton wrote in the second surrealist manifesto, in 1930: "If we cannot find words enough to stigmatize the baseness of Western thought, if we are not afraid to take up arms against logic, if we refuse to swear that something we do in dreams is less meaningful than something we do in a state of waking, if we are not even sure that we will not do away *with time*, that sinister old farce, that train constantly jumping off the track, mad pulsation, inextricable conglomeration of breaking and broken beasts. . . ."[23] The dadaist and surrealist aspiration to simultaneity found its proper field on the stage, the screen, and, most of all, on the printed page, where it could be viewed all at once as a space as well as a time. This is the aspect of the printed word behind the mechanics of the calligram and anagram. Within the boundaries of the text, multiple temporal orders can be entertained. Hence two literary phenomena that were discussed before as examples of play with boundaries and play with infinity can also be seen as devices used to effect simultaneity. These are the devices of incorporation of formal features into the text and the use of intertextual references.

SIMULTANEITY AND FORM

The use of physical trappings in any text is conducive to simultaneity. A preface written at "the conclusion" and placed at the beginning of the text circles it with a temporality that can reverse itself. The voice of the footnote is a voice in simultaneity with the voice of the text. Tables of contents, indexes, chapter headings, all move towards omniscience, towards giving an overview. Consider the tabulation of passages that Carroll made for *Sylvie and Bruno* and *Sylvie and Bruno Concluded*. It stands at the exact center of the two volumes, in the preface to *Sylvie and Bruno Concluded*, and gives the reader an overview in both directions of all the passages in the two books where "abnormal states occur."[24] Butor noted in *Inventory* that "in the most sequential works a table of contents can help recapture the volume's simultaneity."[25]

Novels like Cortázar's *Hopscotch* or Nabokov's *Pale Fire* depend upon the simultaneity of the book's printed features for their ironic inversion of the priority "story" features hold over "formal" features.

Hopscotch, like articles in many popular magazines, uses the simultaneity of the book as book, the possibility of rereading and of "continuing on page X." The pages of the book are available simultaneously. *Pale Fire's* poem, annotations, and index present not only the ironic simultaneity of two contradictory voices, Shade's and Kinbote's talking against each other, but the added simultaneity of the reader's voice, constructing a set of resistances to Shade's and Kinbote's versions. Nabokov's Ada and Van had also spoken simultaneously with the text they were writing, trying to uncover "the texture of time." The movement towards prefaces, notes, afterwards, and indexes is a movement of surface, not of "depth" or hierarchy. Rather than foregrounding the text per se, these physical trappings foreground themselves as text. It is a movement that flattens text into context and all of context into a simultaneous, interpretable surface.

An early literary example of simultaneity is also an example of intertextuality. The cento was an ancient verse form in which, as Ausonius set forth the rules, "the pieces may be taken either from the same poet, or from several: and the verses may be either taken entire, or divided in two; one half to be connected with another half taken from elsewhere, but two verses are never to be taken together."[26] D'Israeli noted that the Empress Eudoxia composed a life of Jesus in centos taken from Homer. The cento flaunts the anachronism of intertextuality, creating a simultaneity of all the texts that it is composed of. The word *cento* means "a cloak made of patches," and the form prefigures not only the modernist collage, but also the quilt— that simultaneity of fabrics out of time with one another.

A cento effect is achieved by any newspaper—a text that coordinates a multiplicity of events that are not necessarily coterminous within the simultaneity of its pages. Joyce made extensive use of this aspect of the newspaper in the Aeolus episode of *Ulysses*. But where a newspaper would impose sequence over disparate events by the use of headlines and captions, Joyce interrupts and negates the sequence of events with his headlines and captions. The entire chapter may be seen as a cento that is a simultaneous and cacophonous exercise in a multiplicity of rhetorical effects. In a further dimension of intertextuality, the debate going on between Crawford, O'Molloy, McHugh, and Stephen is on the topic of the "Ancients vs. the Moderns," which is also the ostensive topic of Swift's *A Tale of a Tub*. Thomas Pynchon uses the simultaneity of the almanac in his novel *V* to present a list of natural disasters. These are events that happen in time but not across space, that at any given moment both happen and do not happen, that can only happen all at once on "record," on the page, as they do in the almanac: "These were the mass deaths. There were also the attendant maimed, malfunctioning, homeless, lorn. It happens every month in a succession of encounters between groups of living and a congruent world which simply doesn't care. Look in any yearly Almanac under 'Disasters'—which is where the figures above come from."[27] The "news" that has become the realism of modernism is as well a matter of disjuncture, of a simultaneity imposed upon events that are discontinuous to experience.

Alicia Borinsky has suggested that the intertextual duplicity of Borges's "Pierre Menard" and Reynaldo Arenas's *Hallucinations* (a rewriting of the *Memorias* and *Apologia* of Fray Servando Teresa de Mier) also present problems of simultaneity: "If the other person is not *you* or *I*, but a constant oscillation of all personal pronouns that simultaneously presents and effaces them, how do you build a discourse that assumes the oscillation?"[28] When the subject and object are written through and by each other, we are confronted with the paradox of simultaneous perception—there cannot be a fixing upon one or the other event(s); one is confronted with an infinite simultaneity, a form without a univocal content. When a text nods to the other writings that speak through it, it nods to the simultaneity of all writing. Writing appears on an infinite surface of writing, which is writing continually rewriting itself. When Joyce, Dos Passos, Eliot, and Pound take passages from other documents and incorporate them into the text, or when *The Unnamable* takes cognizance of its textual neighbors *Molloy* and *Malone*, or John Barth's three-part *Chimera* dissolves in and out of itself, intertextuality becomes a matter of simultaneity rather than causality. Literary "history," like the preface, moves forwards and backwards, inscribing meaning over and over again within the same space of the page.

In all of these literary examples of simultaneity, we can see the lyric impulse of print. Thus the lyric use of simultaneity in modernist and postmodernist poetry like that of Jackson McLow, Ron Silliman, and David Antin, is often an exaggeration of the lyric qualities of the lyric—parataxis, repetition, a fundamental reorganization of *the line*.[29] The very quality of print is paratactic—an infinite use of a finite number of elements. The interchangeability of the letter is the basis for the phenomenon of intertextuality. When Desnos says that slapstick is a lyric mode, or when Breton chracterizes surrealism as a lyric movement, they are saying that these are kinds of discourse that deny the sequentiality of logical, temporal, and causal order. They are kinds of discourse that flaunt a juxtaposition of incongruous worlds, that are reversible and repetitious and thereby move to a spatial order, away from a temporal dimension. And at the same time, they deny the orderliness of this order by celebrating those anomalous categories of everyday life—fate, chance, accident, and hazard, categories that also deny that orderliness. This is how the conversations of *Alice in Wonderland* move towards simultaneity and away from the direction and logic of everyday life. The nonsense conversations are continually halted by gaps in any common stock of knowledge, by a clash between members' biographical situations, and by a systematic use of randomness rather than a purpose at hand. They are like the lyric movement of bumper cars—cars that continually weave in and out and through each other's paths, that celebrate accident over direction, whose activities are marked by absolute spatial boundaries and arbitrary, amorphous temporal boundaries. The difference between the nonsense conversations and everyday-life conversations, bumper cars and ordinary driving, is the difference between juggling and dropping bombs, or a three-ring circus and a tragedy.

DISCONTINUITY

Discontinuity is a way of bringing about simultaneity. The discontinuity of repetition and reversibility moves along a set of axes that begin to define a space as well as a time. Discontinuity of classification brings about an interruption and splitting of hierarchical arrangement. Bergson noted that the reciprocal interference of series is essential to much of what is seen as comic: "A situation is invariably comic when it belongs simultaneously to two altogether independent series of events and is capable of being interpreted in two entirely different meanings at the same time." He concluded that the reciprocal interference of series, inversion, and repetition all consist in "looking upon life as a repeating mechanism with reversible action and interchangeable parts."[30] Bergson's idea of the machine has all the qualities of a metafiction: it is a machine of simultaneous possibilities, a machine that exists in space as well as time; it is a machine that is self-generating and self-perpetuating, that carries instructions for its own operations; and it is a machine that remains only a well-defined possibility, a machine that is a fiction, a machine made out of discourse.

The more extreme the discontinuities of discourse, the more nonsensical the discourse. Discontinuity takes its defining otherness from the categories and hierarchies of everyday life, and as discourse comes to hold within the simultaneity of its textual boundaries a "set" of elements that are increasingly marked by their difference from one another, the gestalt moves to the impossible realm of nonsense, the realm of the immaculate fiction. G. B. Milner, following Bergson, suggested that all "humor based laughter is generated by discrete elements taken, not in isolation, but in conjunction."[31] Within the gestalt of the discourse event, two or more domains take turns appearing and disappearing in the range of vision, and as these domains come to be farther and farther away from each other, the gestalt becomes more nonsensical. This is the nonsensical simultaneity of the list that can be a list of anything, that presents a simultaneity that is dissolvable into its disparate components. The only occasion for the meeting of the elements is a form—the list itself. This is also the nonsensical simultaneity of the pun, which places two or more distinct and disparate meanings within one simultaneous frame. While metaphor may become univocal, dissolving categories into a new category equaling more than the sum of its parts, the simultaneity of the pun is the sum of its constituent parts. The pun carries the comedy of dirt swept under a rug, which, discovered, still consists of dirt under a rug.

Fundamental to much nineteenth-century nonsense literature is a discontinuity brought about by combining elements from disparate domains within the text. As noted earlier, Emile Cammaerts remarked that nonsense's "world of topsyturvydom" was a world that "confused classes and values."[32] Much of Edward Lear's nonsense works this way— the simultaneous confusion of domains in his "Flora Nonsensica," limericks, nonsense cookbooks, and verses like the "Teapots and Quails" series:

> Teapots and Quails
> Sniffers and Snails,
> Set him a sailing
> And see how he sails . . .
>
> Lobsters and owls,
> Scissors and fowls
> Set him a howling
> And hark how he howls[33]

In this type of discourse, any number of elements can serve within the defining list. Rhyme and alliteration bear a list of words linked by sound rather than by common sense. The use of rhyme and alliteration tends toward nonsense and away from common sense. Even in the most logical of discourses, rhyme speaks in an alogical voice. This is the point of Edward Lear's "Epitaph":

> Beneath these high cathedral stairs
> Lie the remains of Susan Pares
> Her name was Wiggs, it was not Pares
> But Pares was put to rhyme with stairs.[34]

Rhyme works as a principle of simultaneity and convergence, just as in numerical compositions a number like thirty-three can serve to converge a great many disparate elements and events. This prose rhyme in Gertrude Stein's "Roast Beef" provides another example of the rhyming simultaneity of disparate domains and her philosophy of "using everything":

Lovely snipe and tender turn, excellent vapor and slender butter, all the splinter and the trunk, all the poisoning darkening drunk, all the joy in weak success all the joyful tenderness, all the section and the tea, all the stouter symmetry.[35]

The paratactic possibilities of rhyme and alliteration bring us back to the idea of a lyric unfolding to infinity. Many jump rope rhymes and hand-clapping rhymes have this quality. We can rarely, if ever, say there is a definitive rhyme, since the text is an abstraction, a simultaneity, of a multiple set of variations that dissolve in and out of each other. The rhyme is the convergence of its versions. In Baltimore, children add an interchangeable number of elements to make up a rhyme:

> I'm goin to Kentucky
> I'm goin to the fair
> To see my sister Rita
> With the flowers in her hair.
> Oh, shake it baby, shake it
> Shake it as you can
> Shake it like a milkshake
> And do the best you can
> Oh, rumble to the bottom
> Rumble to the top
> Turn around and turn around
> Until you make a stop[36]

In this rhyme the narrative of "I'm goin to Kentucky" can be infinitely braided into a set of jump rope rhymes and actions. The order of events is infinitely interruptable and interchangeable. The same phenomenon can be seen in the Anglo-American love lyric, where digressions and elaborations threaten to take over the lyric's logical structure.[37] Any single lyric is a particular combination of a set of elements common to many other lyrics. These genres flaunt their status as performances by defining a spatial and temporal field and systematically incorporating elements from separate domains within them. They take place on a playground of performance whose boundaries are arbitrary in relation to what is enclosed within them, yet definitive and examinable at each instance of performance.

THE CONVERGENCE OF DISPARITY

The surrealists made the simultaneous convergence of disparity into a conscious poetic principle, "Beautiful as the fortuitous meeting on a dissection table, of a sewing machine and an umbrella," wrote Lautréamont.[38] This principle was the basis for Réverdy's famous thesis on imagery: "The image is a pure creation of mind. It cannot be born from a comparison but from a juxtaposition of two more or less distant realities. The more the relationship between the two juxtaposed realities is distant and true, the stronger the image will be—the greater its emotional power and poetic reality."[39] The more disparate the domains, the stronger, the more integral, the image. Breton wrote in "Signe ascendent" (1948) that "only on the analogical plane have I ever experienced any intellectual pleasure. For me, the only real *evidence* is a result of the spontaneous, extra-lucid and defiant relationship suddenly sensed between two things which common sense would never bring together."[40] In Breton's surrealist game, "One in the Other," he played with the possibility that any reality can be described in terms of any other, and that as a result of these descriptions the powers of the image would be shown to be theoretically unlimited. He said, "We had already gone beyond thinking that any object might be described in terms of any other, but rather that any *action* and also any *person* even placed in a precise situation might be described in terms of any object and vice versa."[41] Simultaneity would therefore be effected not only between members of disparate classes, but between types of classes, moving along the vertical hierarchical axis as well as the horizontal axis of the logical type. This is comparable to Bateson's example of the schizophrenic who would include among his class of "not chairs" an abstraction like "tomorrow." The surrealist use of metaphor was a matter not only of a "fresh cut," but a fresh cut across a set of contradictions, a gesture of impossibility. In this sense, the surrealist metaphor works like the riddles of proper nots: "What has eyes but cannot see?", "What has legs but cannot walk?", but goes further in removing the riddle from everyday life. The answers to these riddles restore common sense to the question, restricting the range of simultaneity. But the answers to surrealist riddles restore only the unlimited potential of the image to the question. This emphasizes again the point that metaphor in nonsense is left without a context, without an application to the ongoingness of events. When the Mad Hatter asks, "Why is a raven like a writing desk?"[42] the question is what interests us, the fantastic combination of domains that is implied. The hatter does not bother with an answer to the riddle.

A nineteenth-century parlor game called "What Is My Thought Like?" works the same way as these surrealist and nonsense riddles. One player thinks privately of some object and then asks the other players in succession, "What is my thought like?" Each names some object such as: a rose, a book, a wedding ring, a blister, a pair of boots. The leader then declares what his thought was and calls upon each player to prove the resemblance.[43] Metonymy, relationships of propinquity, are sacrificed to an overwhelming metaphoric dimension whenever nonsensical simultaneity has this unlimited faculty for creating relationships of identity.

Huizinga pointed out in *Homo Ludens* that play interrupts the reasonableness, the logical sequence, of events. One of the favorite rhetorical tricks of the sophists, for example, was the *antilogia*, or double reasoning. Huizinga writes that "apart from giving free reign to play, this form allowed them to hint at the perpetual ambiguity of every judgment made by the human mind; one can put a thing like this or that."[44] The thisness or thatness of things is what makes them susceptible to riddling and puns, for riddling and puns always point to the multivocality of the sign. "Surrealism" itself can be seen as splitting into a pun, or being the answer to a riddle. Breton said, "I believe in the future resolution of these two states, dream and reality, which are seemingly so contradictory, into a kind of absolute reality, a surreality."[45] The effect of the riddle and pun is to dissolve meaning into its constituent and simultaneous parts; the more contradictory those parts, the more nonsensical.

THE TERRIBLE PUN

Puns are "terrible" and "awful" because they split the flow of events in time. Like any intrusion of nonsense into conversation, they are a "trip-up," an impediment to seriousness.[46] This is emphasized by the point that a pun is only terrible if members frame it as a pun, if it is foregrounded and brought to attention. Harvey Sacks has illustrated the extraordinary frequency of puns in "ordinary" discourse, writing, "Puns are recognizable, though not always recognized."[47] Hence the importance of distinguishing between "pun intended" and "no pun intended." When puns go unattended and are unintended, they serve as short cuts, they fit into the prevailing mode of discourse. When they are intended and attended to, they move the discourse to another plane, interrupting the purpose at hand by introducing a universe that "does not count," that does not go or get anywhere. This is the universe of the Alice conversations and most of *Sylvie and Bruno*. Conversations are continually halted by puns, by a splitting of the discourse into two simultaneous and disparate paths, each followed by a respective member of the conversation. While in everyday discourse a pun is attended to and then put aside while the conversation moves on, in Carroll's nonsensical discourse, puns are attended to, but are not recognized as "only puns," and thereby achieve a continual dividing of the conversations they appear in. Bruno's discourse is especially subject to this kind of splitting. When the Professor says that he hopes Bruno had a good night, Bruno answers, "I's had the same night oo've had . . . there's only been *one* night since yesterday." A few paragraphs later, the Warden says of the Professor, "Positively, he runs over with learning." "But he needn't run over me!" Bruno replies.[48] In these works, all short cuts, all usage of idioms, are literalized; all puns are exposed. This is the kind of punning logic that underlies the following jump rope rhyme:

Dr. Brown fell in the well
And broke his collar bone
Why don't he attend to the sick
And leave the well alone.[49]

Much of children's traditional speech play uses the simultaneity of the pun. These forms of speech play often work within the hierarchy of one logical type, systematically exploring the divergences between the meanings of a word. In these two verses, for example, the categories "vegetable names" and "state names" are worked into narratives that divide at every step into a double that is the pun:

Do you carrot all for me?
My heart beets for you.
With your turnip nose
And your radish face
You are a peach.
If we cantaloupe
Lettuce marry
Weed make a swell pear.[50]

Mississippi said to Missouri
If I put on my New Jersey
What will Delaware?
Virginia said, Alaska.[51]

These punning narratives work like Lewis Carroll's "Jabberwocky," making the metaphoric dimension a place of substitution and divergence within the simultaneity of a "grammatical" metonymic dimension. Joyce uses the same technique in this passage from *Ulysses*: "The fashionable international world attended *en masse* this afternoon at the wedding of the chevalier Jean Wyse de Neaulan, grand high chief ranger of the Irish National Foresters, with Miss Fir Conifer of Pine Valley, Lady Sylvester Elmshade, Mrs. Barbara Lovebirch, Mrs. Poll Ash, Mrs. Holly Hazel eyes, Miss Daphne Bays."[52] When a narrative tolerates extensive punning, when it is saturated with puns, the effect is a text that splits itself into simultaneous texts with every step. In surrealism, we see the extended use of Duchamp's punning signature "Rrose Selavy." Seeing it everywhere is a sign that the text has been split, marked, just as a master of graffiti will leave his mark all over the city in a simultaneity of marks while the populace is sleeping and the text of the city is both hidden and vulnerable. The mark of Rrose Selavy is not only in Duchamp's work, but in others' work as well. In Desnos's *Domaine public* it appears and reappears, and while Duchamp is never mentioned, a note at the beginning of Desnos's collection "Rrose Selavy" says to decode the thirteenth verse: "Rrose Selavy connait bien le marchand du sel."[53]

Infante's *Three Trapped Tigers* is another text that has been marked and split by extensive punning.[54] This is discourse that becomes non-sensical because it is organized around puns; it is discourse that stops itself at every step and splits. The puns are not passed by as they are in the conversations of everyday life. Rather, the point of the "narrative" is to get to the next pun, just as the eye goes from item to item in the list, ignoring the space between the items that defines them. John Lennon proved to be another master of this type of continuous punning in his books *In His Own Write* and *A Spaniard in the Works*. In the former book is the following political satire, "You Might Well Arsk":

Why were Prevelant ze Gaute, unt Docker Adenoid getting so friendly? You might well arsk. Why was Seldom Loyled sagged? Why did Harrassed Macmillion go gophing mit Bod Hobe? Why is Frank Cunnings and the T.U.C. against the Commen Margate? You might well arsk. Why is the Duck of Edincalvert a sailing mit Udda Fogs? Why did Priceless Margerine unt Bony Armstrove give Jamaika away? You might well arsk. Why won't Friendly Trumap give his Captive his pension? [55]

THE PORTMANTEAU

The pun involves the simultaneity of two or more meanings within one word. Conversely, the portmanteau involves the simultaneity of two or more words within one meaning. Some forms of children's speech play point to the portmanteau-quality of words that are assumed to be univocal in their everyday use: "Did you ever see the cowslip, the toothpick, the catfish, the chimneysweep, the oceanwave, the moonbeam, the peanutstand?" And many words that are classified as "picturesque" or "strong" language turn out to be portmanteau words. For example, *absquatulate* (abscond and squat), meaning to depart or turn away, and *bodaciously* or *bodyaciously* (bold and audacious).[56] The portmanteau proper is Carroll's invention. As Humpty Dumpty explains in "Jabberwocky," "There are plenty of hard words there . . . slithy means 'lithe and slimy.' 'Lithe' is the same as 'active.' You see it's like a portmanteau—there are two meanings packed up in one word."[57] Another portmanteau proper is the "frumious bandersnatch" of Fit the Seventh in "The Hunting of the Snark." *Frumious* is a word made up of fuming and furious.[58] Gilles Deleuze has discussed these "mots valises" in his *Logique du Sens*, suggesting that they portray a synthesis by disjunction: "Nous découvrons la loi du mot-valise en général, à condition de dégager chaque fois la disjonction qui pouvait être cachée."[59] While we can say that the portmanteau involves the simultaneity of two or more words within one meaning, we can also say that the simultaneity, once attended to, dissolves "the meaning" into its constituent elements, and those constituent elements again split into all the possible combinations of meaning available to their convergence. In the preface to "The Hunting of the Snark," Carroll proposes: "Supposing that, when Pistol uttered the well-known words—'Under which King, Bezonian? Speak or die!' Justice Shallow had felt certain that it was either William or Richard, but had not been able to settle which, so that he could not possibly say either name before the other, can it be doubted that, rather than die, he would have gasped out 'Rilchiam'?"[60]

Joyce made extensive use of the portmanteau, first in *Ulyssses*, and then in *Finnegans Wake*. When Stephen's stream of consciousness in "Telemachus" and "Proteus" reveals phrases like "the pluter perfect imperturbability of the department of agriculture" and "We don't want any of your medieval abstrusiosities"[61] Joyce is already on the way to making the portmanteau a principle of simultaneous composition, as he does in the *Wake*. In *Ulysses*, the use of simultaneity appears as a shifting and reversal of the temporality of everyday life that is largely achieved through techniques like stream of consciousness. The text is broken up into a constellation of simultaneous moments, an infinity of such moments within the space of a single day. Here is Stephen on the beach: "You are walking through it howsomever. I am, a stride at a time. A very short space of time through very short times of space. Five, six: the *nacheinander*. Exactly: and that is the ineluctable modality of the audible. Open your eyes. No. Jesus! If I fell over a cliff that beetles o'er his base, fell through the *nebeneinander* ineluctably, I am getting along nicely in the dark."[62] The text is a game of blind man's bluff, an Odyssean wandering towards, around, and away from a destination within the time of a single day and the space of a single city. The idea of a conjunction of the *nacheinander* and the *nebeneinander* as a method of composition is directly echoed in Robbe-Grillet's recent pronouncement that the contemporary novel arranges metaphors in the order of metonymy,[63] a feat that continually breaks up the temporality and causality of the "narrative" and causes artifice itself to appear on the scene. *Ulysses* and *Finnegans Wake* are novels of hesitancy, novels that do not achieve an arrival or centering.

In the *Wake*, simultaneity is taken on the level of the word itself— each word contains within itself a multiple nest of other words, other meanings, converging into the etymologies and the near-infinite possibilities of their combination. The multiplicity of the word spins in a vortex towards its roots and out towards its borrowings, modifications, and nuances to the multiple form as printed in the text. The word itself becomes a philosophy of history, as the *Wake* speaks its own language made up of what may be all languages. Joyce wrote as an advertisement for *Work in Progress*:

Humpty Dump Dublin squeaks through his norse;
Humpty Dump Dublin hath a horrible vorse;
But for all his kinks English, plus his irismanx brogues
Humpty Dump Dublin's grandada of all rogues.[64]

Joyce manages to disperse the integrity of objects, characters, and events in a movement that threatens the integrity of language, and the status of the text as text as well. The attack on language that the *Wake* presents is an attack on univocality. If Joyce has succeeded in fragmenting English into a set of borrowings that range from Norse to West Indian creoles, he has also succeeded in fragmenting any univocal notion of culture. The British Empire has proved to be less than the sum of its constituent parts. "Il y a chez Joyce, c'est essential dans son oeuvre, des le début, une volonté farouche de détacher la langue anglais de sa nationalité et cela est très important pour nous," wrote Butor in an essay on translating Joyce.[65]

THE MACARONIC

The *Wake* can be seen as part of the tradition of the macaronic text. The macaronic is any literary construction that is written in more than one language. The word is sometimes said to come from *macaroni*, an Italian paté composed of diverse ingredients,[66] or *macarone*, "a lubberly fellow."[67] Although macaronics began to appear in Italy at the close of the fifteenth century, the first great master of the macaronic was Theophile Folengo, better known under his pseudonym of Merlin Coccaie. Folengo was born in Mantua in 1491, and his most famous macaronic, in which the author combined Latin, Italian, and Mantuan dialect words, tells of the adventures of a hero named Balbus. It was published in Venice in 1547 and, according to Lalanne's *Curiosités littéraires*, consists of "tirades full of verve and malice against the great, the defects of men and the vanity of the nobility."[68] The pleasure of macaronic verse is a pleasure in a combination of elements taken from systems conventionally regarded as disjunctive. It was originally a form created by scholars to display a knowledge of two disparate languages, a system of Latin inflections joined to words of a modern vernacular such as English, French, German, or Italian.[69] The form thus had a great deal to do with the rise of the vernacular during the Renaissance. In that momentous first encounter of Pantagruel and Panurge, for example, Panurge spoke German, Italian, Basque, Dutch, Spanish, Danish, Hebrew, Greek, and Latin, as well as several nonsense languages that were Rabelais's/Panurge's invention. Dobson gives an example of a macaronic by a J.A.M. called "St. George and His Dragon" that begins:

Haec fabulum's one of those stories,
Which the Italians say 'ought to be true.'
Sed which modern wiseacres have scattered
Among les Illusions Perdus!

St. George eques errans erat
Qui vibrat a seven-foot sword
Und er wurde eher be all up a tree
Than be caught a-breaking his word.[70]

The macaronic can be distinguished from the kind of hidden juxta-position of languages à la "Mots d'heures gousses, rames," noted in the chapter on boundaries, by the use of two or more languages simul-taneously. In the macaronic, both languages are discrete and identi-fiable. They are allowed to coexist in the simultaneity of the form, creating a voice that is neither here nor there, that splits into a con-tradiction of what it knows. As primarily a scholastic form, the mac-aronic reveals the problem of Bouvard and Pecuchet, the problem of contradictions in knowledge that cannot be reconciled. The macaronic does not effect a synthesis—it is a simultaneity of examinable elements, a conjunction that, like all nonsensical simultaneity, is the sum of its parts and no more. Its movement is perpetual but not hierarchical; it does not rise to a conclusion, it simply keeps going, as this combina-tion of gibberish and macaronic by John Lennon demonstrates:

He is putting it lithely when he says
Quobble in the Grass,
Strab he down the soddie flays
Amo amat amass;
Amonk amink a minibus,
A marmylaidie Moon,
Amikky mendip multiplus
Amighty midgey spoon.
And so I traddled onward
Careing not a care
Onward, onward, onward
Onward, my friends to victory and glory
For the thirty-ninth.[71]

The attack on univocality that the macaronic undertakes has to do with the beginning of a tear in the fabric of any singular way of organ-izing the world, in any ethnocentrism. The confrontation with another language is a confrontation with the limits of the everyday lifeworld. It is an encounter with the possibility of the "unimaginable object" through an alternative organization of the world. The confrontation with the other is one in which the relationship to the other and the con-ditions of the other's existence are systematically explored through manipulation and exaggeration. The medley of languages and cultures seen in the macaronic is an outgrowth of "learning," of confrontation with the disjunctions and convergences, the limitations, of social reality. G. K. Chesterton suggested that the notion of "holiday" is intrinsic to the particular kind of nonsense that developed in English; "The holiday was an essential element in the dream life of the Victorian world."[72] While the reclusive Charles Dodgson limited his holidays to picnics and boating outings, Edward Lear was an inveterate tourist, traveling to India, Ceylon, Egypt, Arabia, Asia Minor, Syria, Palestine, Italy, and Greece and spending much of his life away from his native England.[73]

When another culture is possible, but not able to be experienced, it acquires the status and operations of a fiction, a world existing simultaneously with the everyday lifeworld, yet outside of it. The cultural other becomes a space in which meaning is fabricated and erased, in which features become stereotypic. Writing about this other comes to converge or diverge from the stereotype. The world is seen as a simultaneity, but a controlled simultaneity, the number of elements allowed to appear in each constituent part of the simultaneity depending upon the knowledge at hand at any given time. For an example of the prevalence of this nonsense of the cultural other in nineteenth-century America, one has only to look at the limerick books that were often printed as souvenirs of exhibitions. "The New Book of Nonsense, A Contribution to the Great Central Fair," published in Philadelphia in 1864 by the Ladies of the Sanitary Commission, for example, consists mostly of limericks poking fun at Southerners, "foreigners," blacks, and the inhabitants of Northern cities other than Philadelphia.

With the movements of modernism we see a world increasingly self-conscious about its simultaneity. Marinetti listed among the essential elements of futurism: "a feeling for the great city . . . and the simultaneity that derives from tourism, business and journalism; the passion for success, the keenest instinct for setting records, the enthusiastic imitation of electricity and the machine; essential concision and synthesis; the happy precision of gears and well-oiled thoughts; the concurrence of energies as they converge into a single, victorious trajectory."[74] The futurist's vision is one of speed, of machines that begin to warp time and space into the simultaneity of relativity. Dadaism, too, was a movement characterized by a convergence of languages and cultures. The word *dada* was chosen because of its multivocality—German/French babytalk for a horse, Rumanian for "Yes, Yes," and Kru African for the tail of a cow. The original members of the Zurich movement came from diverse parts of Europe: Tristan Tzara and Marcel Janco from Rumania; Jean Arp and Francis Picabia from France; Hugo Ball, Richard Huelsenbeck, Emmy Hennings, and Hans Richter from Germany; Walter Serner from Austria; Marcel Slodki from the Ukraine; and Sophie Taeuber from Switzerland.[75] From the beginning there was a fascination with "Africanisms," both Huelsenbeck's invented Africanisms and the authentic ones presided over by Jan Ephraim, the Dutch sailor-turned-landlord of the Cabaret Voltaire. It was with African drums that Huelsenbeck wanted to drum Western literature out of existence.[76] Similarly, what are probably modernism's most extensive texts of convergence of languages and cultures, *Finnegans Wake* and *The Cantos*, were written by authors whose position was that of an exile, one who stands outside in order to see. The point of fragmentation in modernism is also the point of convergence.

In summary, the use of simultaneity to transform the everyday, common-sense lifeworld is the use of another paradox in a pattern of paradoxes. Simultaneity takes place in an impossible context, it splits perception into two or more disjunctive axes, yet it presents itself with an integrity that is self-defined. In folkloric forms simultaneity is often an aural convergence, as it is in puns, rhymes, and portmanteau words. In literary forms the quality of print itself gives an added dimension of simultaneity. In printed forms the simultaneity of formal features that are included in the text, allusion, and other aspects of intertextuality become foregrounded. Simultaneity may be characterized as a lyric movement in both folklore and literature to the extent that it is paratactic, involving the convergence of an interchangeable set of elements within the frame of the text that interrupt or deny any logical, temporal, or causal order. Finally, we can see nineteenth- and twentieth-century use of simultaneity as an aspect of a culture that came to see its position as a relative one, simultaneous to other cultures, converging in space and time within an increasingly accessible world. The world thus comes to have the quality of the printed page, the spatial organization of disparity, as much as the page takes on the mode of the world's discourse.

NOTES

1. Schutz, *Collected Works*, 1:230.
2. Quoted in Bigsby, *Dada and Surrealism*, p. 5.
3. Opie, *Lore and Language*, pp. 310–13.
4. M. and H. Knapp, "Tradition and Change in American Playground Language," *Journal of American Folklore* 86 (1973): 138.
5. Butor, *Inventory*, pp. 48–49. The dialogue is in Rabelais, *Gargantua and Pantagruel*, pp. 392–96.
6. Thomas Carlyle, *Sartor Resartus* (New York: Scribner's, 1896), p. 208.
7. See Ronald J. Christ, *The Narrow Act: Borges's Art of Allusion* (New York: New York University Press, 1969), p. 36.
8. Beckett, *Three Novels*, p. 136.
9. Sterne, *Tristram Shandy*, pp. 473–74.
10. Ibid., p. 474.

11. Ibid., p. 475.

12. Barth, *Lost in the Funhouse*, p. 91.

13. Shklovsky, "A Parodying Novel," p. 69.

14. Hugh Kenner, *The Stoic Comedians* (Berkeley: University of California Press, 1962), p. 40.

15. Matthews, *Surrealism and Film*, p. 3.

16. Edmund Wilson, "C. L. Dodgson: The Poet Logician," in *Aspects of Alice*, Phillips, pp. 200-201.

17. Alain Robbe-Grillet, *For a New Novel*, trans. Richard Howard (New York: Grove Press, 1965), pp. 154-55.

18. Butor, *Inventory*, p. 32.

19. Jorge Luis Borges, *Labyrinths* (New York: New Directions, 1962), p. 224.

20. Manuel Grossman, *Dada: Paradox, Mystification, and Ambiguity in European Literature* (New York: Pegasus Books, 1971), p. 55. This experiment is the same as the Hilbert experiment discussed in chapter 1.

21. Bigsby, *Dada and Surrealism*, p. 15.

22. Ibid., p. 29.

23. Breton, *Manifestoes*, p. 128.

24. Carroll, *Complete Works*, p. 513.

25. Butor, *Inventory*, p. 56.

26. D'Israeli, *Curiosities of Literature*, 1:299.

27. Thomas Pynchon, *V* (New York: Bantam, 1964), pp. 270-71.

28. Alicia Borinsky, "Rewritings and Writings," *Diacritics* 4 (1974): 25.

29. For an introduction, see Jerome Rothenberg's anthology, *Revolution of the Word* (New York: Seabury Press, 1974).

30. Bergson, "Laughter," p. 123.

31. G. B. Milner, "Homo Ridens," *Semiotica* 5 (1972): 2.

32. Cammaerts, *Poetry of Nonsense*, pp. 25-27.

33. Lear, *Teapots and Quails*, pp. 15, 22.

34. Lear, *Complete Nonsense Book*, p. 48.

35. Stein, *Selected Writings*, p. 479.

36. Collected at Coppin School, Baltimore, May 1975.

37. For an introduction to this form, see H. M. Belden, *Ballads and Folk Songs Collected by the Missouri Folklore Society*, Columbia: Missouri Folklore Society 15, no. 1, 1 January 1940.

38. See Balakian, *Surrealism*, p. 154.

39. *Nord-Sud*, March 1918, quoted in Breton's 1924 manifesto, *Manifestoes*, p. 20.

40. In André Breton, *La clé des champs* (Paris: Éditions du Sagittaire, 1953), p. 112.

41. This game is described by Roger Caillois in "Riddles and Images," in *Game, Play, Literature*, ed. Ehrmann, p. 148.

42. Carroll, *Complete Works*, p. 75. Carroll did not provide an answer to this riddle for 31 years. In 1896 he wrote that "a raven is like a writing desk because it can produce a few notes, though they are *very* flat; and it is never put with the wrong end in front!" (Fisher, *Magic of Lewis Carroll*, pp. 61-62).

43. Blitz, *Parlor Book of Magic*, p. 34.

44. Huizinga, *Homo Ludens*, p. 152.

45. Breton, *Manifestoes*, p. 14.

46. The *Boston Evening Transcript* for 6 August 1832 stated the following complaint about punning: "Puns, pungently pointed and perpetrated promptly are productive of a proruption of a pretty proportion of piquant pleasure; but puns protracted and in every person's premises, should be punishable by a propulsion of the perpetrator from the punning premises" (Loomis, "Traditional American Wordplay," p. 2).

47. Harvey Sacks, "On Some Puns with Some Intimations," in *Sociolinguistics*, ed. R. W. Shuy (Washington, D.C.: Georgetown University Press, 1973), p. 135.

48. Carroll, *Complete Works*, p. 293.
49. B. R. Buckley, "Jump Rope Rhymes," *Keystone Folklore Quarterly* 11 (1966): p. 110.
50. Withers, *A Rocket in My Pocket*, p. 193.
51. Ibid.
52. James Joyce, *Ulysses* (New York: Vintage Books, 1961), p. 327.
53. Robert Desnos, *Domaine public* (Paris: Gallimard, 1953), p. 40.
54. See, for example, Infante, *Three Trapped Tigers*, pp. 287–89.
55. John Lennon, *"In His Own Write" and "A Spaniard in the Works"* (New York: Signet, 1964), p. 57.
56. Botkin, *A Treasury of American Folklore*, pp. 273–74.
57. Carroll, *Complete Works*, p. 215.
58. Ibid., p. 776.
59. Deleuze, *Logique du Sens*, p. 61.
60. Carroll, *Complete Works*, p. 755.
61. Joyce, *Ulysses*, pp. 33, 95.
62. Ibid., p. 37.
63. Robbe-Grillet, "Order and Disorder," p. 5.
64. See Herbert Gorman, *James Joyce: A Definitive Biography* (New York: Farrar and Rinehart, 1939), p. 340. The quote appears and is discussed in Atherton, *Books at the Wake*, p. 126, and in Anthony Burgess, *Joysprick* (New York: Harcourt, Brace, 1973), p. 136.
65. Michel Butor, "La Traduction," *James Joyce Quarterly* 4 (1967): 216.
66. Similarly, *Finnegans Wake* puns on "Mrs. Houligan's Cake," an Irish Christmas cake so full of ingredients it is nearly inedible.
67. See Wright, *History of Caricature*, pp. 315–23, for a discussion of macaronic verse in fifteenth- and sixteenth-century Italy and France.
68. Lalanne, *Curiosités*, p. 76.
69. Dobson, *Poetical Ingenuities*, p. 59.
70. Ibid., pp. 79–80.
71. John Lennon, "Alec Speaking," in *"In His Own Write" and "A Spaniard in the Works,"* p. 52.
72. G. K. Chesterton, "Lewis Carroll," in *A Handful of Authors*, ed. Dorothy Collins (New York: Sheed and Ward, 1953), p. 119.
73. See Vivien Noakes, *Edward Lear: The Life of a Wanderer* (Boston: Houghton Mifflin, 1968).
74. Filippo Marinetti, "Geometrical and Mechanical Splendor and Numerical Sensibility," in *Selected Writings*, ed. R. W. Flint (New York: Noonday, 1971), p. 97.
75. Bigsby, *Dada and Surrealism*, pp. 14–15.
76. Grossman, *Dada*, pp. 57–58. See also Richard Huelsenbeck's *Memoirs of a Dada Drummer*, ed. H. J. Kleinschmidt, trans. Joachim Neugroschel (New York: Viking, 1974).

7 · arrangement and rearrangement within a closed field

THE PLAYGROUND

Simultaneity is one of the effects of the final nonsense operation I discuss here—arrangement and rearrangement within a closed field.[1] In this method for making nonsense, the boundaries of the event are given by convention while the space within those boundaries becomes a place of infinite substitution. Here an arbitrary relation between form and content is flaunted. This method can be contrasted to the nonsense effected by shifting boundaries, for in the nonsense of shifting boundaries, misdirection by means of a surplus or deficiency of signification makes the conventional boundary of the event inadequate or misleading when juxtaposed with the conditions of the performance at hand. But in nonsense that involves an arrangement or rearrangement within a closed field, the boundaries are fixed and arbitrary, and they surround a permutable and incongruous content. In other words, we could say that the nonsense of shifting boundaries demonstrates a subordination of form to content, while the nonsense of a closed field demonstrates a subordination of content to form.

The dominant spatial dimension of this type of nonsense immediately links it to simultaneity with its convergence of disparate events. Its spatial dimension is also what makes this type of nonsense making clearly a type of play, for as Huizinga noted in *Homo Ludens*, play is defined mainly in space: "More striking even than the limitation as to time is the limitation as to space. All play moves and has its being within a playground marked off beforehand either materially or ideally, deliberately, or as a matter of course."[2] In the chapters on infinity and simultaneity we saw the paradoxes that nonsense

171

displays with regard to time. When arrangement and rearrangement are performed within a closed space, the boundary of that space is both absolute and nonexistent. The boundary is formed on the interface between "the real" and the "not really real." It is a spatial boundary that is not a boundary having to do with relationships of propinquity so far as everyday life determines those relationships. Therefore, what is inside and what is outside the boundary bear no necessary relation to each other from the point of view of the play/fiction. Yet the unnecessary, arbitrary nature of that relationship, from the point of view of "reality," depends upon relationships outside the boundary for the definition of "unnecessary, arbitrary." Simply put, this is a spatial manifestation of the paradox of all nonsense—its status as "not sense" always contingent upon an idea of common sense.

In realism the frame is hidden, as if the shape of everyday events could form a continuum with the shape of fictive events. In reversals and inversions the frame becomes an articulation of exact difference, of a "proper not" relationship between categories. In misdirection the frame is dissolved into content as the fiction appropriates its immediate context. With infinity the frame becomes self-generating and self-perpetuating and reveals the etymological problem of the frame holding another frame. With simultaneity the frame becomes the very shape of infinity, a place where events converge. In arrangement and rearrangement within a closed field, frames are appropriated and made the absolute and arbitrary boundaries of a content that may be incongruous in its relationship to the frame, or in the relationship between its constituent elements. In simultaneity we saw the infinite possibilities of convergence once convergence was permitted; with nonsense made within a closed field, those possibilities of convergence are themselves combined and recombined within a borrowed structure.

A child with blocks and a table top will combine the blocks to exhaustion within the playground of the table top. Playing pick up sticks or throwing dice involve the same movement—a finite number of elements threatening an exhaustion of combinations. Once the elements combined and recombined need not be of the same domain, once they can be cabbages and kings, we have made a further shift away from common sense and towards nonsense. The connection between play and the nonsense of a closed field is made apparent here— a manipulation and transformation of events taking place within a closed frame. While play is fantasy play, those events that are manipulated and transformed are taken from the classes and hierarchies of everyday life. Once play becomes ironic, satiric, and increasingly nonsensical, it takes those events from other universes of discourse, other levels of textuality, arranging and rearranging them according to principles internal to the playground, and the "fit" between play and reality becomes increasingly incongruous. As play moves towards nonsense, context is appropriated within the play frame, play appropriates reality, until reality is incorporated into the surface of nonsense, and form and content are infinitely permutable. Just as in the surrealist game "One in the Other" any object could be depicted in terms of any other, so in the nonsense of a closed field anything can give form to, serve as the scaffolding for, anything else.

THE MEDLEY

To combine a diverse set of elements within a closed field is to create a medley. The word *medley* signifies combat and fighting; a combination; a heterogenous mixture of things or of persons differing in rank and occupation; a cloth woven of different colors; or a musical composition consisting of incongruous parts. A medley can consist of a recombination of elements from the same domain, appearing out of sequence and hierarchy, or a combination of elements from disparate domains enclosed within the frame of the medley. In contrast to the list, the medley is a form that appears within a closed frame—it threatens infinity by combination of elements rather then by addition of elements. The medley signifies nothing beyond itself; its message is "This is a medley." William Willeford, in his study of clowns and jesters, notes that the "Feast of Fools" was characterized by a replacement of the prescribed vespers with a medley of all the vespers used throughout the year, and draws a connection between this type of medley and the motley dress of clowns.[3] Such medleys and motleys return us to Mrs. O'Houligan's cake and the macaroni paté. The boundary of the nonsense event forms a closed field within which a simultaneity of disparate elements is produced.

The picture frame and the printed page form ready-made closed fields. They invite simultaneity by their primary spatial quality and rearrangement by their absolute boundaries. As what is enclosed in the picture frame or the page increasingly flaunts its *arranged* quality, its artifice and contrivance, the message "This is a fiction" becomes increasingly clear. Think of the still life—first as a combination of elements that might really be found together in everyday life. Once Cézanne includes a plaster cupid within those everyday arrangements, confusing the status of the representation of a representation and the representation of "real objects," or when he paints within a single frame leaves that have been printed on a curtain and "real leaves" with the same quality of "realness," he has made a step towards closing the surface of the painting and erasing the hierarchical relationship between reality and the fiction. The dadaist collage was another aspect of this deliberate mixing of categories within a single spatial frame.

Tzara made poems out of words cut from a newspaper and scattered on the ground in chance juxtaposition. The photomontages and rayograms of John Heartfield and Man Ray were a further attack on realism —a manipulation and transformation of the art form most conventionally considered as "real."[4] The surrealists continued this project by including within a single canvas elements of painting, sculpture, and poetry, as well as elements known only in dreams. These experiments with collage may be compared to the arrangement and rearrangement within a closed field that characterizes divination. When Duchamp drops three pieces of thread, a meter long each, and then preserves the resulting shape as "Three Standard Stoppages," or when the dadaists compose poems by pulling words out of a hat, the chance juxtaposition of elements form a message beyond the powers of common sense. Its celebration of fate, chance, accident, and hazard makes this an art of the impossible context.

I have already discussed the convergence of domains typifying simultaneity as printed discourse. Joyce's appropriation of the "Peg's Paper" style in the "Nausicaa" episode of *Ulysses*, and the Gaelic revival style, journalese, the Theosophist style, the political style, and so on in the "Cyclops" section, are examples of the kind of rearrangement and elimination of hierarchy between universes of discourse typical of collage. Including a newspaper article in a novel is tantamount to including a flower woven into fabric among the real flowers in a painting, or a painting among the elements of a painting seen in Magritte's work. When there is a representational "fit" between forms being arranged within other forms—print within print, painting within painting—there is a collapsing of time that erases the boundary between form and content and makes one perceive them as if they were the same. This is what happens when we watch a character read a letter in a film, a letter that we will find ourselves reading at the same speed as the character's reading. It is as if we were able to perceive a set of Chinese boxes, one within the other, all at once. It is perhaps the closest thing we have to experiencing infinity. When John Lennon uses typefaces to parody religious, political, and newspaper discourse, or the dadaists use letters of varying sizes and thicknesses in their optophonic poems to make the page take on the appearance of a musical score, representation is being flattened into a surface of infinitely combinable possibilities. Genres are collapsed into one another; we can no longer say whether the printed page is simulating music or whether music is simulating the printed text as it does in Satie's "Trois morceaux en forme de poire." A convergence of form takes place as well as a juxtaposition of disparate content.

VARIATION AND REPETITION

Robbe-Grillet has suggested that the nouveau roman is typified by the following technique: "Instead of having to deal with a series of scenes which are connected by causal links, one has the impression that the same scene is constantly repeating itself, but with variations."[5] This is the movement of any game that takes the same elements and "throws" them over and over again. With nonsense in a closed space, repetition becomes not only the repetition of particular elements of a series, but repetition of the series itself in all its possible combinations. The reading of Cortázar's *Hopscotch* involves two throws of the elements of the text, the second throw catching the reader in infinity. Gertrude Stein especially was a master of the arrangement and rearrangement of elements within a closed field. For Stein, description consisted in "using everything" and "beginning again and again," the elements of the discourse being combined and recombined until the "face" of the object almost magically appears. In *Lectures in America*, she wrote: "I began to get enormously interested in how everybody said the same thing over and over again with infinite variations, but over and over again until finally if you listened with great intensity you could hear it rise and fall and tell all that there was inside them, not so much the actual words they said or the thoughts they had, but the movement of their thoughts and words endlessly the same and endlessly different."[6] This is the experience of reading the Stein "Portraits." For example, consider the variations in the opening paragraph that constitute "Picasso":

One whom some were certainly following was one who was completely charming. One whom some were certainly following was one who was charming. One whom some were following was one who was completely charming. One whom some were following was one who was certainly completely charming.[7]

Beckett appears as a descendent of this tradition. There is Molloy with sixteen stones in his pocket, trying to figure out every possible procedure that will allow him to suck each stone before sucking any one stone twice. All sixteen stones must be manipulated; his problem is to involve the entire series in repetition and to avoid repeating any single element out of the series. Watt's ponderings of Mr. Knott's movements provide another case in point. Watt calculates to exhaustion all the possible ways for Mr. Knott to move between fire, bed, window, and door. Then he calculates all the possible arrangements of Mr. Knott's furniture—tallboy, dressing table, washstand, bed, and nightstool—in relation to the first series of bed, fire, window, and door. Later he figures the permutations of Mr. Knott's appearance. By conjoining the series "tall, fat, pale, and dark" with the series "thin, small, flushed, and fair" and the series "sturdy, middlesized, yellow, and ginger," he manages to juggle three series within a closed space.

These examples from literature show both arrangement and rearrangement within a closed space. The narrator or character has invented a series, arranging elements into a list, and then computed all the possible relationships the elements of the series can bear to each other. With the creation and conjoining of new series, the possible combinations increase exponentially. While the series threatens infinity arithmetically and truly, the rearrangement of sets of series threatens infinity exponentially, and is only physically impossible. Forming the combinations is possible but approaches the computer's point of exhaustion.

With this type of transformation of common sense, the text consists of a space upon which meaning can be continually traced. The content of the text is never definitive, is always being muted by its own elements. All that is absolute about the text is its boundaries, the elements that are and are not enclosed at any given point. Just as reversibility, simultaneity, infinity, and play with the boundaries of text and context in nonsense can be seen as "discussions" or exaggerations of features involved in the manufacture of any text, so arrangement and rearrangement within a closed field can be seen as symptomatic of all interpretation once the text's physical boundaries are defined. Arrangement and rearrangement of elements goes on with each "reading" of the text, each reencounter with a situation defined through conventional parameters. As this arrangement and rearrangement threatens infinity and arbitrariness, it breaks from everyday life, common sense, and realism and tends towards nonsense.

Among curiosities of literature, the anagram presents one example of the nonsense of arrangement and rearrangement within a closed field. Charles Dodgson was a master of anagrams, coming up with three for William Ewart Gladstone alone:

> Wilt tear down all images?
> Wild agitator! Means well.
> A wild man will go at trees[8]

The anagram, too, finds its tradition intersecting with divination. In the cabalistic tradition, the use of anagrams was known as *themura*, the activity of finding the hidden and mystical meaning of names. Dobson included in *Poetical Ingenuities and Eccentricities* an example of divination by anagram: In the seventeenth century an André Pujom, finding that his name spelled "Pendu à Riom," fulfilled his destiny by cutting someone's throat in Auvergne and by being subsequently hung in Riom, the seat of justice for the province.[9] The Opies record an example of the use of three series in combination with each other to divine the future. The names of a couple are written, one above the other. The letters in common to both names are then cancelled out, and the formula "Love, hate, marry, adore" is checked along the remaining letters of each name, thereby divining the nature of the relationship according to each partner.[10] For example:

Susan Stewart	=	Adore
Daniel Halevy	=	Adore
John Doe	=	Hate
Mary Smith	=	Adore

In literature, the anagram can be used as a symbol of the mystical power of words, the possibilities of the word beyond its everyday meaning when placed on the page as an object of contemplation and manipulation. The anagram comes to represent the interpretability of the text, an infinity by exhaustion, larger than the potential of any single reader. In *Three Trapped Tigers*, Bustrofedon "Bustrofactored" the very word *anagram* into "a ram's song," as he also computed the possibilities of the word *vida*—"the serpent that eats itself . . . a wheel of fortune." He arrives at "David, avida, vida, avi, vid, ida, davida, dad, ad, di, va,"[11] and makes the word into a star. In Nabokov's *Ada*, there are the obvious permutations of the hero and heroine's names, Van and Ada Veen, permutations emphasized by scrabble games in the text. But there is also the hidden anagram of the novel's theme—Ada's entomological interests and Ada's and Van's sexual relationship—the anagrams INSECT and INCEST. Similarly, the "Ithaca" section of *Ulysses* asks "What anagrams had he (Bloom) made on his name in youth," answering:

Leopold Bloom
Ellpod bomool
Moll dope loob
Bollopedoom
Old Ollebo, M.A.

The permutations reveal elements of the plot destined in Bloom's own name—Molly's adultery and his own vulnerability.

Just as lexical units can be broken up into their component letters and rearranged, so can larger syntactical units. Children's cartoon games sometimes consist of sets of heads, bodies, and legs for disparate characters available to be combined and recombined. A nineteenth-century card game called "Mixed Pickles" works the same way, only with syntactical units. In this game, slips of cards are used in three different colors—red, white, and blue. Each of the red cards contains a sentence beginning, each of the white ones a middle, and each of the blue ones, an end. The cards are turned up randomly and combined in the order of red, white, and blue. Sentences like "Nothing is made by—hunting buffalos—in a tub" or "Isn't it dreadful—kissing a weasel—to please the children" result.[12]

TWO TYPES OF ALLUSION

Taking a constant set of elements and repeating them by varying the nature of their combination is one way to arrange and rearrange things within a closed field. Two other devices for rearrangement also have to do with methods of allusion. These devices may be termed paradigmatic and syntagmatic allusion. The first type of allusion consists in keeping constant a metonymic dimension while substituting items in the paradigmatic dimension. The second type of allusion involves appropriating a variety of syntagmatic dimensions by which to arrange and rearrange a constant set of paradigmatic elements.

When Robbe-Grillet suggests that the modern novel is written by arranging metaphors in the order of metonymy, he is suggesting that the syntagmatic dimension of the novel is appropriated from some "external" (external to the text) source and made absolute, while the paradigmatic dimension of the novel is mutable, interchangeable. When the syntagmatic and paradigmatic dimensions of a text are each self-consistent and mutually disjunctive, allegory is the result. The following allegorical riddle provides an example:

> I have a tree of great honor
> which tree beareth both fruit and flower;
> Twelve branches this tree hath make,
> Fifty two nests therein he make,
> And every nest hath birds seven;
> Thank-ed be the King of Heaven;
> And every bird hath a different name:
> How many may all this together frame[13]

The set "tree" (fruit, flower, branches, nests, birds, bird names) and the set of "time measurements" (the year, months, weeks, days) are mutually exclusive and self-consistent. They are made to fit into each other—the apparent form, the tree, subordinated to the hidden form, the measurements of time. Allegory remains serious because it is, in a sense, indexical. The hidden paradigmatic dimension, the dimension that arises from interpretation, is self-consistent and always pointed to. Allegory points in one direction; it displays none of the ambivalence of nonsense forms like the pun. There is a code to be discovered and, once it is discovered, the interpretation continually returns to the "surface" level of the discourse. Hence the "fervor" of allegory, the near-religious devotion with which its surface set of paradigmatic items points to its single set of substitutes. Allegory calls for a continual gesture of good faith towards the hidden set of elements. It is not that the reader reaches this dimension and stays there, but rather, that the reader is called to continually make a gesture in the same direction, over and over again.

But once the paradigmatic dimension or the syntagmatic dimension is not internally consistent, there is a tendency towards nonsense. A shifting paradigmatic dimension juxtaposed with a consistent syntagmatic dimension is not only a characteristic of the modern novel—it is also the basis for Lewis Carroll's "Jabberwocky," which maintains conventional syntactic and phonological rules but dispenses with morphological rules. Similarly, there is Louis Aragon's contention that the surrealists' grammar was "impeccable": "It is not the structure of the sentence which is ambiguous in surrealism, but the mating of words and the incongruous image that results."[14]

In the work of Gertrude Stein, the metonymic dimension is manipulated while the metaphoric dimension remains conventional. Stein's concern was with syntactical limits, the possible permutations of the sentence—her vocabulary remained the vocabulary of common sense. Any transformation of the image that she achieved was done through repetition and denial of sequence, for any manipulation of the metonymic dimension will result in a distortion of time. Another example of the manipulation of the metonymic axis juxtaposed with a constant set of elements from a borrowed metaphoric axis is Merce Cunningham's dance, "Walkaround Time." For this dance, Jasper Johns silkscreened the images of Duchamp's "The Bride Stripped Bare By Her Bachelors, Even" onto seven inflatable vinyl cubes that were scattered on the stage and then reassembled at the close of the dance into an arrangement approximating that of the Duchamp piece. The ambiguity of the dance's title is the ambiguity of the operation involved—for the Duchamp piece had already been a rearrangement of metaphors into a new metonymic dimension. And so we may see the Cunningham dance as a kind of metonymic doubling: It is both outside of the time of Duchamp's metonymic, a walk *around* it, and another, transformed metonymic, a walking around that is itself in time. As does Stein, Cunningham maintains the integrity of Duchamp's images and metaphors as he manipulates their sequence. The entire piece is, however, a reversal of a Steinian sequence—for Stein, like the cubists, moved from an integral object to a split object. But Cunningham begins with a scattered event (that Johns had created from the integrity of the Duchamp piece) and reassembles it according to a new principle—thereby both restoring and destroying the Duchamp event. What has been restored is the paradigmatic dimension of the Duchamp piece; what has been destroyed, what cannot be repeated, is its syntagmatic dimension, its dimension in time. The event that Cunningham offers closure to is and is not "The Bride Stripped Bare By Her Bachelors,

Even," since it has come to be through a new metonymic process, a new time.

Substitution within a metaphoric dimension that is fitted into a constant metonymic dimension is the procedure used whenever a text appropriates and distorts the form of another text. Think of Dali's painting, "Swans Reflecting Elephants," where the syntagmatic dimension of both painting and title is maintained until the substitution, "elephants." Similarly, Magritte's version of David's "Portrait of Madame de Récamier" substitutes a reclining coffin for that lady's position in the picture. In John Barth's story "Title," he writes, "very well: to write this allegedly ultimate story is a form of artistic fill in the blank, or an artistic form of the same if you like. . . . And I mean literally fill in the blank."[15] This is another way to state the procedure of metaphoric substitution—as a random or incongruous method of "filling in the blank." Literal manifestations of this are the nonsensical "forms" that can be found in joke shops. These forms consist of parodies of bureaucratic questionnaires, using either joke questions with their ensuing answers, or real questions with joking answers. "The Most Laughable Thing on Earth; Or, A Trip to Paris" is a nineteenth-century card game that also works this way. The cards for this game each contain the name and a "grotesque sketch" of some object or objects like "a hod of mortar," "a guinea pig," "a basin of gruel," "a wheelbarrow," "a jar of pickles," or "a tub of soft soap." A story is read by the leader of the game, and when he comes to the blanks, he nods at one of the players, who must then show his top card. The story begins like this:

Brown, Jones and Robinson were walking together in the streets of New York, when Brown suddenly exclaimed, "I will go to Paris and return in the personification of ————."

"I, too," said Jones, "should like to see Paris, but I have not got ————."[16]

The secret languages of children's folklore also usually involve a manipulation of morphemic units within the standard metonymic sequence of the base language. The morphemic units are transformed, much in the way in which "Jabberwocky" uses portmanteaus—by the addition or subtraction of syllables. In "Bop talk," for example, the syllable "OP" is added after each consonant.[17] "Pig Latin" works by leaving off the first letter of a word and prefixing it to "ay." "Hog Latin" can be composed by adding the suffix "gree" to each syllable, or adding the suffix "guy" to each syllable, or by taking the first consonant sound of a word, adding "iggity" to it, and prefixing the whole new combination of letters to the remainder of the word. "Egg Latin" adds "egg" as a new syllable before each vowel.[18] Other languages, like the "Tuttin Tongue," involve the substitution of an entire alphabet for the conventional alphabet. What happens in all these secret languages is what happens in "Jabberwocky"—the morphemic units are manipulated and distorted while the syntagmatic sequence is "preserved." The secret language is basically a transformation of the lexeme and a testing of speaking and auditory skills. It, too, can go on theoretically to infinity, but is limited by the exhaustion of its speakers.

The anagram and the secret language have the status of a code. They are forms of discourse that operate according to a general principle of rearrangement (in the case of the anagram) or a specific principle of rearrangement (in the case of the secret language). With the anagram a constellation of messages can be deciphered, for deciphering the anagram moves to a plurality of hidden meanings, moves from the overt to the covert. But deciphering the secret language involves an opposite movement, a movement from the covert to the overt. Once one discovers the metaphoric principle involved, one can strip the secret language of its secret apparatus. The secret language is like the gestalt of puzzles like "Find the faces in the trees," with their surplus of signification. But the secret language is also an example of rearrangement within a closed space, for it takes the metonymic dimension of a closed field, the grammar of the base language, and substitutes an infinity-threatening combination of elements within the form of that dimension.

The secret language promises an optimistic outcome—a "principle uncovered." It is the kind of trick that can be "revealed," a trick in which meaning can be captured and recaptured. With the type of transformation of common sense effected by the juxtaposition and shifting of the metaphoric against the metonymic, or the metonymic against the metaphoric, there is always a juggling of meaning from one dimension to another. In the secret languages a hierarchical organization that gives primacy to the uncovering of hidden meaning stops this shifting. There is a move towards univocality in uncovering the message just as there is in allegory.

But many uses of this juggling move like a shell game; meaning is shifted from one axis to another in a continual and multivocal movement. This is what happens in most uses of syntagmatic allusions, one of the most common forms of intertextual relationship between the texts of folklore and the texts of literature.[19] The paradigmatic allusion is an allusion made by "naming the other," but the syntagmatic allusion is made by appropriating the other's metonymic dimension and substituting a new metaphoric dimension. The text is arranged and rearranged within the closed metonymic field of another text. The procedure escapes plagiarism because nothing is named. Nothing fixed has been taken from the other text except the shape of content. *Ulysses'* use of the *Odyssey*, *The Waste Land*'s use of Jessie Weston's *From Ritual to Romance*, Borges's "The Cult of the Phoenix"'s relation to a passage in De Quincey's "Secret Societies," the relationship between game and ballad structure[20] or riddles and detective stories—all of these are examples of borrowing from one metonymic dimension to another. In this type of operation, a paradox of description is made evident: one can successfully describe the "primary" or "secondary" text in terms of each other, yet all one arrives at is one or the other text, two parts less than their sum. This movement of description is a movement towards origins, towards a place of privileged signification that always returns us to the etymological paradox of infinite regression. If, as Eliot suggested, "the whole of the literature of Europe from Homer has a simultaneous existence,"[21] it is a simultaneity of "stolen telling," of the evolution of generic forms in their manifestations as texts, their continual interborrowing and interrelation. The notion of genre is based on an idea that the class and its members can be articulated from each other, but the kinds of metonymic borrowing noted above show the paradox that a class can become a member of itself—"genre" is a variety of genre and the *Odyssey* can become, through tradition, synonymous with the epic much in the same way that cellophane tape has become "Scotch tape" or "Kleenex" the word for tissue. Metonymic borrowing thereby presents a problem of abstraction, the problem of distinguishing the text from its "principle of generation," the problem of distinguishing the treasure from the key to the treasure.

When a text appropriates the metonymic structure of a game for its own metonymic structure, it has chosen a rule from a set of rules; for the game is abstract, systematic, self-perpetuating by turns, throws, and plays, and reversible to infinity in its consequences. This type of arrangement and rearrangement within a closed field is perhaps the most nonsensical, for the metonymic structure that is being borrowed is already one of flaunted artifice. The text as game most clearly illustrates the idea of nonsense as a surface, as a system of absolute resistances to common-sense interpretive procedures. Consider some textual uses of playing cards, for example. In seventeenth-century France, playing cards were used to provide instruction to children, and soon after, in England, they became a means of portraying and spreading political caricatures. The earliest known pack of such cards is one that appeared at the time of Charles II's restoration. It contains a series of caricatures of the principle acts of Commonwealth and the leaders of Parliament.[22] Here the characters satirized take the literal form of playing cards, and their machinations become the machinations of the game. It is the content of the card face that becomes interchangeable. The metonymic of political events is turned into the metonymic of a card game.

With Carroll's games of cards, chess, and croquet, the metonymic of the game is maintained, and, at the same time, is traversed by a substitution of elements that are incongruous with both game and plot.

Enough of the game structure is given to present a closed field, yet the game is never "played out." The game is interrupted continually by the plot, and the plot is interrupted by the game. The structure of the game and the narrative events is always deferred in Carroll's nonsense. We should remember that the croquet game in *Alice in Wonderland* is being played by a pack of cards; one game is imposed over another. If the inanimate elements of the game are animals, it is only "proper" in a game where the animate elements, the players, are inanimate objects made animate. And if the players all play at once without waiting for turns, it may be because they are used to games where "all of the cards" are out on the table at once.

Carroll not only appropriated game structures; he invented them as well. One of his games, "doublets," involves the conversion of one word into another by means of the rearrangement of one letter at a time. Here is how Carroll transformed "Head" into "Tail" in his introduction to the game in *Vanity Fair*, March 1897:

HEAD
HEAL
TEAL
TELL
TALL
TAIL[23]

The boundary of the game remains constant and closed while the elements within are transformed. The game resembles a ladder with a fixed top and bottom rung and interchangeable rungs in between. Substitution can go on indefinitely in the middle, but the object is to reach the closure of the desired word within as few moves as possible. Thus, doublets presents another example of closed forms like the shaggy dog story or "Why are fire engines red?" type of riddles, but its specification of a minimal number of moves keeps it from threatening infinity and makes it an example of arrangement within a closed space. It is this procedure for making doublets that Raymond Roussel appropriated as a technique for making a novel. Roussel chose two similar words, like *billard* (pool table) and *pillard* (plundered). Then he added to them words that are alike, but that can be taken in two different senses, such as:

1. Les lettres du blanc sur les bandes du vieux billard
2. Les lettres du blanc sur les bandes du vieux pillard

In the first sentence "lettres" is taken as typographical signs and "blanc" is taken as cue chalk, "bandes" are taken to mean "cushions" on a pool table.

In the second sentence "lettres" is taken to mean "missives" and "blanc" is taken to mean "a white man," and "bandes" is used as "warrior hordes."[24]

The problem that Roussel set before himself was to begin a story with the first sentence and end it with the second.

The doublet is a plot made with letters. Like any plot, it involves a beginning and a conclusion whose nature may be generically determined by a rearrangement of the elements between, according to some guiding principle. With doublets that principle is "one letter at a time." In realism it may be "one event at a time," for in realism, the object is to arrive at the point by going the most direct route. With novels such as Roussel's, the object is to accomplish the doublet, to make plot be a matter of discourse in a position that threatens a plenitude of elegant and ornamental moves.

To make the game's structure the structure of the fiction has been a frequent project of Robbe-Grillet as well. If his film *Après Eden* uses the plot of *Alice in Wonderland*, it is the gamelike elements of that plot that are appropriated: the circularity, the repetition, the use of series, and the symmetry. Similarly, *Last Year at Marienbad* sparked a controversy between author, director, mathematicians, and critics as to the nature and history of the game it was based upon. Robbe-Grillet's first plan for a novel involved a plot organized according to a hermetic series of 108 scale drawings made by medieval alchemists of the snake Ouroboros, the snake who swallows his tail. This plan is based on a diagram of a wheel with 108 spaces placed around the circumference in such a way that at any given point the sum of two numbers on opposite sides of the circle would be 108. Robbe-Grillet hoped that he thereby would create a fiction whose apparent randomness of structure would conceal secret principles of organization hermetic to reader and critic.[25] The irony of this plan is the irony of the notes to *The Wasteland*, or the irony of the hints regarding *Work in Progress* that Joyce dropped to Stuart Gilbert et al.: The text is reduced to an application of the hidden rule, and yet is both more and less than this rule. The discovery of the secret principle underlying the text does not close down the interpretation of the text. Rather, it opens up a new plane of significance and divergence. The hermeticism of all nonsense is interpretable as well as decipherable, and so threatens infinity.

The collage and the page present examples of arrangement and rearrangement within a closed field—the use of the absolute and arbitrary parameters of such a field to give integrity to the convergence of disparate domains. Their very disparity invites rearrangement, the possibility of reversal and inversion. Metaphoric substitution within a given metonymic dimension shows the arrangement of one text within the fixed dimension of another text, thereby constituting an arrangement within a closed field, but also providing a rearrangement of the appropriated text by eliminating some of its elements.

TRAVESTIES

Another way to transform a text by rearrangement within its boundaries is to "pervert" it, to twist its elements into a different conclusion from the one it conventionally effects. Proverbs, those last bastions of common sense, are often the victims of this technique. This perversion can be done by rearranging the elements of the sentence: "Better never than late," "Time wounds all heels." Or by eliminating elements of the proverb: "All work and no play makes Jack." Or by metaphoric substitutions: "Cast thy bread upon the waters and it will come back moldy," "An apple a day keeps the fingers sticky." Or by the rearrangement of two or more proverbs within one closed field: "A stitch in time is worth two in the side." "A stitch in time gathers no moss."[26] All of these perversions depend upon a knowledge of the text being manipulated and an inversion of the metaphorical power of the proverb to the literal power of nonsense. In his little review, *Proverbe*, Paul Eluard hoped to destroy the metaphorical short cut aspect of the proverb and restore to it the power of a fresh cut. He would take commonplaces and transform them by the use of puns, spoonerisms, or the reversal of their elements in the same way the tradition of "the perverted proverb" does.[27] Beckett is also a practitioner of this art, with phrases like "Where a scout's knife is, there will his heart be also," "When you have the will you do not have the way," and "Saying is inventing" sprinkled throughout *Molloy*.[28]

These "perversions" can be seen as forms of parody, for parody is a matter of substituting elements within a dimension of a given text in such a way that the resulting text stands in an inverse or incongruous relation to the borrowed text. If a parody substitutes a metonymic dimension within the metaphoric dimension of the parodied text, parody is effected by caricature. An example would be the kind of nonsense-photography studios often found at fairs and carnivals. Here, the subject stands behind a screen so that only his face appears through a hole which is surrounded by a mock-up of a cowboy or astronaut or hillbilly scene. More often, parody works by the substitution of the metaphoric dimension within the metonymic of the travestied text. Children sometimes do this by parodying their own tradition:

Roses are red
Cabbages are green:
My face is funny
But yours is a scream[29]

Yankee Doodle went to town
A riding on a stage coach
Hit a bump and skinned his rump
And landed in the city dump[30]

Literary parodies play an important part in *Alice in Wonderland*, as noted in the discussion of reversals and inversions. They play a similar role in Infante's *Three Trapped Tigers*, which includes a parody "Poe(t)'s Ravings" that is a parody of "The Raven," and a parody of *Alice in Wonderland*. Infante's parody of a translation of the popular song "Guantanamero" presents a miniature of the text of *Three Trapped Tigers* as a whole, of the constraints and license of a text that is itself merely a version of its original, a dispersal of that original within the elements of another language:

> Yo soy un hombre sincero
> I'm a man without a zero
>
> De donde crece la palma
> From the land of the pawn-trees
>
> Y antes de morirme quierro
> And 'fore lay dying I xerox
>
> Hechar mil voces del alma
> One thousand copies of me.[31]

Parody can only survive so long as there is common sense, so long as there is discourse that takes itself seriously. From this comes the contention that nonsense, as the outer space of the intertextual universe, cannot be parodied. Chesterton moaned in his study of Carroll that once *Alice in Wonderland* became a classic, it was no longer funny. That people had tried to parody *Alice* was symptomatic of this, and analogous to "the comic comic strip."[32] And Stephen Heath has suggested that it is impossible to parody *Finnegans Wake*: "La parodie, évidement, est un mode de la stylistique; le rassemblement des marques d'une individualité (le style de l'Auteur) suivi de la reproduction de cette individualité. Or, dans l'oeuvre de Joyce, la parodie ne trouve aucun point d'attache. . . . A la place d'un style, le plagiat."[33] Nonsense can only be parodied when its hermeticism is broken, when it shows some attachment to everyday life. So long as nonsense remains a closed field, a surface that refers to itself, any attempt to parody nonsense will result in imitation, in the generation of more nonsense. Here again is the self-generating, and self-perpetuating, power of nonsense. Parody becomes symptomatic of the intertextual feature of the text attaching itself to, appropriating, another text, not to reify that primary text, but in order to transform it, to reduce it to a set of elements available to an alternative order or to an order available to an alternative set of elements.

READY-MADE SYSTEMS

At times nonsense will effect a traversal that depends upon the availability of a given, or ready-made, system from common sense. The common-sense system provides the closed form within which nonsense effects its rearrangement or substitution of elements. One such use of the play of rearrangement within closed fields is the mnemonic device. Here a structure is used to incorporate all the elements of what is desired to be remembered. For example, there is the mnemonic for the colors of the rainbow (red, orange, yellow, green, blue, indigo, and violet), "Roy G. Biv," which appears in *Ulysses*, and another mnemonic for the same elements, "Read Over Your Greek Books In Vacation." Another mnemonic is this one for the spectral classification of stars (O,B,A,F,G,K,M,R,N,S): "Oh, be a fine girl, kiss me right now smack."[34] The mnemonic is knowledge centered in itself; it has no meaning outside of its use. It is purely "a device," for it does not "count" on its own. The mnemonic thus bears an intrinsic resemblance to nonsense. When the mnemonic attempts to account for the entire world, to encompass elements beyond any "useful knowledge," incorporating heterogenous domains within its structure, its nonsensical quality becomes evident. Bouvard's and Pecuchet's attempt to use their house as a mnemonic base results in a nonsensical surplus of signification; the elements being rearranged overrun and dissolve the closed space:

For greater clearness, they took, as a mnemonic base, their own house, where they were living, attaching to each one of its parts a distinct event—and the courtyard, the garden, the surroundings, the entire district, had no other meaning than to jog their memory. The boundary-posts in the country limited certain epochs, the apple trees were genealogical trees, the bushes were battles, the world became a symbol. They sought, on the walls, a quantity of things that were not there, and ended by seeing them, but no longer knew the dates that they represented.[35]

The same thing happens in Marquez's *One Hundred Years of Solitude* to the victims of the "insomnia plague." Trying to establish a mnemonic system as a stay against their deteriorating memories, they are caught in an infinite regress of explanation. And the same thing happens whenever we remember the mnemonic and forget what it stands for, as is frequently the case.

The nonsense of the search for a comprehensive mnemonic is the nonsense of any attempt to use a system to account for all universes, to enclose the infinite within the finite. "Funes the Memorius" in Borges's story of the same name is dissuaded from classifying all of his past experience numerically by "the thought that the task was interminable and the thought that it was useless."[36] The task is interminable because our access to the interminable world is terminable, and the task is useless because it has no use outside of itself, it is classification for classification's sake. It was Borges who invented the wise residents of Tlön, who "consider metaphysics a branch of fantastic literature.

They know that a system is nothing more than the subordination of all the aspects of the universe to some one of them. Even the phrase 'all the aspects' can be rejected, since it presupposes the impossible inclusion of the present moment, and of past moments."[37] The problem is one of a system that can account for the hierarchical arrangement of domains as well as domains of the same logical type. Systems like "Mineral, Animal, and Vegetable," or "Bird, Beast, and Fish,"[38] work so long as one stays within one logical type. Once Borges's "present" or the schizophrenic's "tomorrow" intrude, the world has slipped beyond the boundaries of the field of the system.

Thus the enclosure of the world within a closed space is always an illusion, is always a fiction made by flattening the world to one variety of elements—a use of systems regardless of the contingencies of the everyday lifeworld. The uses of such closed spaces are the uses of any textual boundaries: the enclosure of a set of elements, possibly from disparate domains, within a play context, a context where those elements may be manipulated and explored at the same time that the activity of boundary making itself is being manipulated and explored. Because of this relation between text making and play, it is not surprising that one of the first and most pervasive ways to rearrange elements within a closed field is to arrange a text within the closed field of the body, or to arrange the elements of the body within the closed field of a text. Examples of the first type of arrangement include the sayings adults use to distinguish the parts of the face for a child: "Bo Peeper" (eye), "Nose Dreeper" (nose), "Chin Chopper" (chin), "White Lopper" (tooth), "Red Rag" (tongue), "And Little Gap" (mouth).[39] Other rhymes use the elements of the body within a narrative, as the "This little pig" rhyme does with toes. Here is an example that uses the parts of the face in this way:

> Ring the bell (tug at a lock of the child's hair)
> Knock at the door (tap forehead)
> Peep in (peer into his eyes)
> Lift up the latch (tilt his nose)
> Walk in (open his mouth)
> Go way down in the cellar and eat apples (tickle throat)[40]

Fingers and toes and elements of the face are given names and thereby given identity. Once this is accomplished, they can be used as elements in another text, or their relationship as series can be appropriated by another text. Tristan Tzara's play "Le Coeur à Gaz" is an example of this kind of arrangement and rearrangement. The characters of the play include "Eyebrow, Eye, Mouth, Nose, and Neck."[41] Joyce uses the same technique in this passage from *Finnegans Wake*: "Brow, tell man; eye, feign sad; mouth, sing mim."[42]

G. B. Adams has contended that the use of fingers in counting has a bearing upon the kind of numerical system that will develop among a people. For example, the words *five*, *fist*, and *finger* all have a common English root. Adams found that not only fingers and toes, but other parts of the body as well have been incorporated into service among different peoples to provide forms for the numerals themselves, or to provide mnemonics to "help recall a particular sequence in counting up to a particular total which is required to be remembered for some special reason."[43] Thus the origin of numbers may have to do with a perception of the body itself as repeatable and infinite in its possibilities of arrangement and rearrangement.

In the chapter on infinity I discussed the use of numbers as a ready-made infinite system. The coordination of the numerical series with a series of elements was one way to threaten infinity. Another method was to take a single numeral and align it to a set of disparate elements (one cabbage, one king, etc.). Swift suggests in *A Tale of a Tub* that one should pick any number and insist that all things in the world can be explained by it. These uses of numbers may also serve as an example of arrangement and rearrangement within a closed field. Although they do not involve a field that is by definition closed, they can involve a field that is arbitrarily closed. The number can serve as the organizing principle for a set of incongruous elements. Flann O'Brien's *At Swim-Two-Birds* ends with a reflection on this type of nonsense:

Numbers, however, will account for a great proportion of unbalanced and suffering humanity. One man will rove the streets seeking motor-cars with numbers that are divisible by seven. Well known, alas, is the case of the poor German who was very fond of three and who made each aspect of his life a thing of triads. He went home one evening and drank three cups of tea with three lumps of sugar in each, cut his jugular with a razor three times and scrawled with a dying hand on a picture of his wife good-bye, good-bye, good-bye.[44]

Terms or letters can be used as the organizing principle of a set of elements in the same way as numbers are used in the O'Brien example. D'Israeli tells of a poet named DeSaussay who wrote a folio volume consisting of panegyrics to persons of eminence whose Christian names were Andrew because Andrew was his own name.[45] The ball bouncing rhyme

> A my name is Alice
> I live in Alabama
> My husband's name is Alfred
> And we sell Apples

or Alice's "I love my love with an H because he is Happy. I hate him with an H because he is Hideous. I feed him Ham Sandwiches and Hay"[46] use the same technique. Similarly, Tzara's "Grains et issues" has six consecutive lines, each beginning with a *p*, and Breton suggested that as a method of composition: "Following a word the origin of which seems suspicious to you, place any letter whatsoever, the letter 'l' for example, always the letter 'l', and bring the arbitrary back by making this letter the first part of the following word."[47]

With alphabetical order we have access to a closed field as well as to a set of elements. Alphabetical order provides us with the convention of conventions, for it is a finite and fixed order that is both arbitrary and sequential. As Butor has noted, "It is the only way to create a truly amorphous enumeration, to suspend all conclusions which might be drawn from the relations of proximity among the various elements on the page."[48] Alphabetical order epitomizes the elimination of hierarchy, the leveling of the elements of the list. It provides a gesture of resistance to any attempt to interpret significance in the particular arrangement of textual elements. It presents us with a time without order, a sequence where before and after hold no hierarchical import.

The alphabet is one of the most common systems used to organize the text in children's folklore. For example, in this ball-bouncing game, players recite in sequence a sentence with exactly ten words belonging to the letter that comes up on their turn. The player turns a foot over the ball on each word:

Anna and her adorable brother Alvin ate apples at their Aunt Alice's apartment.

Betty Boop bought a big batch of bitter butter from her brother, Bobbie Boop.

"Can Cousin Carol cook a good dinner for Cecil, who is a captain in the army?" asked cute baby Caroline as she ate a colored cookie.[49]

Edward Lear was an expert at nonsense alphabets, as is demonstrated in his verses constituting "An Alphabet with Consonance." These verses include "The Absolutely Abstemious Ass," "The Bountiful Beetle," "The Perpendicular Purple Polly," and "The Visibly Vicious Vulture."[50] The surrealist E.L.T. Mesens also constructed an alphabet in verse. This was his "Alphabet sourd aveugle," which was made up of a series of twenty-six poems, one for each letter of the alphabet, and each poem incorporating a number of lines, all of which began with the same letter.[51] This method for organizing the poem is arbitrary and systematic, thus merging the greatest principle of surrealism with the greatest principle of nineteenth-century nonsense verse.

Alphabetical order is what gives those two great nonsensical enterprises, the dictionary and the encyclopedia, any pretense to formal integrity.[52] The dictionary's attempt to capture language and the encyclopedia's attempt to capture knowledge are both forms of arrangement and rearrangement within a closed field. They are attempts to organize the world within the text analogous to the attempt to invent an all-inclusive mnemonic—they reduce the world to discourse. While the Red Queen in *Through the Looking Glass* says, "I've heard nonsense, compared with which that would be as sensible as a dictionary,"[53] her words have a profoundly ironic ring, for there is nothing that is so nonsensical as the dictionary, the telephone book, or the encyclopedia—all of them texts that arrange the world within the hermetic surface of an arbitrary convention, a convention without the hierarchy or values of the everyday lifeworld. The encyclopaedism of Joyce or Pynchon[54] may be seen as an attempt to capture the quality of this enterprise in a fiction. Rabelais and Borges have also made ironic comments about the nature of alphabetical order by constructing alphabetical arrangements of imaginary creatures: Rabelais in his alphabetical list of monsters in *Gargantua and Pantagruel*, and Borges in his *Book of Imaginary Beings*.[55] The monster and the imaginary being are anomalous, things that do not exist because they cannot be classified, because they stand ambiguously between categories or as the impossible merger of categories. Such creatures defy nature and the organization of nature that is culture. To then array them according to the arbitrary convention of the alphabet, a convention borrowed from discourse, is to emphasize their status as fictions and the very status of fictions as paradoxes of classification.

Other arbitrary and sequential orders are the names of the days of the week and the names of the months. These two orders are appropriated by nonsense to provide a closed field as well. I have already mentioned the use of the days of the week and the months of the year as "tags" for jump rope rhymes. Here they act as a series, a way of counting, of distinguishing each jump. In children's folklore, they appear attached to arbitrary but determining events, a way of divining by the almanac:

> Monday for health
> Tuesday for wealth
> Wednesday the best day of all
> Thursday for losses
> Friday for crosses
> Saturday no luck at all[56]

Philippe Soupault's poem "The Life of Philippe Soupault" uses the same structure:

> Philippe Soupault in his bed
> born a Monday
> baptized a Tuesday
> married a Wednesday
> sick a Thursday
> dying a Friday
> dead a Saturday
> buried a Sunday
> that's the life of Philippe Soupault.[57]

Christian Morgenstern used the months of the year as a closed field within which he was able to arrange the names of animals, explaining that this is a mnemonic, "Wie sich das Galgenkind die Monatsnamen Markt":

Jaguar
Zebra
Nerz
Mandrill
Maikäfer
Ponny
Muli
Auerochs
Wespenbär
Locktauber
Robbenbär
Zehenbär[58]

These are further examples of nonsense appropriating the form of a conventional system and rearranging its content in an incongruous way. This, again, is nonsense as "the last word in stolen telling," nonsense's absolute reliance upon convention and intertextuality for each of its inventions. Fortunately for nonsense, the formalities of everyday life are easily stripped and appropriated. Bergson contended that the ceremonial side of social life always included a latent comic element: "For any ceremony to become comic it is enough that our attention be fixed on the ceremonial element in it and that we neglect its matter, as philosophers say, and think only of its form."[59] Hence the importance of the tea party in the very British nonsense of Monty Python and Lewis Carroll. The courtroom provides another ready-made structure for nonsense; the law is stripped to a set of arbitrary rules. In addition to the "sentence first, verdict afterwards" variety of justice that Alice encounters, there is Rabelais's Judge Bridlegoose, the trial of HCE in *Finnegans Wake* for crimes in Phoenix Park, the trial of Bloom in the Nighttown episode of *Ulysses*, and the trial of Dermott Trellis by his characters in *At Swim-Two-Birds*. All of the values of the courtroom—the "weighing" of evidence, the resort to a hierarchical arrangement of values, the importance of precedent, of previous interpretations, the drawing of conclusions—are inverted and rearranged in the nonsense courtroom. In nonsense the law becomes a procedure without content, the systematic and arbitrary application of rule without regard to context. Victorian nighthouses, like Renton Nicholson's "Judge and Jury Society," often staged burlesque reenactments of famous trials for libel and criminal conversation,[60] thereby playing with the same type of rearrangement as is found in the fictions of nonsense. Similarly, in 1921 the dadaists staged a trial, "The accusation and judgment of Maurice Barrés for a crime against the safety of the mind."[61] This trial marked the first confrontation between Breton and Tzara, for Breton, as self-appointed judge, wanted "a serious parody" of a court trial to be enacted, while Tzara wanted to present "a legal circus," a trial that would more closely approximate the dada program of antiorder.

These examples of nonsense appropriating the institutions of every-day life and rearranging them according to another, incongruous, set of principles are a further extension of the kind of manipulation of common sense that appeared in the perverted proverb and the parody. In summarizing this chapter, we can conclude that the kinds of arrangement and rearrangement that nonsense effects within a closed field have to do with distinguishing the boundaries of the text, with the process of making texts as distinguished from making what is in-side of them. They are a radical shifting of form away from its content. Nonsense of this variety points to an intertextual dependence that is characteristic of all uses of systems. The page and the picture frame, the word and the proverb, the narrative and the ceremony, all become elements that can be combined and recombined, or a scaffolding upon which anything can be hung. This nonsense operation, like Gertrude Stein's directive, says that performance can and should "use every-thing," and that anything can be used to arrange anything else.

NOTES

1. The term "closed field" in relation to fictions has been used by Hugh Kenner, "Art in a Closed Field," *Virginia Quarterly Review* 38 (1962): 597–613, and in chapter 3 of *The Stoic Comedians*.
2. Huizinga, *Homo Ludens*, p. 10.
3. Willeford, *Fool and His Scepter*, p. 16.
4. See Bigsby, *Dada and Surrealism*, and Herbert Gershman, *The Surrealist Revolution in France* (Ann Arbor: University of Michigan Press, 1969).
5. Robbe-Grillet, "Order and Disorder," p. 5.
6. Gertrude Stein, *Lectures in America* (Boston: Beacon Press, 1957), p. 138.
7. Stein, *Selected Writings*, p. 333.
8. Sutherland, *Language and Lewis Carroll*, p. 23.
9. Dobson, *Poetical Ingenuities*, p. 194.
10. Opie, *The Lore and Language*, pp. 336–37.
11. Infante, *Three Trapped Tigers*, p. 221.
12. Blitz, *Parlor Book of Magic*, p. 65.
13. L. Morrison, *"Black Within and Red Without": A Book of Riddles* (New York: Crowell, 1953), p. 108.
14. Balakian, *Surrealism*, p. 133.
15. Barth, *Lost in the Funhouse*, p. 108.
16. Blitz, *Parlor Book of Magic*, p. 58.
17. Rochelle Berkovits, "Secret Languages of Schoolchildren," *New York Folklore Quarterly* 26 (1970): 127–52.
18. Eugenia Millard, "What Does It Mean? The Lore of Secret Languages," *New York Folklore Quarterly* 10 (1954): 104.
19. The term that is sometimes used in literary criticism for this type of allusion is "paradigmatic allusion," meaning a paradigm is taken from one text and trans-ferred to another. Since this is not the linguistic notion of *paradigmatic*, which I have been using throughout the essay, I have tried to use *syntagmatic* for allusion

that preserves the metonymic dimension of the text, reserving *paradigmatic* for metaphoric allusions, the kinds of intertextual allusions discussed along with quotation in chapters 5 and 6 of this essay.

20. See A. G. Gilchrist, "Notes on Children's Game Songs," *Journal of the Folk Song Society* 19 (1915): 221-39.

21. Quoted in F. O. Matthiessen, *The Achievement of T. S. Eliot* (London: Oxford University Press, 1958), p. 35.

22. Wright, *History of Caricature*, pp. 371-73.

23. Fisher, *Magic of Lewis Carroll*, p. 131.

24. Roussel, *How I Wrote Certain of My Books*, pp. 3-4. Joyce also uses doublets in *Wake*, always in passages where "Dodge the Father" is being alluded to in some way: "Item . . . Utem . . . Otem . . . Etem . . . Atem" (pp. 223-24). "Tumbaldum, tambaldam to his tembledem tambaldoom" (p. 258). "He he hi ho hu" (p. 259). "Denary, danary, donnery" (p. 261). "I'll tall tale tell" (p. 366). "To tell how your mead of, mard, is made of" (p. 377).

25. Bruce Morrisette, "Games and Game Structures in Robbe-Grillet," in *Games, Play, Literature*, ed. Ehrmann, pp. 160-61.

26. From C. G. Loomis, "Traditional American Wordplay," *Western Folklore* 18 (1959): 353-54, and "Perverted Proverbs From the UCLA Folklore Archives," *Western Folklore* 20 (1961): 200.

27. Maurice Nadeau, *The History of Surrealism* (New York: Macmillan, 1965), pp. 61-62.

28. See Dina Sherzer, "Gnomic Expressions in *Molloy*," in *Speech Play*, ed. Kirshenblatt-Gimblett, pp. 163-71.

29. David Winslow, "An Introduction to Oral Tradition among Children," *Keystone Folklore Quarterly* 11 (1966): 47.

30. R. M. Atkinson, "Songs Little Girls Sing: An Orderly Invitation to Violence," *Northwest Folklore* 2 (1967): 3.

31. Infante, *Three Trapped Tigers*, p. 217.

32. Chesterton, *Handful of Authors*, ed. Collins, p. 115.

33. Stephen Heath, "Ambiviolences," *Tel Quel* 50 (1972): 24.

34. See Alan Dundes, "Mnemonic Devices," *Midwest Folklore* 11 (1961): 139-47.

35. Flaubert, *Bouvard and Pecuchet*, pp. 140-41.

36. Borges, *Ficciones*, p. 114.

37. Ibid., p. 25.

38. For examples of these games, see Alice Bertha Gomme, *The Traditional Games of England, Scotland, and Ireland*, 2 vols. (New York: Dover, 1964), 2:388, and Brewster, *American Nonsinging Games*, pp. 34-35.

39. J. O. Halliwell, *Popular Rhymes and Nursery Tales* (London: Bodley Head, 1970), p. 94.

40. Paul Brewster, "Rope Skipping, Counting Out and Other Rhymes of Children," *Southern Folklore Quarterly* 3 (1939): 183.

41. J. H. Matthews, *Theatre in Dada and Surrealism* (Syracuse, N.Y.: Syracuse University Press, 1974), pp. 31-33.

42. Joyce, *Wake*, pp. 366-67.

43. G. B. Adams, "Counting Out Rhymes and Systems of Numerations," *Ulster Folklife* 11 (1965): 87.

44. O'Brien, *At Swim-Two-Birds*, pp. 217-18.

45. D'Israeli, *Curiosities of Literature*, p. 399.

46. Carroll, *Complete Works*, p. 223.

47. Breton, *Manifestoes*, p. 30.

48. Butor, *Inventory*, p. 47.

49. Withers, *A Rocket in My Pocket*, p. 55.

50. Lear, *Complete Nonsense Book*, pp. 345-58.

51. J. H. Matthews, *An Anthology of French Surrealist Poetry* (Minneapolis: University of Minnesota Press, 1966), p. 20.

52. Hugh Kenner discusses extensively the importance of the encyclopedia for the works of Flaubert and Joyce in *The Stoic Comedians*, chapters 1 and 2.

53. Carroll, *Complete Works*, p. 163.

54. See Edward Mendelson, "Encyclopedic Narrative: From Dante to Pynchon," *MLN* 9 (1976): 1267-75.

55. Rabelais, *Gargantua and Pantagruel*, pp. 588-89, and Jorge Luis Borges, *The Book of Imaginary Beings* (New York: Avon, 1969).

56. William S. and Ceil Baring-Gould, *The Annotated Mother Goose* (New York: Bramhall House, 1962), p. 218. This is a rhyme for determining on which day of the week one should get married.

57. Philippe Soupault, *Poésies Complètes* (Paris: Gallimard, 1937), p. 139.

58. Morgenstern, *Gallows Songs*, p. 54. I have left the poem untranslated, since the translation is obviously another poem in this case.

59. Bergson, "Laughter," p. 89.

60. D. Gray, "The Uses of Victorian Laughter," *Victorian Studies* 10 (1966): 148-49.

61. Recounted in Nadeau, *History of Surrealism*, pp. 64-65, and Gershman, *Surrealist Revolution in France*, p. 217.

III · conclusion

8 • change's sensibility

THE RELATIONSHIPS OF RELATIONSHIPS

The preceding chapters have explored the idea that making nonsense is an outcome of the use of a set of interpretive procedures. I have suggested that the texts of nonsense are produced by appropriating the vertical and horizontal (or any other) organization of categories common to common sense and traversing that organization through procedures such as reversing or inverting them, shifting their boundaries, repeating them to infinity and/or exhaustion, conjoining them in time, or fracturing them into their members and recombining them according to some "contra-sensible" principle. By investigating how nonsense making works rather than what it is about, I have tried to emphasize that the "nature" of nonsense—nonsense's target and focus—is something that is ongoing and emergent in social process. The set of operations itself does not suggest exhaustiveness or universality, since it obviously depends upon a "culture"-specific set of logical principles. Nor are the operations *in themselves* sufficient to produce nonsense. The five operations I have considered are contingent upon a message "This is play," a message that recognizes the contextual parameters of the playground. Through repeated use, such operations themselves, or a combination of them, can become contextual markers for play. Repetition, for example, seems to be a marker for play performance whenever its threat of infinity is recognized. As in the case of counting out rhymes and lullaby choruses, an exaggeration of a nonsense feature may be typical of gestures effecting absolute breaks from "reality" to the domain of play. Because such nonsense operations cannot be definitive, they further point to the paradox of logical types intrinsic in any message "This is play."

The movement to talk about "operations" rather than "content" in this essay may be seen as a common-sense gesture, since it implies that operations transcend their particular historical occasions of use. However, the operation itself is another category of behavior, the "being in between categories" it poses is another category related to "pure theory," "abstraction," and "nonsense." Just as the theory of logical types did not escape the implications of its position as a meta-theory, and was thereby caught up in an infinite regress of classes, and just as it was impossible to talk about common sense in part 1 of this essay without recourse to the typifications of common sense, so talking about the "operations" of nonsense presents us with another paradox of process and product: the world reversed, shifted, multiplied, and split, becomes another world—a world tending towards the "achieved" (that is, assumed to be achieved) status of common sense. And this world is further reversed, shifted, multiplied, split, or manipulated in some other way by ongoing contexts of playfulness. This was the process described at work in the trick with its perpetual search for new victims, new contexts. And it is also the process at work in the inter-textual phenomenon of parody. Parody reveals the ongoing nature of the appropriation of one text by another, and shows that that appropriation is often a traversal or violation of the principles of the text that has been appropriated. Once irony makes a split with reality by means of its double voices, parody can step in, opening the wound between discourse and the world, between discourse and discourse.

As levels of the intertextual construct tend towards nonsense, they become increasingly critical and, particularly, self-critical. Nonsense as a critical activity is and is about change; is an aspect of and is about the ongoing nature of social process. The congruence or divergence that the fictions of nonsense display in relation to other domains of social life recalls once again Bateson's dictum that conformity or non-conformity between parts of a patterned whole may be informative of some still larger whole. The paradox of logical types, the paradox of an existence that simultaneously is and is not, was seen to be also the paradox of the message "This is play," and the paradox of the simultaneous is/is not status of metaphors and fictions. While realism stands in a metonymic relationship to the common-sense world and thereby attempts to make continuous, to "smooth over," the break between "real" and fictive domains, the fictions of irony, parody, and nonsense flaunt the paradox of the break between those domains. Furthermore, nonsense operations make apparent other paradoxes that common sense smooths over in everyday life. While common sense minimizes contradiction, nonsense makes it gigantic. Thus the paradox of simultaneity undermines the focus and relativity that common sense has accomplished by resort to typification. Reversals and inversions emphasize the paradoxical status of fictions and point to the irony of all definitions—that categories are defined in terms of their "proper nots" and that definition is a relationship of intolerance and an avoidance of anomaly, ambiguity, and ambivalence. Categories stand in relation to that which they "cannot stand," and systems of categorization avoid what they cannot categorize. Shifting boundaries points to the paradox of the message "This is play"—the ambiguous status of the frame both in and out of the world of "reality," the frame as a gesture made *between*. These nonsense operations focus upon, discuss, and often exaggerate problems within common sense and problems arising from the relationships between common sense and other universes of discourse.

Play with infinity, simultaneity, and rearrangement within a closed field point to features of language that are potentially nonsensical by virtue of their capacity for repetition and, consequently, their capacity for infinity. Coordination and subordination are grammatical devices and—at the same time—when unrestrained by everyday events, they can be devices for playing with infinity. They are ways of linking elements together. Coordination allows us to connect things by means of open form—one cabbage plus one king plus one anything else, to infinity. Subordination allows us to connect things by means of closed form—for instance, embedding in the sentence, or we might think of shaggy dog stories—and thereby allows us to digress to infinity between a fixed beginning and ending. Predication is another feature of grammar that can become a nonsense feature.[1] Predication enables us to say "John hit the ball, Mary hit the ball, Spot hit the ball" or "John hit the ball, John went upstairs, John made his bed, John bumped his head." The simultaneity and rearrangement characterizing predication and paraphrasing are focused in everyday life by a sense of what Joyce called the *nacheinander* and *nebeneinander*, the short spaces of time and short times of space that characterize immediate situations. But in nonsense, predication and paraphrasing threaten an infinity of time and space. The gesture of nonsense is away from a center of predication and towards an ever-dissolving perimeter. Thus nonsense not only exaggerates features of common-sense reasoning to make them problematic, it also exaggerates aspects of the language in which that common sense is constructed, pointing to the arbitrary and potentially "traitorous" nature of language as pure form.

The accomplishment of nonsense by means of these operations is not a clear matter of one operation accomplishing one aspect of nonsense. Rather, the relationships between the nonsense operations are often contradiction producing and nonsensical. Play with infinity will always be characteristic of the uses of simultaneity because of common sense's concept of "infinite space." And arrangement and rearrangement within a closed space will always have to do with infinity and simultaneity because of the common-sense operations of predication and paraphrasability. Play with infinity and simultaneity present a paradox of limitedness and limitlessness, the impossible boundary by which infinity and simultaneity are defined. Similarly, nesting inverts the common-sense procedure of definition by closure. Nesting presents closure *repeated*, an anticlosure enclosed by infinity. Nesting threatens infinity, that which by definition cannot be "nested." The common-sense conception of discrete and mutually causal events is thereby turned inside out; in nonsense each event potentially carries and causes an infinity of events. Thus while nonsense can reverse or invert common-sense procedures, it can also point to contradictions within common-sense procedures and appropriate the devices of common sense for its own purposes: nesting to infinity provides an example of the inversion of a common-sense procedure, play with simultaneity and infinity point to the contradictions between everyday and "ideal" conceptions of time and space and appropriate—liberate—grammatical devices used in the multiplication, splitting, and rearrangement of categories in everyday life.

Because of this array of relationships between the universe of common sense and the universe of nonsense and between the nonsense operations themselves, we cannot say that nonsense is simply the "proper not" of common sense. Not every feature of common sense is always inverted by nonsense. Rather, these nonsense operations present a repertoire of procedures for manipulating common sense that can be used singly or in combination. Forthright appropriation takes place when there are intrinsic contradictions in common sense. Inversions and manipulations of various part/whole features present other aspects of the repertoire. These aspects of the relationships between nonsense and common sense emphasize the point that nonsense is emergent in common sense itself, both on the level of content and method. Just as reality-generating conversation is threatened by the potential puns it bears within itself, just as any text carries the seeds, the structure, of its own parody, so all common sense is potential nonsense. Nonsense emerges by a continual process of fissure and reflexivity within the ongoing accomplishment of common sense. When, in everyday-life conversations, we say, "Cut out the nonsense," it is a gesture that preserves the integrity of common sense in two ways: this gesture both *points to* and *places* nonsense outside the situation at hand, as if that is where it had been all along. The gesture not only "preserves" the integrity of common sense; it *gives* an integrity to common sense.

NONSENSE AND LEARNING

Nonsense is a threat to this integrity and to the univocality of common sense, and is thus articulated as a separate, impossible, or unrealizable, domain. Nonsense is thereby a domain between realizable domains, a domain that does not count, and we have seen that its status *between*—its liminal status—is important for members making a transition between realizable domains. It is a place to stand in the middle of change. Here again, we can see the importance of nonsense and other "impossible contexts" for getting from one state of things to another, the motion that is characteristic not only of change, but of learning as well.

Even "stimulus-response" models of learning—what Jerome Bruner has called "operational learning" or Bateson has called "Learning I," for example—involve a fundamental reflexivity and an ability to recognize the sequential nature of a sequence. Jerome Bruner has suggested that the following two abilities are prerequisites to observational learning, learning that involves a matching-to-model or congruence: (1) there must be an ability to differentiate or abstract oneself from a task, and (2) there must be an ability to construct an action pattern by the appropriate sequencing of a set of constituent subroutines to match a model.[2] The first ability involves a self-consciousness regarding the activity at hand, and a recognition of the boundary between self and task, task and immediate environment. The second ability involves arranging and rearranging a set of elements in light of a given model. Thus even observational learning involves what Bateson has called Learning II—learning about learning. Learning about learning depends upon an ability to classify contexts, to recognize and organize contextual markers. In Bateson's words, it is "a corrective change in the set of alternatives from which choice is made, or it is a change in how the sequence of experience is punctuated."[3] This type of learning is contingent upon the organism's ability to respond to a stimulus, to engage in "zero learning," Learning I. Once the organism is able to respond to the context of the stimulus, the contextual marker that classifies the stimulus, learning about learning is possible; the organism begins to recognize and classify contexts of learning.

In terms of Bruner's concept of operational learning, we can say that once one becomes aware of the possibilities of infinite repetition in any "imitation," one has shifted away from a simple "response" to an ability to recognize and organize the conditions of response. A discrimination is made between "the same context," context as repeatable, and the "instance of context," context as singular. And what becomes of interest is the recognition of the former—the idea of context as a reapplicable interpretive procedure. This discrimination is a separating-out of contextual markers from their origin in social process. It is the process of textuality, of making texts, emergent in social process.

For learning about learning to be achieved, there must be a decontextualization of the message, a discrimination of the message from its particular instances of use. Learning depends upon freeing the message from the constraints of the situation at hand. This is the idea at the center of Bruner's work on learning and play, following the "DeLaguna" dictum which says: "The evolution of languages is characterized by a progressive freeing of speech from dependence upon the perceived conditions under which it is uttered and heard and from the behavior that accompanies it."[4] Thus learning comes to be associated with the "impossible context" of nonsense by a progressive decontextualization, a freeing of the message from the situation and purpose at hand. As is nonsense, this process is marked by an increasing formality. "It is not too serious an oversimplification to say that it is precisely such a process of reorganizing knowledge into formal systems that frees it of functional fixedness. By using a system of notation that redefines functional requirements in formal terms, far greater flexibility can be achieved," writes Bruner.[5] The "uselessness" of nonsense is replicated in the "freed-from-contextual-and-functional constraints" status of learning. Learning is seen as a process that works most efficiently in a play context—a context independent of the everyday lifeworld.

But to say that learning is "free of context" may be to confuse levels of analysis. The play context is contingent upon the everyday lifeworld as much as it is "freed" of it; play depends upon a fiat by framing, not a fiat by content. Thus we must keep in mind the idea that learning about learning has to do with discriminating and classifying contextual markers that "frame" the situation. The contextual marker is an abstraction only in the eyes of common sense. In terms of Gödel's proof, abstraction is another category, not a category outside of the process of categorization. Abstraction, like play, fictions, and other paradoxes, becomes contingent upon a reflexivity by which consciousness can be split and maintained simultaneously. Without this flexibility, this fundamental reflexivity, we are locked into the "double bind" of the schizophrenic. To say that abstraction is a context freed from this paradox is to engage in the common-sense procedure that allows us to reconcile the paradox, but it does not free learning as a category of activities from being caught up in, and implicated in, this infinite set of self-conscious activities. Decontextualization may be seen as a necessary fiction by which fictions are engaged in and common sense is given integrity. Any theory of learning as "leisure" is suspect in that it is another way of removing change—ongoingness—from the everyday lifeworld and placing it in another domain. It is the same gesture that removes nonsense and play from such ongoingness, and that places a concern with learning, play, and nonsense within the social enclaves of the child, the mad, and the chronically foolish. Just as Garfinkle emphasized that every instance of "context" is itself indexical, so can we say that every use of abstraction is indexical.

Abstraction becomes a style, a contextual marker to be discriminated among other contextual markers. As a variety of metacommunication, it is isomorphic with this same *procedure* of discrimination. Like other forms of metacommunication, it is what it is about.

Metacommunication does not involve a decontextualization so much as a recontextualization. Decontextualization is the reappearance of the myth of the "frameless activity." In metacommunication there is a paradox in framing brought about through reflexivity, and this paradox points to other paradoxes in communication. This is the critical aspect of the varieties of discrimination taking place in any act of metacommunication. Rather than freeing the act of framing from its context, we can say that the act of framing becomes increasingly self-conscious regarding its context and regarding the procedures for interpretation—the contextual markers—by which such a context comes to be. Simultaneity and infinity, for example, are not ideas that are independent of common sense so much as they are paradoxes potential and emergent in common sense—paradoxes that are actualized through the paradox of a metacommunication that threatens spatial and temporal infinity. Thus when we say that children's acquisition of performance "competence" involves an ability to deal with abstraction, we are saying that this is a development of an ability to reflexively discriminate between contextual markers, arranging them according to a socially manufactured hierarchy of relevance. Consider what has been assumed to be the developmental path of riddling and joking, for example, a movement from a concern with problems of description and problems of classification of internal elements to a reflexive concern with problems of classifying utterances and situations.[6] While the developmental pattern may be seen as one of increasing competence with forms of metacommunication and an ability to discriminate between contexts, to be self-conscious about performance, we may also assume that the ability to frame a performance as a performance depends *from the outset* upon competence with using metacommunication, with classifying the utterance and with classifying contexts.

Nonsense seems to have a great deal to do with the exercise of these metacommunicative abilities. The paradox of metacommunication is articulated over and over again by nonsense's activities: the ambiguous status of fictive events underlies the exercise of reversibility; simultaneity and repetition are nonsense features emphasizing an isomorphism with other forms of metacommunication; playing with boundaries is always playing with, and honing, an ability to discriminate between contextual markers; and rearrangement within a closed field may be construed as an exercise in varying the historical occasions of the marker's use, in moving an articulated space through time. To engage in nonsense, one must already have the ability to learn about learning; nonsense not only engages this ability, nonsense itself may be seen as an exploration of the parameters of contexts of learning. First of all, nonsense making is often about the discrimination of contextual markers, hence its characteristic tendency towards "formalization." Secondly, nonsense often involves a kind of flaunted, a *skilled*, incompetence, an incompetence that depends upon a consciousness of the boundary between incompetence and competence. The nonsense device of incompetence *repeated*—the child who, having fallen down, gets up and falls down again and again just to show that he fell down the first time on purpose—is a reflexive gesture that reframes the incompetence as purposeful and accomplished. This brings us again to the uses of the fiction, "practice," the domain of reversibility where mistakes "do not count." The other face of this device is the mistake-on-purpose, the planned mistake that does count, that, indeed, counts as skill in the fictive domain. In nonsense, the mistake repeated is not evidence of an inability to "learn from one's mistakes," but rather a play gesture, a gesture that effects a reversible world where mistakes are their proper nots, a gesture that promises mastery and threatens infinity.

While we may see nonsense as a form of "adaptive potentiation," as Sutton-Smith has termed it, a place where an orientation to novelty may be prepared freed from the constraints of the everyday lifeworld,[7] we can also say that the devices of nonsense are emergent in that lifeworld and are a critique of the very process by which they have emerged—the process of learning. Nonsense is not simply a safe place to work out a response to the world of common sense, as it might be in simple reversals and inversions, it is also a field where one can critique the interpretive procedures used in manufacturing that world, and, with increasing self-consciousness, a critique of the interpretive procedures by which nonsense itself has come to be. The flaunted incompetence of nonsense presents a further play with paradox, this time a paradox involved in determining the parameters of learning: nonsense as a *mistake-on-purpose*.

PARADOX REGAINED

This paradox of the mistake made on purpose is only one in a series of paradoxes that nonsense discusses and exaggerates. While nonsense makes apparent paradoxes in common sense and thereby weakens the premises by which common sense is manufactured, nonsense also reveals a pattern of paradox—a set of paradoxes that are isomorphic with one another and thereby appear to have some sense, some method, to their seeming madness. Here it might be helpful to review some of the paradoxes that nonsense flaunts. First of all, there is the problem of reflexivity, of talking about something while one is, in fact, that something. This is the paradox of Epimenides, the paradox of any metacommunicative message, and the paradox of the mistake-on-purpose. Secondly, there is the paradox of inclusion and exclusion apparent in anything that both "is and is not" by virtue of belonging to two contradictory sets. This is the paradox of the classes that are and are not members of themselves in the theory of logical types. It is the paradox of any definition by means of "proper nots." Both of these paradoxes are paradoxes of simultaneity; paradoxes of multiple and coterminous identity, an identity that is *diffuse* and thereby paradoxical by refusing closure. Finally, nonsense makes manifest the paradox of infinity implicit in common-sense reasoning, the paradox of measuring a measureless amount of time and space, and the paradoxical possibilities of repetition and quotation.

Whenever paradoxes play with terminal and categorical boundaries in these ways, there is a comment made about the nature of interpretation itself. To "resolve" (in other words to live with) the paradox is to come to decide upon a context—a boundary—for the paradox itself. The paradox is first and foremost about paradox, about "leaks" in the interpretive process. Paradox takes as its subject and object itself, and is thereby always about itself.[8] Paradox thereby is not merely a feature of all metacommunication; its reflexivity is isomorphic with that of metacommunication. As is the case with the categories of nonsense, fate, chance, and accident, paradox is a defining characteristic of all impossible contexts—contexts that can never be contextualized, categories outside the scheme of categorization.

To say that nonsense reveals a pattern of paradox is to say that nonsense discusses a set of incongruities by means of a redundant set of contextual markers. Paradoxes appear on the level of content, for they are often what nonsense is about. And paradox is the mode of presentation, for nonsense points to the paradox of the fictive frame. Furthermore, the social use of nonsense is paradoxical; nonsense presents the uncategorizable category, the context that cannot be contextualized. This is why we can suspect that nonsense is not necessarily *about* previous aspects of social life (although it may be, especially if those aspects are not congruent with the prevalent organization of experience), and that nonsense is not necessarily a *preparation* for future contexts, since from the standpoint of present "reality," nonsense contexts are now, and forever shall be, impossible. If nonsense has to do with learning, it has this status most likely as a pattern of incongruity, teaching the nature and uses of incongruity, and a set of procedures for making things incongruous. Nonsense does not teach us to recognize contextual markers so much as it teaches a set of procedures for manipulating, for erasing and reforming, contextual markers. Nonsense gives information on the level of learning about learning, presenting a critique of learning manifested on the level of the "mistake-on-purpose." Convention proceeds not merely according to an organization of social life, but according to the shape of mistakes in such an organization. Nonsense gives us information regarding this shape of mistakes; it gives us information about paradox, reflexivity, and the processes of interpretation by which it (nonsense) is manufactured.

The contrasts between common sense and nonsense are not so much contrasts of content as of procedure. Common sense proceeds by maximizing pattern. All social meaning is created by means of redundancy, and the verification of patterns of meaning is also the verification of patterns of social relationships. To borrow an example from Bateson, when someone says "It's raining," one expects the audience to look out the window and confirm that the statement is correct, for "few people in this situation restrain themselves from seemingly duplicating this information by looking out the window. We like to prove that our guesses are right, and that our friends are honest. Still more important, we like to test or verify the correctness of our view of our relationship to others."[9] This is how any truism, like the proverb, works. The utterance of "A stitch in time saves nine" or "You know what I mean" is a metonymic gesture, confirming an assumed-to-be-shared social meaning. Whether such meaning is actually shared or not is not the point; the point is the assumption and the way the assumption allows one to continue through the various dimensions of experience with privileges of signification.

Nonsense both depends upon and interrupts this metonymy. In nonsense, a statement that "It's raining" could result in the audience holding out their hands and looking at the ceiling. This nonsense gesture would depend upon the pattern "It's raining"/"look outside" to effect its mistake-on-purpose, "It's raining"/"look inside." The nonsense gesture interrupts not only the metonymy of common sense, but also the metonymy of social relationships verified through common sense. Thus, although nonsense may be insulated through framing, through its status as an impossible context, its contexts are at the same time fields for the manipulation and recreation of social relationships. We have only to think of the anomaly of carnival or rites of inversion, or the calculated chaos of the "reign of terror." Nonsense challenges any idea of tradition as stable, as having integrity and coherence through time. This idea of tradition is manufactured by common sense with a vested interest in its own part in such a tradition. In tradition are emergent processes that are themselves counter-traditional and ambivalent, and nonsense's emergence from common sense in a replication of this process. In nonsense, hierarchies of relevance are flattened, inverted, and manipulated in a gesture that questions the idea of hierarchy itself—a gesture that celebrates an arbitrary and impermanent hierarchy. Hence the danger of nonsense not only as a valueless activity, but as an activity "without values." The evidence for this valueless state ranges from Colonel Streamer's "Ruthless Rhymes for Heartless Homes" to Trotsky's worrying about the "Bohemian nihilism" of futurism.[10]

In nonsense, purpose becomes a continual and pleasurable movement away from itself, a reflexive gesture that spirals away from any point of privileged signification or direction. Both "author" and "audience" are continually fractured and rearranged. While all language assumes a possible society, while all language is *utopian*, all nonsense divides and rearranges any idea of society as coherent and integral. Nonsense threatens the disintegration of an infinite "making conscious," an infinite movement of undercutting the world all at once and over and over again. It refuses the uplifting note by which the world assumes a happy ending.

NOTES

1. See Jerome Bruner, "Nature and Uses of Immaturity," in *Play*, ed. Bruner, Sylva, and Jolly, pp. 36, 43.

2. Ibid., pp. 35-56.

3. Bateson, *Ecology of Mind*, pp. 279-308.

4. Bruner, "Nature and Uses of Immaturity," p. 57. See also G. A. DeLaguna, *Speech: Its Function and Development* (Bloomington: Indiana University Press, 1963).

5. Bruner, "Nature and Uses of Immaturity," pp. 54-55.

6. See Brian Sutton-Smith, "A Developmental Structural Account of Riddles," in *Speech Play*, ed. Kirshenblatt-Gimblett, pp. 11-19, and Martha Wolfenstein on the development of "the joke facade" in *Children's Humor: A Psychological Analysis*.

7. See Brian Sutton-Smith and David M. Abrams, "The Development of the Trickster in Children's Narrative," *Journal of American Folklore* 90 (1977): 29-48, and Sutton-Smith, "Play As Adaptive Potentiation," *Sportswissenschaft* 5 (1975): 103-18.

8. Colie, *Paradoxica Epidemica*, p. 7.

9. Bateson, *Ecology of Mind*, p. 132.

10. Leon Trotsky, *Literature and Revolution* (New York: Russell and Russell, 1957).

bibliography

Abrahams, Roger. "The Complex Relations of Simple Forms." *Genre* 2 (1969): 104-28.

Adams, G. B. "Counting Out Rhymes and Systems of Numerations." *Ulster Folklife* 11 (1965): 85-97.

Adorno, Theodor. "Society." *Salmagundi* 10-11 (1969-1970): 140-53.

Ainsworth, C. H. "Jump Rope Verses around the United States." *Western Folklore* 20 (1961): 179-99.

Arieti, Sylvano. *Interpretation of Schizophrenia.* New York: Robert Brunner, 1955.

Atherton, James. *The Books at the Wake.* Carbondale: Southern Illinois University Press, 1959.

Atkinson, R. M. "Songs Little Girls Sing: An Orderly Invitation to Violence." *Northwest Folklore* 2 (1967): 2-8.

Austin, J. L. *How to Do Things with Words.* New York: Oxford University Press, 1962.

Babcock, W. H. "Games of Washington Children." *American Anthropologist* 1 (1888): 243-84.

Babcock-Abrahams, Barbara. "A Tolerated Margin of Mess: The Trickster and His Tales Reconsidered." *Journal of the Folklore Institute* 11 (1975): 147-86.

Bakhtin, Mikhail. *Rabelais and His World.* Translated by Helene Iswolsky. Cambridge, Mass.: MIT Press, 1968.

Balakian, Anna. *Surrealism: Road to the Absolute.* New York: Noonday, 1959.

Banning, Kendall. *Censored Mother Goose Rhymes.* New York: privately printed, 1926.

Baring-Gould, Sabine. *A Book of Nursery Songs and Rhymes.* London: Methuen, 1895.

Baring-Gould, William S., and Baring-Gould, Ceil. *The Annotated Mother Goose.* New York: Bramhall House, 1962.

Barth, John. *Chimera.* Greenwich, Conn.: Fawcett, 1972.

———. *Lost in the Funhouse.* New York: Bantam, 1969.

Barthes, Roland. "L'Effet de réel." *Communications* 11 (1968): 84-89.

———. *S/Z.* Translated by Richard Miller. New York: Hill and Wang, 1974.

Bascom, William. "The Four Functions of Folklore." *Journal of American Folklore* 67 (1954): 333-49.

Bateson, Gregory. "The Message 'This is Play.'" In *Conferences on Group Processes*, edited by Bertram Schaffner, pp. 145-242. New York: Columbia University Press, 1955.

————. *Steps to an Ecology of Mind*. New York: Ballantine, 1972.

Bateson, Gregory, and Ruesch, Jurgen. *Communication: The Social Matrix of Psychology*. New York: Norton, 1968.

Bauman, Richard. "The Development of Competence in the Use of Solicitational Routines: Children's Folklore and Informal Learning." *Working Papers in Sociolinguistics*, no. 34. Austin, Tex.: Southwest Educational Development Laboratory, May 1976.

Beaujour, Michel. "The Game of Poetics." In *Game, Play, Literature*, edited by Jacques Ehrmann. *Yale French Studies* 41 (1968):58–67.

Beckett, Samuel. *Three Novels*. New York: Grove Press, 1955.

————. *Watt*. New York: Grove Press, 1955.

Beckett, Samuel; Brion, Marcel; Budgen, Frank; Gilbert, Stuart; Jolas, Eugene; Llona, Victor; McAlmon, Robert; McGreevy, Thomas; Paul, Elliot; Rodker, John; Sage, Robert; and Williams, William Carlos. *Our Exagmination Round His Factification for Incamination of Work in Progress*. New York: New Directions, 1972.

Belden, H. M. *Ballads and Folk Songs Collected by the Missouri Folklore Society*. Columbia: Missouri Folklore Society 15, no. 1, 1 January 1940.

Ben-Amos, Dan. *Folklore Genres*. Austin: University of Texas Press, 1974.

Berger, Peter, and Luckmann, Thomas. *The Social Construction of Reality*. Garden City, N.Y.: Anchor Books, 1977.

Bergson, Henri. "Laughter." In *Comedy*, edited by Wylie Sypher, pp. 61–190. Garden City, N.Y.: Anchor Books, 1956.

Berkovits, Rochelle. "Secret Languages of Schoolchildren." *New York Folklore Quarterly* 26 (1970):127–52.

Berlyne, D. E. *Conflict, Arousal, and Curiosity*. New York: McGraw Hill, 1960.

————. "Laughter, Humor, and Play." In *Handbook of Social Psychology*, 5 vols., edited by G. Lindzey and E. Aronson, 3:795–852. Reading, Mass.: Addison-Wesley, 1969.

Bersani, Leo. *Balzac to Beckett: Center and Circumference in French Fiction*. New York: Oxford University Press, 1970.

Bigsby, C. *Dada and Surrealism*. London: Methuen, 1972.

Blake, Kathleen. *Play, Games, and Sport: The Literary Works of Lewis Carroll*. Ithaca, N.Y.: Cornell University Press, 1974.

Blitz, Signor, ed. *The Parlor Book of Magic and Drawing Room Entertainments*. New York: Hurst, 1889.

Bolton, H. C. *The Counting Out Rhymes of Children*. London: Elliot Stock, 1888.

————. "More Counting Out Rhymes." *Journal of American Folklore* 10 (1897): 318–19.

Bombaugh, C. C. *Facts and Fancies for the Curious from the Harvest Fields of Literature*. Philadelphia: Lippincott, 1905.

Boole, George. *An Investigation of the Laws of Thought, On Which Are Founded the Mathematical Theories of Logic and Probability*. London: Walton and Maberly, 1854.

Borges, Jorge Luis. *The Book of Imaginary Beings*. New York: Avon, 1969.

————. *Ficciones*. Edited by Anthony Kerrigan. New York: Grove Press, 1962.

————. *Labyrinths*. New York: New Directions, 1962.

Borinsky, Alicia. "Rewritings and Writings." *Diacritics* 4 (1974):22–28.

Botkin, Benjamin. *A Treasury of American Folklore*. New York: Crown, 1944.

Breton, André. *La Clé des champs*. Paris: Éditions du Sagittaire, 1953.

————. *Manifestoes of Surrealism*. Translated by Richard Seaver and Helen Lane. Ann Arbor: University of Michigan Press, 1972.

Brewster, Paul. *American Nonsinging Games*. Norman: University of Oklahoma Press, 1953.

——. "Rope Skipping, Counting Out and Other Rhymes of Children." *Southern Folklore Quarterly* 3 (1939):173-85.

——. "Spelling Riddles from the Ozarks." *Southern Folklore Quarterly* 8 (1944): 301-3.

Browne, E. B. "Southern California Jump Rope Rhymes: A Study in Variants." *Western Folklore* 14 (1955):3-22.

Bruner, J., Jolly, N., and Sylva, K., eds. *Play: Its Role in Development and Evolution*. Middlesex: Penguin Books, 1976.

Buckley, B. R. "Jump Rope Rhymes." *Keystone Folklore Quarterly* 11 (1966): 99-111.

Bulmer, R. "Why Is the Cassowary Not a Bird?" *Man* 2 (1962):5-25.

Burgess, Anthony. *Joysprick*. New York: Harcourt, Brace, 1973.

Burridge, K.O.L. "A Tangu Game." In *Play, Its Role in Development and Evolution*, edited by J. S. Bruner, N. Jolly, and K. Sylva, pp. 364-66. Middlesex: Penguin Books, 1976.

Butor, Michel. *Inventory*. Translated by Richard Howard. New York: Simon and Schuster, 1961.

——. "La Traduction." *James Joyce Quarterly* 4 (1967):215-26.

Caillois, Roger. *Man, Play, and Games*. New York: Free Press of Glencoe, 1961.

——. "Riddles and Images." In *Game, Play, Literature*, edited by Jacques Ehrmann. *Yale French Studies* 41 (1968):148-58.

Cammaerts, Emile. *The Poetry of Nonsense*. New York: Dutton, 1925.

Carlyle, Thomas. *Sartor Resartus*. New York: Scribner's, 1896.

Carroll, Lewis. *The Complete Works of Lewis Carroll*. New York: Vintage Books, 1976.

Chesterton, G. K. "Lewis Carroll." In *A Handful of Authors*, edited by Dorothy Collins, pp. 112-19. New York: Sheed and Ward, 1953.

Christ, Ronald J. *The Narrow Act: Borges's Art of Allusion*. New York: New York University Press, 1969.

Colie, Rosalie. *Paradoxica Epidemica: The Renaissance Tradition of Paradox*. Princeton, N. J.: Princeton University Press, 1966.

Cortázar, Julio. *Hopscotch*. New York: Avon, 1975.

Csikszentmihalyi, Mihaly. *Beyond Boredom and Anxiety: The Experience of Play in Work and Games*. San Francisco: Jossey-Bass, 1975.

Curtius, Ernst Robert. *European Literature and the Latin Middle Ages*. New York: Harper and Row, 1953.

DeLaguna, G. A. *Speech: Its Function and Development*. Bloomington: Indiana University Press, 1963.

Deleuze, Gilles. *Logique du sens*. Paris: Editions de Minuit, 1969.

Derrida, Jacques. *Of Grammatology*. Translated by G. Spivak. Baltimore: Johns Hopkins University Press, 1974.

——. "Signature, Event, Context." Translated by Tzvetan Bogdanovich. Paper given at the Congrès International des Sociétés de philosophie de langue française, August 1971, at Montréal.

——. "Structure, Sign, and Play." In *The Structuralist Controversy*, edited by Richard Macksey and Eugene Donato, pp. 247-64. Baltimore: Johns Hopkins University Press, 1972.

Desnos, Robert. *Domaine public*. Paris: Gallimard, 1953.

D'Israeli, Isaac. *Curiosities of Literature*. 3 vols. London: Routledge, Warnes and Routledge, 1859.

Dobson, W. T. *Literary Frivolities, Fancies, Follies, and Frolics.* London: Chatto and Windus, 1880.

——. *Poetical Ingenuities and Eccentricities.* London: Chatto and Windus, 1882.

Dorson, Richard. "The Identification of Folklore in American Literature." *Journal of American Folklore* 70 (1957): 5-7.

Douglas, Jack. *Understanding Everyday Life.* Chicago: Aldine, 1970.

Douglas, Mary. *Purity and Danger.* New York: Penguin Books, 1966.

——. "The Logical Basis of Constructed Reality." In *Rules and Meanings*, edited by Mary Douglas, p. 27. Middlesex: Penguin Books, 1977.

Douglas, Mary, ed. *Rules and Meanings.* Middlesex: Penguin Books, 1977.

Dundes, Alan. "The Study of Folklore in Literature and Culture: Identification and Interpretation." *Journal of American Folklore* 78 (1965): 136-42.

Dundes, Alan, and Georges, Robert. "Some Minor Genres of Obscene Folklore." *Journal of American Folklore* 75 (1962): 221-26.

Durkheim, Emile, and Mauss, Marcel. *Primitive Classification.* London: Routledge and Kegan Paul, 1963.

Ehrmann, Jacques. "*Homo Ludens* Revisited." In *Game, Play, Literature*, edited by Jacques Ehrmann. *Yale French Studies* 41 (1968): 31-57.

Elliot, Henry. "Similarities and Differences between Science and Common Sense." In *Ethnomethodology*, edited by Roy Turner, pp. 21-26. London: Penguin Books, 1971.

Emrich, Duncan. *The Nonsense Book of Riddles, Rhymes, Tongue Twisters, Puzzles and Jokes.* New York: Four Winds Press, 1970.

Fernandez, James. "The Mission of Metaphor in Expressive Culture." *Current Anthropology* 5 (1974): 119-45.

——. "Persuasions and Performances: Of the Beast in Every Body . . . and the Metaphors of Everyman." In *Myth, Symbol, and Culture*, edited by Clifford Geertz, pp. 39-60. New York: Norton, 1971.

Fink, Eugen. "The Oasis of Happiness: Toward an Ontology of Play." In *Game, Play, Literature*, edited by Jacques Ehrmann. *Yale French Studies* 41 (1968): 19-30.

Fisher, John. *The Magic of Lewis Carroll.* New York: Simon and Schuster, 1973.

Flaubert, Gustave. *Bouvard and Pecuchet.* Translated by T. W. Earp and G. W. Stonier. New York: New Directions, 1954.

Flescher, Jacqueline. "The Language of Nonsense in *Alice*." In *The Child's Part*, edited by Peter Brooks, pp. 128-44. Boston: Beacon Press, 1969.

Foreman, Richard, and Mannheim, Kate. "Blvd. de Paris (I've Got the Shakes)." New York, 1977 (handout for play).

Foucault, Michel. *The Order of Things.* New York: Random House, 1970.

——. *Raymond Roussel.* Paris: Gallimard, 1963.

Fry, William. *Sweet Madness: A Study of Humor.* Palo Alto, Calif.: Pacific Books, 1963.

Gadamer, Hans George. "The Historicity of Understanding." In *Critical Sociology*, edited by Paul Connerton, pp. 117-33. New York: Penguin Books, 1976.

Garfinkle, Harold, ed. *Studies in Ethnomethodology.* Englewood Cliffs, N.J.: Prentice-Hall, 1967.

Garvey, Catherine. "Some Properties of Social Play." In *Play, Its Role in Development and Evolution*, edited by J. Bruner, A. Jolly, and K. Sylva, pp. 570-83. Middlesex: Penguin Books, 1976.

Geertz, Clifford. *The Interpretation of Cultures.* New York: Basic Books, 1973.

Gershman, Herbert. "Children's Rhymes and Modern Poetry." *French Review* 44 (1971): 539-48.

———. *The Surrealist Revolution in France.* Ann Arbor: University of Michigan Press, 1969.

Gifford, Don, and Seidman, Robert. *Notes for Joyce.* New York: Dutton, 1974.

Gilbert, Stuart, and Ellman, Richard, eds. *Letters of James Joyce.* 3 vols. London: Faber, 1957–1966.

Gilchrist, A. G. "Notes on Children's Game Songs." *Journal of the Folk Song Society* 19 (1915):221–39.

Goffman, Erving. *Frame Analysis: An Essay on the Organization of Experience.* New York: Harper and Row, 1974.

Goldman, Lucien. *The Human Sciences and Philosophy.* London: Cape Editions, 1973.

Gomme, Alice Bertha. *The Traditional Games of England, Scotland, and Ireland.* 2 vols. New York: Dover, 1964.

Goodman, Felicitas D. *Speaking in Tongues: A Cross-Cultural Study of Glossolalia.* Chicago: University of Chicago Press, 1972.

Gorman, Herbert. *James Joyce: A Definitive Biography.* New York: Farrar and Rinehart, 1939.

Gray, D. "The Uses of Victorian Laughter." *Victorian Studies* 10 (1966):145–76.

Grossman, Manuel. *Dada: Paradox, Mystification, and Ambiguity in European Literature.* New York: Pegasus Books, 1971.

Guirard, Pierre. *L'Étymologie.* Paris: Presses Universitaires de France, 1972.

Gumperz, John, and Hymes, Dell, eds. *Directions in Sociolinguistics.* New York: Holt, Rinehart, Winston, 1972.

Halliday, M. K. "Anti-language." *American Anthropologist* 78 (1976):170–83.

Halliwell, J. O. *Popular Rhymes and Nursery Tales.* London: Bodley Head, 1970.

Hatch, Evelyn, ed. *A Selection from the Letters of Lewis Carroll to His Child-Friends.* London: Macmillan, 1933.

Heath, Stephen. "Ambiviolences." *Tel Quel* 50 (1972):22–43, and *Tel Quel* 51 (1972):64–76.

Heck, J. O. "Folk Poetry and Folk Criticism." *Journal of American Folklore* 40 (1972):1–77.

Hickerson, Joseph, and Dundes, Alan. "Mother Goose Vice Verse." *Journal of American Folklore* 75 (1962):249–59.

Hilbert, Richard. "Approaching Reason's Edge: 'Nonsense As the Final Solution to the Problem of Meaning.'" *Sociological Inquiry* 47 (1977):25–31.

Holquist, Michael. "How to Play Utopia." In *Game, Play, Literature*, edited by Jacques Ehrmann. *Yale French Studies* 41 (1968):106–23.

———. "What Is a Boojum?" In *The Child's Part*, edited by Peter Brooks, pp. 145–64. Boston: Beacon Press, 1969.

Huelsenbeck, Richard. *Memoirs of a Dada Drummer.* Edited by H. J. Kleinschmidt. Translated by Joachim Neugroschel. New York: Viking, 1974.

Huizinga, Johann. *Homo Ludens: A Study of the Play Element in Culture.* Boston: Beacon Press, 1955.

Husserl, E. "Lived Experiences of Time." In *Rules and Meanings*, edited by Mary Douglas, pp. 73–74. Middlesex: Penguin Books, 1977.

———. "The Possibility of Cognition." In *Rules and Meanings*, edited by Mary Douglas, pp. 197–220. Middlesex: Penguin Books, 1977.

Hymes, Dell. *Foundations in Sociolinguistics.* Philadelphia: University of Pennsylvania Press, 1974.

———. "'The Wife Who Goes Out Like a Man': A Reinterpretation of a Clackamas Chinook Myth." In *Structural Analysis of Oral Tradition*, edited by Pierre

Maranda and Elli Köngas-Maranda, pp. 49-80. Philadelphia: University of Pennsylvania Press, 1971.

Infante, G. Cabrera. "Revelations of a List Maker." *New Yorker*, 19 September 1977, pp. 32-35.

——. *Three Trapped Tigers*. Translated by Donald Gardner and Suzanne Jill Levine. New York: Harper and Row, 1971.

"Interview with Julio Cortázar." *Diacritics* 4 (1974):35-40.

Jakobson, Roman. "Two Aspects of Language and Two Fundamental Types of Disturbance." In *Fundamentals of Language*, edited by Roman Jakobson and Morris Halle, pp. 67-96. The Hague: Mouton, 1956.

James, William. *Principles of Psychology*. 2 vols. New York: Dover, 1950.

Jameson, Fredric. *The Prison-House of Language: A Critical Account of Structuralism and Russian Formalism*. Princeton, N.J.: Princeton University Press, 1972.

Joyce, James. *Finnegans Wake*. New York: Viking, 1939.

——. *Selected Letters*. Edited by Richard Ellman. New York: Viking, 1957.

——. *Ulysses*. New York: Vintage Books, 1961.

Keith-Spiegel, Patricia. "Early Conceptions of Humor: Varieties and Issues." In *The Psychology of Humor*, edited by J. Goldstein and P. McGhee, pp. 4-34. New York: Academic Press, 1972.

Kellock, Harold. *Houdini: His Life Story, from the Recollections and Documents of Beatrice Houdini*. New York: Blue Ribbon Books, 1928.

Kenner, Hugh. "Art in a Closed Field." *Virginia Quarterly Review* 38 (1962): 597-613.

——. *The Stoic Comedians*. Berkeley: University of California Press, 1962.

Kirshenblatt-Gimblett, Barbara, ed. *Speech Play: Research and Resources for the Study of Linguistic Creativity*. Philadelphia: University of Pennsylvania Press, 1976.

Knapp, M. and H. "Tradition and Change in American Playground Language." *Journal of American Folklore* 86 (1973):131-41.

Köngas-Maranda, Elli. "Riddles and Riddling." *Journal of American Folklore* 89 (1976):127-38.

Kreitler, Hans, and Kreitler, Shulamith. *Psychology of the Arts*. Durham, N.C.: Duke University Press, 1972.

Kristeva, Julia. *Sēmiōtikē: Recherches pour une sémanalyse*. Paris: Editions du Seuil, 1969.

——. *Le Texte du Roman*. The Hague: Mouton, 1970.

Kuhn, Thomas. *The Structure of Scientific Revolutions*. Chicago: University of Chicago Press, 1962.

Lacan, Jacques. "Of Structure As an Inmixing of an Otherness Prerequisite to Any Subject Whatever." In *The Structuralist Controversy*, edited by Richard Macksey and Eugene Donato, pp. 186-94. Baltimore: Johns Hopkins University Press, 1972.

Lalanne, L. *Curiosités littéraires*. Paris: Paulin, Libraire-Éditeur, 1845.

Leach, Edmund, "Anthropological Aspects of Language: Animal Categories and Verbal Abuse." In *Reader in Comparative Religion*, edited by William Lessa and Evon Vogt, 3rd ed, pp. 206-20. New York: Harper and Row, 1972.

——. "Magical Hair." *Journal of the Royal Anthropological Institute* 88 (1958): 147-64.

Leacock, Stephen Butler. *Nonsense Novels*. New York: Dodd Mead, 1929.

Lear, Edward. *The Complete Nonsense Book*. Edited by Lady Strachey. New York: Dodd Mead, 1912.

———. *Teapots and Quails and Other New Nonsense.* Edited by Angus Davidson. Cambridge: Harvard University Press, 1953.

Lennon, John. *"In His Own Write" and "A Spaniard in the Works."* New York: Signet, 1964.

Lévi-Strauss, Claude. "L'Analyse morphological des contes russe." *International Journal of Slavic Linguistics and Poetics* 3 (1960):122–49.

———. *The Savage Mind.* Chicago: University of Chicago Press, 1966.

———. *Totemism.* Translated by Rodney Needham. Boston: Beacon Press, 1963.

Lévi-Strauss, Claude, and Ricoeur, Paul. "A Confrontation." *New Left Review* 62 (1970):57–74.

Lewis, David. *Convention: A Philosophical Study.* Cambridge: Harvard University Press, 1969.

Liede, Alfred. *Dichtung als Spiel, Studien zu Unsinnspoesie an den Grenzen der Spräche.* 2 vols. Berlin: Walter de Gruyter, 1963.

Lomax, Alan, and Trager, Edith Crowell. "Phonotactique du chant populaire." *L'Homme* 4 (1964):5–55.

Loomis, C. G. "Jonathanisms: American Epigrammatic Hyperbole." *Western Folklore* 6 (1947):211–27.

———. "Traditional American Wordplay." *Western Folklore* 18 (1959):348–57.

———. "Traditional American Wordplay, Wellerisms, or Yankeeisms." *Western Folklore* 8 (1949):1–21.

———. "Wellerisms in California Sources." *Western Folklore* 14 (1955):229–45.

McDowell, John. "Riddling and Enculturation: A Glance at the Cerebral Child." *Working Papers in Sociolinguistics* no. 36. Austin, Tex.: Southwest Educational Development Laboratory, July 1976.

Mack, Dorothy. "Metaphoring As Speech Act: Some Happiness Conditions for Implicit Similes and Simple Metaphors." *Poetics* 4 (1975):221–56.

Marinetti, Filippo. "Geometrical and Mechanical Splendor and Numerical Sensibility." In *Selected Writings,* edited by R. W. Flint, pp. 97–103. New York: Noonday, 1971.

Maryott, Florence. "Nebraska Counting Out Rhymes." *Southern Folklore Quarterly* 1 (1936):39–62.

Matthews, J. H. *An Anthology of French Surrealist Poetry.* Minneapolis: University of Minnesota Press, 1966.

———. *Surrealism and Film.* Ann Arbor: University of Michigan Press, 1971.

———. *Theatre in Dada and Surrealism.* Syracuse, N.Y.: Syracuse University Press, 1974.

Matthiessen, F. O. *The Achievement of T. S. Eliot.* London: Oxford University Press, 1958.

Mendelson, Edward. "Encyclopedic Narrative: From Dante to Pynchon." *MLN* 9 (1976):1267–75.

Mercier, Vivian. *The Irish Comic Tradition.* London: Oxford University Press, 1962.

———. *The New Novel from Queneau to Pinget.* New York: Farrar, Straus, Giroux, 1971.

Merriam, Alan. *The Anthropology of Music.* Chicago: Northwestern University Press, 1964.

Millar, Susanna. *The Psychology of Play.* Baltimore: Penguin Books, 1969.

Millard, Eugenia. "What Does It Mean? The Lore of Secret Languages." *New York Folklore Quarterly* 10 (1954):103–10.

Milner, Florence. "The Poetry of *Alice in Wonderland.*" In *Aspects of Alice,* edited by Robert Phillips, pp. 245–52. New York: Vintage Books, 1971.

Milner, G. B. "Homo Ridens." *Semiotica* 5 (1972):1-30.

Morgenstern, Christian. *Galgenlieder/The Gallows Songs*. Translated by Max Knight. Berkeley: University of California Press, 1966.

Morrisette, Bruce. "Games and Game Structures in Robbe-Grillet." In *Game, Play, Literature*, edited by Jacques Ehrmann. *Yale French Studies* 41 (1968):159-67.

Morrison, L. *"Black Within and Red Without": A Book of Riddles*. New York: Crowell, 1953.

Motherwell, Robert. *The Dada Painters and Poets: An Anthology*. New York: Viking, 1951.

Nabokov, Vladimir. *Ada*. New York: McGraw Hill, 1969.

———. *Lolita*. New York: Putnam, 1955.

———. *Pale Fire*. New York: Putnam, 1962.

———. *Pnin*. New York: Avon, 1969.

Nadeau, Maurice. *The History of Surrealism*. New York: Macmillan, 1965.

Newell, W. W. *Games and Songs of American Children*. 1903. Reprint. New York: Dover, 1963.

Nisbet, Robert. *Social Change and History: Aspects of the Western Theory of Development*. New York: Oxford University Press, 1968.

Noakes, Vivien. *Edward Lear: The Life of a Wanderer*. Boston: Houghton Mifflin, 1968.

Nolton, Lucy. "Jump Rope Rhymes As Folk Literature." *Journal of American Folklore* 61 (1948):53-67.

O'Brien, Flann. *At Swim-Two-Birds*. Middlesex: Penguin Books, 1967.

Opie, Iona and Peter. *The Lore and Language of Schoolchildren*. London: Oxford University Press, 1959.

Oring, Elliott. "Three Functions of Folklore: Traditional Functionalism As Explanation in Folkloristics." *Journal of American Folklore* 80 (1976):67-80.

The Compact Edition of the Oxford English Dictionary. New York: Oxford University Press, 1971.

Partridge, Eric, ed. *A Dictionary of Slang and Unconventional English*. 7th ed. New York: Macmillan, 1970.

Paulhan, Jean. *La Preuve par l'étymologie*. Paris: Éditions de Minuit, 1953.

Peirce, Charles S. *Philosophical Writings of Peirce*. Edited by Justus Buchler. New York: Dover, 1955.

"Perverted Proverbs from the UCLA Folkore Archive." *Western Folklore* 20 (1961): 200.

Phillips, Robert, ed. *Aspects of Alice*. New York: Vintage Books, 1971.

Pollner, Melvin. "Sociological and Common Sense Models of the Labelling Process." In *Ethnomethodology*, edited by Roy Turner, pp. 27-40. London: Penguin Books, 1971.

Polyani, Michael. *Meaning*. Chicago: University of Chicago Press, 1974.

Pynchon, Thomas. *V*. New York: Bantam, 1964.

Rabelais, François. *The Histories of Gargantua and Pantagruel*. Translated by J. M. Cohen. Baltimore: Penguin Books, 1955.

Radin, Paul. *The Trickster*. New York: Schocken Books, 1972.

Reed, Langford. *A Book of Nonsense Verse*. New York: Putnam, 1926.

Richards, I. A. *How to Read a Page*. New York: Norton, 1942.

———. *The Philosophy of Rhetoric*. Oxford: Oxford University Press, 1936.

Richter, Hans. *Dada: Art and Anti-Art*. New York: McGraw Hill, 1965.

Ricoeur, Paul. "The Model of the Text: Meaningful Action Considered As Text." *New Literary History* 5 (1973):91-117.

Robbe-Grillet, Alain. *For a New Novel*. Translated by Richard Howard. New York: Grove Press, 1965.

———. "Order and Disorder in Film and Fiction." *Critical Inquiry* 4 (1977):1–20.

Rothenberg, Jerome. *Revolution of the Word*. New York: Seabury Press, 1974.

Roussel, Raymond. *How I Wrote Certain of My Books*. Translated by Trevor Winkfield. New York: Sun, 1977.

Russell, Bertrand, and Whitehead, A. N. *Principia Mathematica*. Cambridge: At the University Press, 1910.

Sacks, Harvey. "On Some Puns with Some Intimations." In *Sociolinguistics*, edited by R. W. Shuy, pp. 135–44. Washington, D.C.: Georgetown University Press, 1973.

Sapir, David, and Crocker, J. Christopher, eds. *The Social Use of Metaphor*. Philadelphia: University of Pennsylvania Press, 1977.

Schiller, Paul. "A Configurational Theory of Puzzles and Jokes." *Journal of Genetic Psychology* 18 (1938):217–34.

Schutz, Alfred. *Collected Papers*. 3 vols. The Hague: Mouton, 1964.

Searle, John. *Speech Acts: An Essay in the Philosophy of Language*. Cambridge: At the University Press, 1969.

Seitel, Peter. "Proverbs and the Structure of Metaphor among the Haya of Tanzania." Ph.D. dissertation, University of Pennsylvania, 1971.

Sewell, Elizabeth. *The Field of Nonsense*. London: Chatto and Windus, 1952.

———. "Lewis Carroll and T. S. Eliot As Nonsense Poets." In *T. S. Eliot: A Symposium for His 70th Birthday*, edited by Neville Braybrooke, pp. 49–56. New York: Farrar, Straus and Cudahy, 1958.

Sherzer, Dina. "Gnomic Expressions in *Molloy*." In *Speech Play*, edited by Barbara Kirshenblatt-Gimblett, pp. 163–71. Philadelphia: University of Pennsylvania Press, 1976.

Shklovsky, Viktor. "A Parodying Novel: Sterne's *Tristram Shandy*." In *Laurence Sterne: A Collection of Critical Essays*, edited by John Traugott, pp. 69–89. Englewood Cliffs, N.J.: Prentice-Hall, 1968.

Smith, Barbara Herrnstein. *Poetic Closure*. Chicago: University of Chicago Press, 1968.

Soupault, Philippe. *Poésies complètes*. Paris: Gallimard, 1937.

Spencer, Robert F., ed. *Forms of Symbolic Action*. Proceedings of the Annual Spring Meeting of the American Ethnological Society. Seattle: University of Washington Press, 1969.

Starkman, Miriam, ed. *Swift: Gulliver's Travels and Other Writings*. New York: Bantam, 1962.

Stein, Gertrude. *Lectures in America*. Boston: Beacon Press, 1957.

———. *Selected Writings*. Edited by Carl Van Vechten. New York: Vintage Books, 1945.

Sterne, Laurence. *Tristram Shandy*. Edited by James Work. Indianapolis: Bobbs Merrill, 1940.

Streamer, Colonel D. *Ruthless Rhymes for Heartless Homes*. Boston: R. H. Russell, 1901.

Sutherland, Robert. *Language and Lewis Carroll*. The Hague: Mouton, 1970.

Sutton-Smith, Brian. "Boundaries." In *Child's Play*, edited by R. Herron and B. Sutton-Smith, pp. 103–9. New York: John Wiley, 1971.

———. "A Developmental Structural Account of Riddles." In *Speech Play*, edited by Barbara Kirshenblatt-Gimblett, pp. 111–19. Philadelphia: University of Pennsylvania Press, 1976.

———. "The Game As a School of Abstraction." In *The Folkgames of Children*, edited by B. Sutton-Smith, pp. 442–49. Austin: University of Texas Press, 1972.

——. "Piaget on Play: A Critique." In *Child's Play*, edited by R. Herron and B. Sutton-Smith, pp. 326–36. New York: John Wiley, 1971.

——. "Play As Adaptive Potentiation." *Sportswissenschaft* 5 (1975):103–18.

——. "A Syntax for Play and Games." In *Child's Play*, edited by R. Herron and B. Sutton-Smith, pp. 298–307. New York: John Wiley, 1971.

Sutton-Smith, Brian, and Abrams, David. "The Development of the Trickster in Children's Narrative." *Journal of American Folklore* 90 (1977):29–48.

Synge, John. *The Aran Islanders*. Boston: Brice Humphries, 1911.

Tambiah, S. J. "Animals Are Good to Think and Good to Prohibit." *Ethnology* 42 (1969):4–57.

Taylor, Archer. *English Riddles from Oral Tradition*. Berkeley: University of California Press, 1951.

——. "Wellerisms and Riddles." *Western Folklore* 19 (1960):55–56.

Todorov, Tzvetan. *The Poetics of Prose*. Translated by Richard Howard. Ithaca, N.Y.: Cornell University Press, 1977.

Tomaševsky, Boris "Literature and Biography." In *Readings in Russian Poetics*, edited by Ladislav Matejka and Krystyna Pomorska, pp. 47–55. Cambridge, Mass.: MIT Press, 1971.

Trotsky, Leon. *Literature and Revolution*. New York: Russell and Russell, 1957.

Turner, Roy, Ed. *Ethnomethodology*. London: Penguin Books, 1972.

Turner, Victor. *Dramas, Fields, and Metaphors*. Ithaca, N.Y.: Cornell University Press, 1974.

——. *The Forest of Symbols*. Ithaca, N.Y.: Cornell University Press, 1967.

Urban, W. M. *Language and Reality*. London: G. Allen and Unwin, 1939.

Uspensky, Boris. *The Poetics of Composition*. Translated by V. Zavarin and S. Wittig. Berkeley: University of California Press, 1973.

Utley, Frances Lee. "The Study of Folk Literature: Its Scope and Use." *Journal of American Folklore* 71 (1958):139–48.

Van Rooten, Luis. *Mots d'heures: gousses, rames*. London: Angus and Robertson, 1968.

Vološinov, V. N. *Freudianism: A Marxist Critique*. Translated by I. R. Titunik. New York: Academic Press, 1976.

Weber, Samuel. "Saussure and the Apparition of Language: The Critical Perspective." *MLN* 91 (1976):913–39.

Willeford, William. *The Fool and His Scepter: A Study of Clowns and Jesters*. Evanston, Ill.: Northwestern University Press, 1969.

Williams, Raymond. *Communications*. Middlesex: Penguin Books, 1962.

——. *Culture and Society, 1780–1950*. New York: Harper and Row, 1958.

——. *Keywords*. London: Oxford University Press, 1976.

Williams, William Carlos. *Paterson*. New York: New Directions, 1963.

Wilson, Edmund. "C. L. Dodgson: The Poet Logician." In *Aspects of Alice*, edited by Robert Phillips, pp. 198–206. New York: Vintage Books, 1971.

Winslow, David. "An Annotated Collection of Children's Lore." *Keystone Folklore Quarterly* 11 (1966):151–202.

——. "An Introduction to Oral Tradition among Children." *Keystone Folklore Quarterly* 11 (1966):43–58.

Withers, Carl. *A Rocket in My Pocket*. New York: Henry Holt, 1948.

Withers, Carl, and Benet, Sula. *The American Riddle Book*. London: Abelard Schuman, 1954.

Wittgenstein, Ludwig. *The Philosophical Investigations*. Translated by G. E. M. Anscombe. New York: Macmillan, 1953.

Wittgenstein, Ludwig. *The Philosophical Investigations.* Oxford: Oxford University Press, 1958.

Wolfenstein, Martha. *Children's Humor: A Psychological Analysis.* Glencoe, Ill.: Free Press, 1954.

Wood, Robert. *How to Tell the Birds from the Flowers: A Revised Manual of Flornithology for Beginners.* New York: Duffield, 1917.

Worthington, Mabel. "Nursery Rhymes in *Finnegans Wake.*" *Journal of American Folklore* 70 (1957):37–48.

Wright, Thomas. *A History of Caricature and Grotesque in Literature and Art.* 1865. Reprint. New York: Ungar, 1968.

Znaniecki, Florian. *The Method of Sociology.* New York: Farrar and Rinehart, 1934.

index

223

WIDENER UNIVERSITY
WOLFGRAM
LIBRARY
CHESTER, PA.

Library of Congress Cataloging in Publication Data

Stewart, Susan.
   Nonsense: aspects of intertextuality in folklore and literature.

   Bibliography: p. 211
   Includes index.
   1. Discourse analysis. 2. Folk literature—History and criticism. I. Title.

P302.S69   808   79–4950
ISBN 0–8018–2258–0